The Illustrated
Book of
BIRDS

The Illustrated Book of

BIRDS

Text by Dr J. Felix

Illustrations by K. Hísek

Text: Dr. Jiří Felix
Illustrations: Květoslav Hísek
Translated by Olga Kuthanová

English version first published 1978 by
Octopus Books Limited
59 Grosvenor Street, London W1
Reprinted 1978, 1979, 1980, 1981, 1982,
1983 (twice), 1984, 1985

ISBN 0 7064 0766 0

Printed in Czechoslovakia

3/13/01/51-11

Contents

Foreword

Birds are an inseparable part of the world of nature, which so generously gives her gifts to all who use their eyes and ears in the environment in which they live. These small, lively creatures, many brightly coloured, others having beautiful voices, have long endeared themselves to man and it is no wonder that he wants to know their names, where they live and what they feed on, the type of nest they build, and eggs they lay and what their enemies are.

Every nature lover will therefore welcome this book which includes many birds that breed in our hemisphere. With its help he will learn to identify them by their song and other calls as well as by their flight silhouette. He will also learn how to care for birds and help them, for instance by providing food for them in winter or putting up nest boxes.

The book contains colour pictures of 256 birds. In many instances these are accompanied by a line drawing of the bird in flight as well as by a colour depiction of the egg. Birds' nests and eggs, of course, are not objects to be collected, for many of them are such rare species nowadays that destroying a single clutch might have an adverse effect on the entire population. Besides, most species of birds, including their nests and eggs, are now protected by law and any infringement is severely punished. Every nature lover will surely be satisfied with learning about and just observing the life of birds and will himself strive to protect them.

The birds depicted in this book are arranged according to the presently accepted classification. The text accompanying each plate acquaints the reader with the given bird's distribution, its habitat, whether it migrates or stays the winter, where it flies to and when it departs for its winter quarters, when it returns to its nesting grounds, and other biological data such as its average length, wingspan (in the case of raptors), etc. The male of the species is designated by the symbol ♂, the female by the symbol ♀.

About Birds in General

Birds are higher vertebrates with a constant and fairly high body temperature ranging from 38 °C to 44 °C. They have two pairs of limbs, the front pair being in the form of wings which are usually used for flying. Some species of birds, however, have frail wings incapable of supporting them in flight, for example in the case of the ostrich, or adapted only for swimming, as in the case of penguins. All the birds depicted in this book are capable of flight.

Birds evolved over millions of years from reptiles, with which they share many common features to this day. For instance, some reptiles and all birds lay eggs and have a comparable arrangement of the reproductive and excretory organs, the ducts of which share a common opening with the gut — the cloaca. The development of their embryos is also similar.

The first creatures to develop characteristic avian features such as feathered wings appeared about 150 million years ago, in the Jurassic period of the Mesozoic. These primitive birds, about the size of a pigeon, possessed a bill provided with teeth, had three free fingers terminating in claws on the fore limbs and a long tail composed of 23 vertebrae with feathers arranged in two rows on either side. These primitive birds were called *Archaeopteryx*. Perfect fossil remains were found in Upper Jurassic slate formations in Bavaria.

These birds were incapable of strong flight, mostly climbing trees and using their wings for 'parachuting' or gliding.

The fossil remains of another extinct bird, *Hesperornis*, were also found in the North American Chalk of western Kansas. This bird was incapable of flight, had finely toothed jaws, and resembled the present-day divers. It lived between 70 and 140 million years ago. Other primitive birds living at this time included *Ichthyornis, Apatornis*, etc. None of these primitive birds survived the end of the Cretaceous period which marked the end of the Mesozoic and onset of the Tertiary, which brought with it many genera and species of birds that later likewise became extinct, but also species greatly resembling those of the present day and from which the present species evolved.

Because the taste buds are located quite deep inside the mouth on the soft upper palate and on the mucous membrane underneath the tongue and because birds, unlike mammals, do not chew their food but swallow it quickly they have little sense of taste. In most birds the sense of smell is also very poorly developed and they are not aware of scent at all.

The sense of touch is developed in varying degrees. Birds generally have such sensory organs inside the bill and on the tongue, but some also have them at the base of certain feathers and on the legs, etc. Birds that obtain their food from the ground even have these organs at the tip of the bill.

A bird's most perfect and important sensory organ is the eye. Birds see far better than other animals. The eye is large and focuses not only by means of muscles squeezing the lens as in the case of mammals, but also by flattening or bulging. The eyes can also be moved independently and thus each can be looking at a different object at one and the same time. The eyes are usually located on either side of the head and thus each has its own field of vision. Some birds, such as owls, however, have both eyes facing forward, but they are able to turn their head a full 180° each way. Colour vision in birds is about the same as in man. In addition to the upper and lower eyelid birds have another special lid called the nictitating membrane which extends from the inner corner and can cover the entire eye. The retina has a greater density of sensory cells than the eye of man, more than five times as many in the case of raptors, thus enabling them to see their prey even from a great height.

Another important sensory organ is the ear, even though of less perfect structure and still resembling that of the reptiles. There is only one earbone, corresponding to the stirrup in the human ear, and the external ear channel is comparatively short. Despite this a bird's hearing is very good and in some species, such as the owls, it is excellent and put to good use in hunting prey at night. The outer ear of birds has no lobe and is usually covered with feathers.

The vocal organs, located at the lower end of

the trachea, likewise play an important role in the life of birds. This organ, called the syrinx, is remarkably well developed in songbirds, but less so in other groups of birds which usually have a monotonous call or produce only raucous sounds. Some, such as the white stork, have no vocal organs and communicate by clapping their mandibles together.

The bird skeleton is not only strong but also light, because most of the bones are hollow and filled with air. The long bones, in particular, are tubular and very strong, and their inner pneumatic filling greatly reduces the weight of the whole skeleton — a very important factor in flight. Birds' feathers are also very light and arranged to form an impermeable surface that traps 'cushions' of air. The breastbone is remarkably well developed and anchors the powerful muscles which raise and lower the wings.

Structure of the Bird

The shape of a bird in flight is often characteristic and the flight silhouette is an important means of identification. The form of flight often differs greatly between species of birds and is allied to the general shape of their wings and wing surface. Birds capable of rapid and sustained flight have long, narrow wings, e. g. the common swift, hobby, terns, etc. These birds have a slender body that offers minimum resistance to the air. The swift has even lost the ability of movement on the ground and must take to the air by dropping from an elevated position. Ground birds, such as those of the order Gallinae, on the other hand, have fairly short, broad wings and plump bodies. Apart from a few exceptions, gallinaceous birds are poor fliers. Some birds, such as the kestrel, can remain hovering in the air over a single spot for a long time.

Others like the stork and swan fly with neck outstretched. The herons carry theirs bent into the shape of an S.

Feathers

The body of a bird is covered with feathers arranged in most birds in definite tracts called the pterylae. The bare spaces between the feathered tracts are called apteria, but these are very small and masked by the surrounding feathers. The feathers that give the body its typical shape are called contour feathers, e. g. the flight feathers, tail feathers, etc. Such a feather has a long, firm yet flexible shaft bordered on both sides by a web composed of separate individual barbs, which in turn have rows of smaller barbules supplied with hooklets. If the web is damaged in any way, the bird strokes it with its bill or claws, thus causing the hooklets to catch and restore the web again. The part of the feather embedded in the skin is called the quill.

Underneath the contour feathers the body is usually covered with a layer of fine down feathers with a short, fine quill but without a shaft and with barbules that do not possess hooklets. In many birds, e. g. ducks, these down feathers are very important during the nesting period for they are used to line the nest. Down feathers prevent the loss of heat and keep the eggs from becoming cold even during the absence of the duck, who covers the eggs before leaving. The young of many species of birds, e. g. raptors, owls and ducks, are also covered with a thick coat of down feathers.

Another type is the filament feather which is thin, almost hair-like, and is generally found growing immediately next to the contour feathers. Then there are the bristle feathers, growing at the gape of certain birds, which have a short quill and are webless and serve mainly as tactile organs when catching prey.

In water birds the feathers are close-packed and grow thickly over the body thus serving as good heat insulation. In ducks the flight feathers, when the bird is not airborne, are furthermore protected and kept from becoming waterlogged by a sort of feathered pocket into which the bird slips its wings. In most water birds the feathers are also oiled by a fluid secreted by the uropygial gland located on the back at the base of the tail feathers. The oily fluid is spread over the feathers by the bird with its bill thus keeping them perfectly impregnated. Those covering the

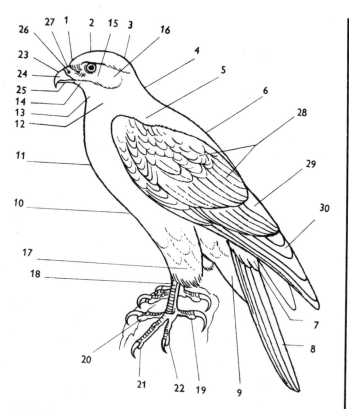

1/ **Bird topography**

1 forehead, 2 crown, 3 hind neck, 4 nape, 5 shoulder, 6 back, 7 upper tail coverts, 8 tail feathers, 9 under tail coverts, 10 belly, 11 breast, 12 neck, 13 throat, 14 chin, 15 cheek, 16 ear region, 17 thigh, 18 tarsus, 19 hind toe, 20 inner toe, 21 middle toe, 22 outer toe, 23 bill ridge, 24 upper mandible, 25 lower mandible, 26 nostril, 27 cere, 28 wing coverts, 29 secondaries, 30 primaries

It is interesting to note that when wetting their feathers ducks and geese perform what might be termed group games, ruffling their feathers and slapping the water with their wings so that it penetrates more easily to the skin, and also diving below the surface. When they have finished their bath they climb out of the water onto dry ground, where they shake and pinch their feathers with their bills to remove the water. Ducks also make jerking movements with their partly-spread wings to dry the feathers, after which they oil and then smooth and trim them.

The feathers of all birds are replaced regularly by the process called moulting. Old feathers are shed and new ones grow in, pushing the old ones out. Whereas in most birds, such as songbirds, pigeons, gallinaceous birds, raptors and owls, the flight and tail feathers are shed successively so that the bird does not lose the power of flight, in many species of water birds, such as ducks, geese and crakes, the flight feathers are shed all at once so that the birds are incapable of flight

head are oiled by rubbing the head over the back feathers. Water birds repeat this process several times a day. This, however, is not the only care given to feathers. Water birds as well as many other birds bathe regularly to keep the feathers from drying out. Water birds bathe thoroughly several times daily. Also the young of many water birds are often introduced to water the second day after hatching. However, their uropygial gland does not begin to function until their contour feathers begin to grow. Their down feathers, of course, would soon become waterlogged if they were not oiled regularly and so they climb through the feathers of their parents, which are more intensively oiled at this time, thereby lubricating their own down. Besides, the habit of preening is an innate one which they possess from birth and so they spread their parents' oil evenly over their whole bodies.

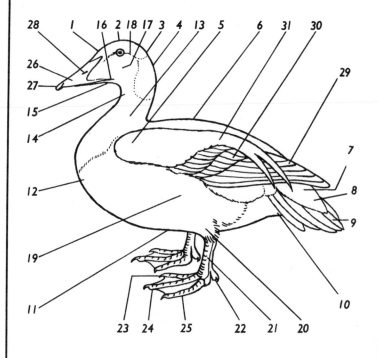

2/ **Topography of the eider**

1 forehead, 2 crown, 3 nape, 4 hind neck, 5 shoulders, 6 back, 7 rump, 8 upper tail coverts, 9 tail quills, 10 under tail coverts, 11 belly, 12 breast, 13 neck, 14 throat, 15 chin, 16 lores, 17 cheek, 18 ear region, 19 flank, 20 shank, 21 tarsus, 22 hind toe, 23 inner toe, 24 middle toe, 25 outer toe, 26 bill, 27 nail, 28 nostrils, 29 primaries, 30 secondaries, 31 shoulder coverts

for a certain period, usually three to seven weeks. During this time they must conceal themselves in reeds and rushes and forage for food on the water. Such birds, however, do not all shed their flight feathers all at the same time. Thus, for instance, drakes, which do not take care of the young, moult sooner than ducks, who shed their feathers after the young have reached maturity. On the other hand, in the case of swans where both partners attend the young, it is the female that moults first while the male protects the cygnets, then he moults, his new flight feathers attaining their full length at the same time as those of the offspring after which, in the case of wild swans, the whole family is able to set out on its migratory flight south.

In some species the male and female have the same coloration throughout the year, e. g. tree creepers, tits, rooks, geese, storks and some warblers, while in others the colour and sometimes the shape of various feathers of the male are markedly different, e. g. most pheasants, ducks, finches and buntings, etc.; this is known as sexual dimorphism. An unusual example of sexual dimorphism is that found in the phalaropes and dotterel where the female is larger and more brightly coloured than the male, who has drabber plumage and therefore is the one who performs the task of incubation.

Some species of birds have two differently coloured sets of plumage a year, which means that they moult twice yearly, the first being a complete and the second a partial moult. Ducks shed both the contour as well as flight feathers in summer. The change is most marked in the drake who loses his bright nuptial plumage at this time and resembles the female. However, the newly emerging flight feathers are again brightly coloured, thus making it possible to distinguish between the two. Ducks moult a second time in the autumn, when they once more shed the small contour feathers but not the flight feathers. At this time the male acquires a new, bright nuptial garb, which he retains until the summer of the following year. In some individuals the moult takes longer than in others and thus in the autumn one may often see amongst the brightly coloured drakes of a given species ones that have not yet completed their moult.

Other birds, such as many species of waders, have a different winter plumage, the difference

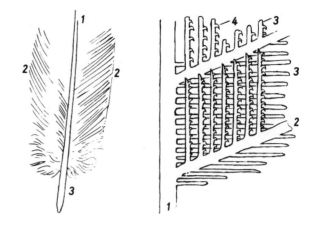

3/ Contour feather
    1 rachis, 2 vane, web, 3 quill

4/ Arrangement of hooklets of a bird feather
    1 rachis, 2 barbules, 3 barbicels, 4 hooklets

being particularly striking in the case of the ruff. The nuptial dress of the male is very colourful as he sports a broad, brightly coloured collar or ruff, hence his name. In summer, however, he sheds his bright plumage as well as the long feathers of the ruff and by autumn he acquires a new garb resembling that of the female. Some species of grebes also have brightly coloured nuptial plumage, but this is worn by both the male and female. The little gull has a nuptial as well as non-breeding plumage; in winter its black head turns white but in spring the white feathers are soon shed and replaced by the characteristic black ones. Also certain herons have a brightly coloured breeding plumage.

The Bill

The bill, covered by a thick and strong horny sheath, is another important part of the bird's body. The individual bird groups exhibit marked variation in the shape of the bill depending on the kind of food they eat. Warblers have a long, narrow, pointed bill so that they can easily catch small insects and their larvae. Flycatchers have a flat bill that is broader at the base making it easier for them to catch insects in flight. Tits have a strong bill to break hard seed coverings. Tree creepers have a long, downcurved bill that is very slender at the tip to help them extricate small insects, and their eggs and larvae from cracks in the bark of trees. The hawfinch has an unusually stout bill that enables it to crack even the hardest shells. Crossbills have bills with overlapping tips to facilitate the extraction of seeds from the cones of conifers. Corvine birds, which are omnivorous, have an extremely large and stout bill. The nightjar, on the other hand, has a short but very wide bill with stiff bristles at the gape, which serve as sensory organs that help it catch insects while in flight. The bills of owls are downcurved and stout, similar to those of raptors, where the upper mandible is not only remarkably strong and downcurved but also sharp on the edge, which enables the birds to rip and tear the flesh of animals and to 'cut off' softer pieces. Some raptors, such as members of the family Falconidae, also have a horny 'tooth' in the upper bill which further facilitates the tearing of flesh. Those of gallinaceous birds are comparatively short but stout, in some species even shovel-shaped to facilitate turning of the earth in which the birds seek their food. Pigeons have short bills with swollen ceres at the base. Woodpeckers have bills specially adapted for chiselling wood and uncovering concealed grubs. The bills of many species of marshland and water birds are also specially adapted to the kind of food they eat. Members of the Anatidae family have a characteristic nail, or horny plate, at the tip of the bill, the upper and lower edges of which are serrated. The notches on the edges of the bills of geese are very hard and short, useful for nipping off plants, which form a large part of the goose's diet. The serrated edge of the duck's bill serves to sieve food. As the duck dabbles its bill in mud or water it moves its tongue in such a way as to create a vacuum and as the water flows in the small crustaceans, worms, insects, etc. are sieved and trapped. Then with its sensitive tongue the duck picks out the edible bits while the mud and water flow out again. There may be a great many such notches on the edges of the bill. The shoveler has as many as 180 on the upper bill alone. They begin to develop in young birds at about the age of one week. Mergansers have long, narrow bills with sharp, hooked notches that enable the birds to get a better grasp on the small fish they eat. Herons have a long, pointed

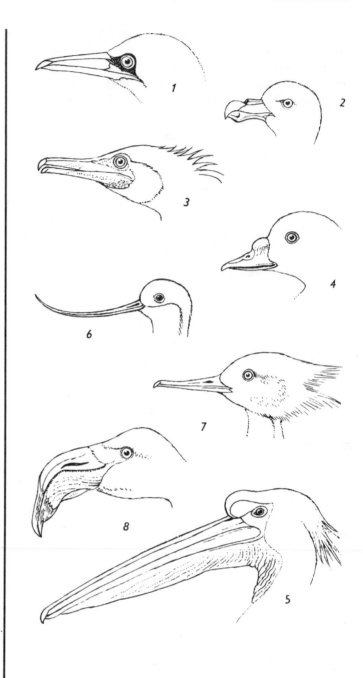

5/ Types of bills
1 gannet, 2 fulmar, 3 cormorant, 4 common scoter, 5 white pelican, 6 avocet, 7 red-breasted merganser, 8 greater flamingo

bill which they often use as a spear when hunting. Storks, too, have a long, straight and pointed bill. The spoonbill's is rather unusual. It has a long spoon-shaped bill wide and flattened at the tip which enables it to dabble in mud or water rather like a duck. Grebes have a sharply pointed bill especially adapted for catching fish.

The bills of waders are for the most part fairly long, which enables them to forage for food in deep mud and water. The oystercatcher's bill is very strong, quite long and compressed at the sides and is used to open the shells of bivalve molluscs or plunged into mud to bring up various worms, etc. Plovers, unlike most other waders, have a fairly short bill. The snipe's bill is very specialized. Its tip is equipped with tactile cells which make it possible for the bird to probe deep in the mud and capture its prey without seeing it. Curlews have a long bill curved like a sabre. The avocet's bill is long and thin with a slight upward curve which it swings from side to side in the shallows to stir up the water for small crustaceans which it then skillfully catches. Striking, because of its peculiar shape, is the bill of the pelican. It is very long and slightly downcurved, the lower mandible consisting of two struts joined at the tip from which hangs a large, distensible pouch. It is excellent for catching fish and the pouch is used by the bird to carry food to the nest.

The large parrot-like bill of the common puffin grows nine superficial scales during the breeding season, six on the upper mandible and three on the lower; these are a brilliant red, blue and yellow but after the breeding season the bright coloration is shed. This moulting of beak scales seems to be a primitive characteristic like the shedding of reptilian scales.

Feet

Birds' feet also have varied shapes, depending on the way of life of the given species. The tree creepers have toes with long, sharp claws that grip the bark as the bird climbs, as do woodpeckers, which furthermore have strong and sturdy tail feathers that serve as an additional support. The toes of woodpeckers are further adapted for climbing, two pointing forward and two backward. The feet of the nightjar are short, making it almost impossible for the bird to move on the ground. It is also incapable of grasping a branch in the usual manner which is why it perches lengthwise and not crosswise. Birds of prey have huge claws on all four toes. Those of

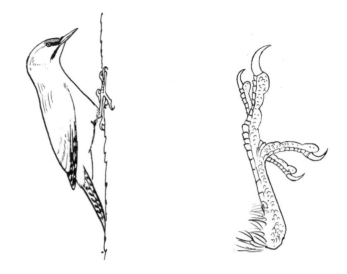

6/ *The grey-headed woodpecker climbing a tree*

7/ *Foot of the black woodpecker*

some, such as eagles, falcons and goshawks, are extremely long, curved and sharp. Vultures, on the other hand, have straight and blunt toes because their legs are adapted to movement on the ground where they seek their food — carrion. Specially adapted are the toes of the osprey, which has a reversible outer toe thus enabling it to catch fish between opposite-facing claws — two pointing forward and two backward. Similarly adapted are the toes of owls, with their long, sharp claws; they, too, have a reversible outer toe. Gallinaceous birds have large, strong feet with blunt but strong claws that serve to dig up food from the ground.

The feet of birds that spend most of their time in the water are also adapted to their environment and vary according to the way of life of the given species. Typical are the feet of the Anatidae family (swans, geese and ducks), which have the three front toes connected by a broad web and a fourth, hind toe located somewhat higher than the others. When swimming, the feet move alternately backward and forward; during the backward movement the webbed toes are spread far apart, whereas when the foot moves forward the toes are drawn together and the toe joints bend so that the surface, and thus the resistance to the water, is as little as possible. When diving, however, e. g. in the case of diving ducks, the feet work differ-

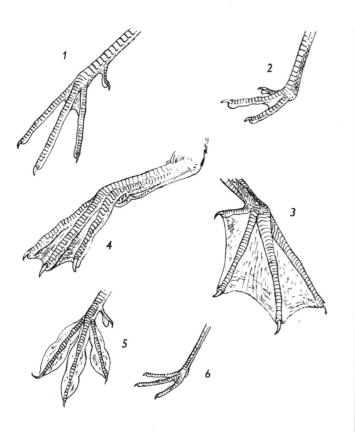

8/ *Types of feet*
  1 spotted redshank, 2 oystercatcher, 3 cormorant, 4 guillemot,
  5 red-necked phalarope, 6 Kentish plover

disappear below the surface in a flash and stay under for up to a minute, swimming as much as fifty metres in that time. Unlike members of the Anatidae family the web of the grebe's foot is not complete; each of the three front toes are fringed separately.

Members of the rail tribe, such as the coot which spends most of its life on water, also have separately fringed toes. Other species of rail have fairly long legs with long toes adapted for running over the leaves of aquatic plants. Moreover, their bodies are very slim to enable them to move with ease through reeds and dense vegetation. All rails, of course, can also swim.

Waders are generally adapted to life at the water's edge, in shallows, swamps and mud flats. Some species, however, inhabit dry localities far from water. These birds often have legs that are very long in proportion to the body. Most have webless toes, though some have a small web at the base of the toes and others have a fairly well developed web, e. g. the avocet.

Very long legs are a characteristic of some of the Ciconiiformes, which include the herons, storks, ibises and spoonbills. Some, such as the white stork or grey heron, can easily stand and feed in quite deep water.

Gulls, skuas and terns have also developed webs and move well on the water's surface; however, they do not float as low down in the water as ducks.

With the three front toes of their large feet connected by a web the divers are superbly adapted for a permanent life on water and only climb out onto dry land during the nesting period. Divers are very awkward on land, dragging themselves along on their bellies rather than walking, the reason for this is that the legs which serve as oars in the water are located at the very rear of the body.

Birds of the group known as totipalmate swimmers (all four toes connected by a web), are also superbly adapted to aquatic life. These include the pelicans, cormorants and gannets.

ently. Because the duck is lighter than water it must overcome the upward hydrostatic pressure. Before submerging it exhales and presses its feathers tightly to its body to squeeze out air remaining in the plumage. Then it gives a sharp push with both legs, jumps above the surface of the water and slips down under, keeping its feet above the body and propelling itself downward by kicking the legs outward and backward, somewhat as in the breast-stroke, with the webbed toes spread wide, then moving them back under the body with the toes drawn together, and again kicking them outward and backward.

It is interesting to note that the ducklings of non-diving ducks are also good at diving and do so when danger threatens.

The grebes are completely adapted to a permanent life on water. They dive well and to great depths. Even a day-old nestling dives adroitly. When swimming grebes float fairly low down in the water. From this position they can

The Mystery of Migration

Birds are divided into the following basic groups, depending on whether they remain in their breeding grounds throughout the year or leave for the winter:

Resident birds — that stay close to the general area of their nesting grounds

Migratory birds — that leave their nesting grounds each year in the autumn or late summer, fly to warmer quarters for the winter, and return again in spring.

Transient migrants or dispersive birds — that range far afield, often hundreds of kilometres, in all directions from their nesting grounds after the breeding season, depending on the weather and available food supply.

There may, however, be various transitional stages between these three basic groups and, sometimes, contrary classification for members of one and the same species. For example, some birds that nest in northern Europe, such as the peregrine falcon and kestrel, are migratory, whereas those of western and central Europe are resident. In other species, some members are migratory and others resident. There are also species which, in general, are classed as migratory but some of their members remain in their nesting grounds for the winter. Sometimes birds that are otherwise resident will suddenly set out in large flocks on a long journey south or southwest; these are called invasional migrations. One example is the nutcracker, normally a resident or dispersive bird, which sometimes, however, travels in large flocks to central Europe from the north or northeast. There are also the birds which are regular winter visitors, migrants who have left their breeding grounds in the far north to spend the winter in central or western Europe.

The answer to why some birds migrate and others stay the winter is not as simple as it seems. Ornithologists have studied the phenomenon for many years and still have not come up with a clearcut explanation.

In some species the primary reason is a short supply of food; typical insectivorous birds would not find enough to subsist on in northern and central Europe during the winter. Swallows and martins depart when insects start becoming scarce. Why, however, do some birds, such as the common swift, leave as early as the end of July, when insects are still plentiful, remaining in their nesting grounds a mere three months? Then there are the birds that were originally migratory, e. g. the European blackbird, but have since become resident, increasingly settling in the vicinity of man.

What causes migratory birds to fly south or some other direction, depending on the species, at a certain time of the year? One factor is almost certainly the changing hours of daylight which bring about an alteration in the bird's hormonal balance. For example, in autumn the rapidly shortening days affect the activity of the sex organs which triggers the migratory instinct. In the more northerly parts of Europe there are fourteen to eighteen hours of daylight during the nesting period and birds have plenty of time to forage for food for their offspring. However, their broods are reared just as successfully by birds that breed in the tropics, where there are only twelve hours of daylight. And the crossbill even nests in Europe during the winter season when there is even far less daylight, the determining factor, apparently, being the abundance of food. As one can see there can be no clearcut answer to all the many questions. One thing that is certain, however, is that migration in various species of birds is triggered by various combinations of external events.

Another theory about bird migration is based on the presumption that migrant birds originally lived only in tropical and subtropical regions. Here they bred and raised their offspring and when they overmultiplied they set out for more northern parts in search of food for their families, returning south again when the young were fully grown. This, however, may be the case with only a few species of birds native to the

9/ *Flight pattern of woodpeckers*

13/ *Common starlings flying in formation*

goal? This problem has been studied by many scientists for years. One theory states that birds are directly influenced by the earth's magnetic field whereby they are able to distinguish the various points of the compass. Complex experiments, mostly with homing pigeons, did not prove the truth of this theory. Modern instruments revealed that the earth's magnetic field has only a slight influence on animals.

The latest theory is the one that believes birds navigate by means of light, or rather by the position of the sun as well as the position of the moon and stars. This theory was substantiated by experiments with many species of birds. In the spring and autumn migration periods captive starlings placed in a round aviary flew in the same direction as when migrating, being able to orientate themselves only by the heavens, which they could see from their cage. The birds orientated themselves precisely according to the position of the sun and at night by the position of the stars. When the apparent position of the sun was altered by a suitable arrangement of mirrors the starlings made corresponding changes in their position. Observations with radar equipment also showed that many birds migrate according to the position of the stars. Nowadays we know that other animals, such as sea turtles, likewise navigate primarily according to the position of the sun and stars. Birds can orientate themselves by the position of the sun even when the sky is overcast, but not in very foggy conditions.

Though the light theory was substantiated in many birds, in others it may be presumed that they can orientate themselves in part also by the earth's magnetic field, etc. This, however, would have to be substantiated by further complex experiments.

At the nesting site and in the surrounding neighbourhood birds find their way mainly by their memory of various landmarks. Many birds move in regular circuits, somewhat like mammals along certain trails, and these are firmly fixed in their memory. When they have fledged, young birds usually remain for a time with their parents thus learning to know the surroundings of their nest. Birds that become independent shortly after fledging get to know the countryside through their own observations. This, however, does not fully explain the problem of orientation. Birds captured by their nests and released several hundred kilometres away returned to their home site, yet they couldn't possibly know the countryside such a distance from their nest. One starling taken by plane 341 kilometres north of its nest returned within several days; captured once again it was taken 500 kilometres south of its nest and was back once more within five days. The same thing happens in the case of many other birds. It is evident from these experiments that long-distance orientation is not limited to migration but comes into play also during the nesting period. It is even developed in birds that are resident and remain in their nesting grounds throughout the year. In experiments with swallows, birds taken thirty-five kilometres from the nest returned within 2.5 to 8 hours. The reason it took them so long to travel a distance which could easily

14/ *A flock of geese in their typical flight formation*

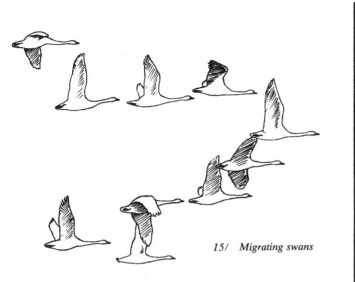

15/ *Migrating swans*

have been covered in an hour was because they no longer knew the landmarks that far away from their home base and had to orientate themselves approximately by the position of the sun. They probably did not fly a direct course at the start but only after they reached ground with familiar landmarks.

The distances some birds travel when migrating are almost unbelievable. Many European birds such as the swallow, cuckoo, nightjar and hobby, fly as far as southern Africa, a distance of about ten thousand kilometres which they travel twice a year, in spring and autumn. The record journeys, however, are those made by the arctic tern which breeds from the coast of Germany and England north as far as the arctic regions of Europe, Asia and North America. Birds from northern Europe travel along the coast of western Europe and are joined by individuals from Greenland and the eastern nesting grounds of North America. They continue along the west coast of Africa to the tip of South Africa whence many individuals continue on to circle the Antarctic, returning again to the tip of South Africa. When the time comes they fly back to their European and other nesting grounds. It is unbelievable that such a small bird, weighing only 90 to 120 grams, flies a distance of 36,000 kilometres to its winter quarters and back every year. Long journeys are also made by the fulmars, shearwaters and petrels. The fulmar, for example, is both a dispersive as well as a migratory bird, some individuals flying as far as the shores of Brazil and Argentina south of the equator. One bird ringed in Stockholm was recovered even as far away as the coast of southern Australia.

Flight is the general method of travel in the bird kingdom but some birds travel long distances by swimming. These, of course, include penguins, which have lost the power of flight. Some birds, however, even though able to fly, swim part of the way when migrating. The young of the gannet, for example, abandon the nest at the age of about 75 days and leap into the sea, swimming in the direction of migration until they are able to fly, which is at the age of 95 to 107 days. The eider, as well as some divers and Brunnich's guillemot sometimes journey hundreds of kilometres in this manner.

Only very occasionally are birds known to migrate in part by walking. In one instance thousands of American coots *(Fulica americana)* were observed walking for three days in the direction of their winter quarters.

The migration of birds of the southern hemisphere is naturally in the opposite direction, that is from the south northward to the equator.

16/ *Spoonbills flying in formation*

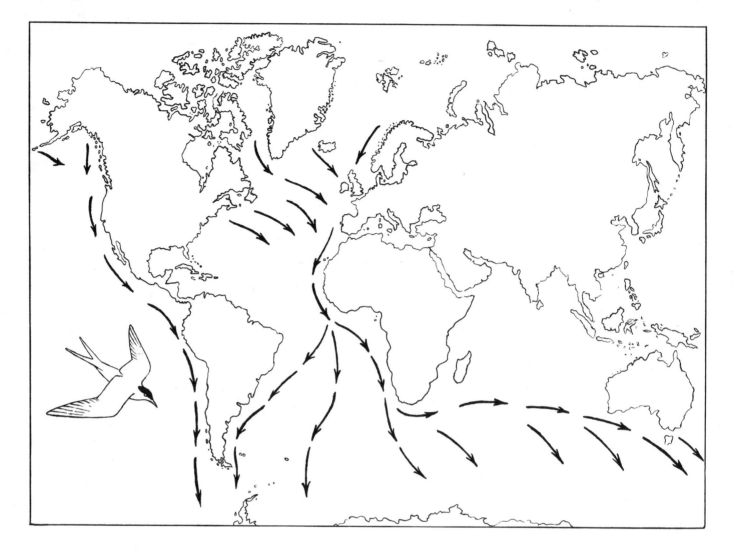

17/ *Migration routes of the arctic tern*

Breeding and Nesting

Courtship

Courtship usually begins after the birds' arrival at their nesting grounds, but in some species it begins in their winter quarters or during the return flight. The males' behaviour is marked by agitation and excitement as they try to attract a partner. Each species has a characteristic manner of courtship; in some it is fairly inconspicu-ous while in others it is quite noticeable, often including intricate antics and loud cries. The courtship display may take place on the ground, among the branches of trees or bushes, as well as in the air and on water. In some species several males participate in the display simultaneously and even engage in duels, which, however, rarely end in blood. One example is the black grouse, the males of the species converging in a single open space for a mass display. The capercaillie, on the other hand, performs its antics at a higher level, usually on tree branches, and the ceremony consists of several stages. Well-known, also, is the courtship display of cooing pigeons, which bow and strut about, and drag their wings along the ground. The male pheasant stands on the ground, stretches its neck upward and rapidly whirs its wings, at the same time uttering crowing sounds. The males of most songbirds sing when courting. Woodpeckers select part of a tree which has good resonance and drum on it with their strong bills.

The courtship display of many species of birds includes spectacular flights. This is especially the case with the raptors, which sometimes perform fantastic acrobatic feats. These aerial displays begin when the bird circles to gain height, then plummets downwards making all kinds of turns and somersaults and providing a magnificent display of its flying skill and artistry only to soar high again to repeat the display.

In the courtship display of the white stork both partners clatter their bills loudly while laying their heads on their backs. Also striking are the courtship antics of the larger grebes; the two partners swim towards each other, stretch their necks upwards and shake their heads briskly, then raise themselves erect above the water with chests pressed together, sometimes holding bits of water plants, for which they dive to the bottom and collect in their beaks. The courtship performance of cranes is also interesting. They hop about and leap into the air, flap their wings and run rapidly around in circles, while making trumpet-like sounds. Their courtship is a veritable dance. As for cormorants, the male sits on the nest, raises his beak and tail straight up in the air, jerks his wings, and as soon as a female approaches throws his head on his back and utters a hollow groan. The female then comes closer with inflated throat pouch and head feathers erect, continuously uttering croaking sounds. The male heron holds himself erect, ruffles his

19/ *White storks greeting each other during the courtship display*

feathers and snaps at the empty air with his beak making a loud clicking sound. Courting swans swim towards each other and when close submerge their necks in the water a number of times, often intertwining them. The courtship of ducks, too, is very striking. In some species the male and female swim around each other, dive, surface, shake their heads rapidly, immerse their bills in the water, jerk themselves erect, lift their wings, lay their necks outstretched on the water, etc. There are many stages to the courtship performance of ducks. At one stage of the goldeneye's courtship, the drake throws his head on his back, jerks it rapidly back and forth a number of times and often kicks up a spray of water with his feet. The courtship performance of the eider is also noteworthy. It usually takes place in the daytime, but often also on clear nights. The drake jerks his head up and down, then suddenly throws it on his back with bill pointing upward at an angle. Often he sprays water in front of him or on his back, preens his feathers and beats his wings against the water. Sometimes he also submerges. In group performances the males stage fights, often adopting threatening postures. During the courtship the duck stretches her neck out over the water (the females of many other species of ducks do this

18/ *Two male black grouse engaged in a 'duel'*

20/ *Various stages of the great crested grebe's courtship display*

21

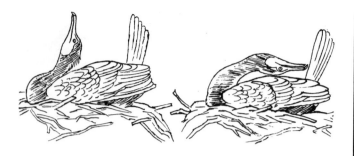

21/ Characteristic phases of the cormorant's courtship display

23/ Various stages of the goldeneye's courtship display

too). The courtship of divers is also interesting. The partners swim slowly side by side, rapidly jerk the tips of their bills in and out of the water, submerge for a moment, and then surface to preen their feathers. The partners then 'separate' with partly spread wings, raise themselves erect and run over the water's surface in a wide circle to the sound of loud cries. Often they also fly up and circle above the water.

An interesting sight is the courtship display of the ruff. The males or ruffs, whose nuptial plumage includes a broad ruff of feathers, wage symbolic duels during which they spread these coloured neck feathers wide. The male snipe flies high in the air during courtship and then swoops down with tail feathers outspread; the loud drumming sound which can be heard far away as he plummets downward is caused by the vibration of air through the outer tail feathers. Gulls,

too, have their characteristic courtship performance, during which the partners stand facing each other, raise their heads upwards, open their bills wide and utter loud calls, bow to each other, shift their weight from one foot to the other, etc. It is interesting to note that at first they sometimes adopt threatening postures. In general, however, the courtship of most birds consists of certain ritualistic performances such as preening, carrying nesting material, passing food, etc.

The Nesting Territory

Birds are not as carefree and independent as most people think. During the breeding season each pair of birds claims and defends a nesting ground or territory. These are specifically delimited areas, that can be compared to the garden or lot on which man builds his house, and their boundaries are generally respected by other birds. Soon after the whole area has been divided up into individual territories the boundaries become established and if some bird trespasses then it is usually ousted by the established owner.

Sometimes, however, a bird of the same species penetrates deep into the established territory and tries to take it over. In such a case the result is a fierce battle, as may be often seen in the case of blackbirds. Birds normally defend their territory only against others of the same species so as to assure enough food for their own family.

Single birds of other species may usually trespass without notice because they are not direct rivals. Even if they seek food on the same terri-

22/ Herons greeting each other during the courtship performance

tory they either collect food of a different kind or in other places. Song thrushes, for example, seek their food chiefly on the ground, tits on the branches of trees and tree creepers seek insects in the crevices of bark. All these birds, then, can live together without any conflict whatsoever.

Nesting territories vary in size, even amongst birds of the same species. The area may be determined by the abundance of food and the degree of competition for territories. In gardens territories tend to be smaller than those situated in woods. Small birds naturally have smaller nesting territories than larger species, e. g. woodpeckers, and those of large raptors can be very large indeed. The territory of small song-birds may extend outwards some forty to seventy metres from the nest; the nest need not be located in the exact centre of the territory, which is often of irregular shape, not round. The location of the nest depends on where the suitable sites are, particularly in the case of birds that nest in tree cavities or nest boxes.

Some birds, even songbirds, breed in colonies, siting their nests close together or immediately above one another, e. g. the house martin. In such cases the birds' nesting territory is so small that it is limited just to the nest and its immediate vicinity. These birds, however, are not in competition for food as they are excellent fliers and fly as much as several kilometres from the nest in search of food. Living in colonies has certain advantages, such as joint protection against enemies. Birds that form colonies include swifts, rooks, jackdaws as well as gulls,

25/ Oystercatchers in a group courtship display

terns, cormorants, auks and many other species. Some form mixed colonies, e. g. grey herons together with night herons, spoonbills or gulls together with terns.

How can birds tell if a certain territory is already occupied? Songbirds advertize ownership by song. The male often sings from some elevated post before he starts to build the nest, thus notifying other males of the same species that the place is taken. In the case of songbirds it is usually the male that seeks and occupies a territory, those of some species arriving from their winter quarters some days ahead of the females. The song in young, unpaired males has another purpose — namely of attracting a mate. At the same time it is also intended to serve the purpose of frightening off other males in the vicinity. A strong, healthy bird has a loud, rich song thus demonstrating his 'superiority' over the weaker individuals of his kind. It is typical that a weaker bird in the neighbourhood often falls silent as soon as a strong male commences his song.

Some birds, such as raptors, advertise their ownership of a territory with sharp cries, male cuckoos with their 'cuckoo' note, woodpeckers by drumming on a resonant tree with their bills.

24/ Courtship flight of the male snipe

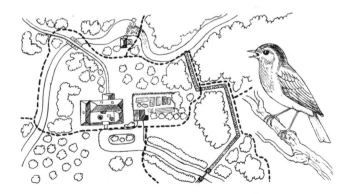

26/ Territories of individual male robins

27/ *Tree pipit's courtship flight*

Besides song most birds also produce other sounds typical for the given species. Most important of these is the call note, used by both sexes to communicate amongst themselves even out of the nesting season, when, as a rule, the males do not sing. In addition to this there are other sounds expressing fright or warning. All these various sounds are innate to the given species and produced even by young birds reared in captivity which have never heard the voices of their parents; in the case of song, however, the young of many species have to learn it from their elders. Some birds, such as the red-backed shrike, also mimic phrases from other species. The call note and sounds expressing fright or warning are signals to which other birds react.

The Nest

Prior to actual nesting the birds form pairs. Some species pair only during the courtship, after which each individual goes its own way, e. g. the cuckoo. In other species the partners remain together, some only for the duration of the nesting period, e. g. wrens, others for life, e. g. the greylag goose and mute swan. In such species if one of the partners dies the other often remains alone. Young birds, however, usually find themselves a new mate. In some species the birds form pairs already in their winter quarters or during migration.

Before nesting, birds usually build a new nest where the eggs are incubated and the young nestlings reared. Building a nest is an inherited trait and birds do not need to be taught how. Each species builds a particular type of nest which can generally be easily identified. Some, mostly songbirds, build very complex structures. Others, such as pigeons, build simple nests of only a few sticks. Woodpeckers hollow out cavities, whereas other birds seek out a ready-made cavity, e. g. starlings and most tits. In some species the nest is built by the female, and only on rare occasions by the male alone. In most species both partners share the task of construction, which in the case of small birds takes about a week and in the case of larger birds up to several weeks. Many birds build a new nest before every breeding season, others use the same nest for a number of years, adapting or adding to it every year, e. g. the white stork and white-tailed eagle. Birds dependent on water in one way or another often build their nests on or near it. Some, for instance grebes, build their nests directly on water, usually concealed in reeds and rushes. Most birds, even waterfowl, build their nests so that the eggs remain dry. Ducks build their nest on a dry foundation even though it may be situated above water, e. g. on bent and broken reeds. Ducks'

28/ *The European bee-eater excavates a nesting tunnel with its beak*

24

nests may also be located quite a distance from water and some species even lay their eggs in tree hollows, sometimes more than twenty metres above the ground, or in the old nests of raptors. Swans build their nests on bent reeds and also on islets, as does the greylag goose, which on rare occasions may also build its nest in a tree, e. g. in a pollarded willow, usually in locations where regular spring floods might damage nests on water. Herons and their allies normally build their nests in trees. Some species, however, sometimes nest in reed beds. The spoonbill also builds its nest on bent reeds, but sometimes also in thickets or even in tall trees. Some gulls build floating structures directly on water, but most species nest on small islets and rocks. Most waders build their nests, often only sparsely lined, on the ground. In some species the nest is merely a shallow depression or else the eggs are laid on bare ground or rock. Some species, e. g. the green sandpiper, lay their eggs in trees in the old nests of other birds. Brunnich's guillemot and the razorbill lay a single egg on bare rock, only sometimes placing a small stone or some grass stems round the egg. For this reason the eggs of these birds are pear-shaped so that they spin round rather than roll off the rock ledge. Striking nests of mud, sand and twigs are built in shallows by the flamingoes; these are tall structures up to half a metre in height. Many birds dig burrows in the ground, e. g. puffins, or in mud or sand banks, e. g. the sand martin, European bee-eater and kingfisher.

The Eggs

The colouring, shape and usually also the number of eggs laid are characteristic for the given species. Some species, however, show a marked variation in the colouring of the eggs. For example the eggs of gulls, terns and above all some birds of prey and auks show a great diversity of colour. Other species of birds, on the other hand, have eggs of a single colour. Birds nesting in cavities or those that cover their nests on leaving them, e. g. ducks, do not need their eggs to have cryptic colours. On the other hand, in the case of those species that lay them in the open and leave them uncovered the eggs are

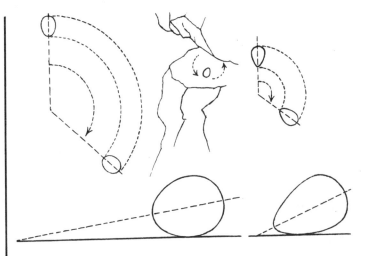

29/ *Pear-shaped alcid's egg rotates in a much smaller circle than eggs of most other birds*

spotted, streaked, speckled, and the like, to merge with their surroundings and escape the notice of enemies. For example, the eggs of the Kentish plover are practically impossible to spot amongst the surrounding pebbles. The same is true of the eggs of the other species of waders. Owls, storks and pelicans have pure white eggs. These, however, lose their whiteness during incubation, sometimes acquiring even a dark brown hue, such as the eggs of the black-necked grebe, which become stained by the damp decaying vegetation in the nest. The eggs of cormorants and pelicans become coated with a chalky layer during incubation.

Some birds lay a specific number of eggs that is usually constant. The avocet, curlew, lapwing and many other waders lay four eggs, the Kentish plover usually only three. In the case of gulls the full clutch contains three eggs, divers usually lay only two, as do pigeons. The gannet and razorbill lay only a single egg. Ducks, on the other hand, lay a great number of eggs, usually about ten, sometimes more. In some species the number of eggs laid depends on the abundance of food. Thus, the snowy owl generally lays four to six eggs; when food is scarce, however, it lays only about three or does not nest at all, whereas when lemmings, the owl's chief food, are plentiful, the clutch may contain ten to fifteen eggs. Thrushes lay about five eggs, but tits lay from six to fourteen, sometimes even more.

Some birds have only one brood a year, others two, e. g. tits. Still others, such as the house sparrow, and the collared turtle dove, may have several broods a year.

The size of the eggs of each species varies within certain limits that generally do not deviate much from the average.

How Birds Incubate

Many birds start incubating after the last egg has been laid, e. g. songbirds, ducks and gallinaceous birds. Some species, such as owls, however, begin incubating as soon as the first egg is laid and the young then hatch successively.

In some species of birds only the female incubates, e. g. ducks, geese and gallinaceous birds; in others the duties of incubation are shared by both partners, e. g. some songbirds, woodpeckers, pigeons, terns and gulls. Only in rare instances is this task performed solely by the male — of European birds the red-necked phalarope and the dotterel. Some birds, however, do not incubate their eggs themselves, either depositing them in the nests of other birds, e. g. the cuckoo (this is known as social parasitism), or burying them in mounds or in sand beside hot springs, e. g. the megapodes of Australia, the best known of which is the mallee fowl.

The length of the incubation period, i. e. the time when the birds sit on the eggs until they hatch, varies, depending chiefly on the size of the bird. In case of small birds it is from twelve to fifteen days, in larger birds it is about twenty days; ducks incubate about twenty-six days, geese twenty-eight days, auks about thirty-five days, gannets forty days, shearwaters and petrels even more than sixty days, and albatrosses as long as about eighty days.

The young peck their way out of the egg with the aid of the so-called 'egg-tooth', a projection on the upper mandible. It is used to cut away a small part of the egg shell. The 'tooth' disappears shortly after hatching.

Leaving the Nest for the World Outside

Birds are divided into two basic groups according to the degree of their development at birth. The young of the first group are independent at birth and follow their parents about within a few hours after hatching. They feed themselves immediately and the parents merely provide them with protection against enemies, cold, rain, etc. They also guide them to food, e. g. gallinaceous birds and ducks. The species belonging to this group are called nidifugous birds.

Birds of the second group are called nidicolous species and in the beginning their young are fully dependent on the care of the parents which provide them with food and feed them for a certain period of time. In many species the young are generally without feathers on hatching and the parents must also keep them warm, e. g. songbirds and cormorants. In other species, for instance in gulls, raptors and owls, the young are hatched with a thick coat of down which keeps the cold out.

As a rule the young of the nidicolous species are fed and cared for by both parents, but in the case of certain species, e. g. many raptors, the male hunts for the food and it is portioned and fed to the young by the female.

The young of nidicolous species demand food in various ways that urge the parents to greater activity. The most common method is by uttering loud cries. Another is visual; the young of many species have bright yellow gapes, coloured spots on the bills or brightly coloured warty protuberances. The third method is tactile — the young grasping at the beaks of the parents bringing them food, e. g. in herons. The adult birds of some species place the food directly into the beaks of their offspring; in other species, e. g. herons, the young take the food from their parents' beaks themselves, and still other species regurgitate partially digested food from the crop into the nestlings' beaks or else into the nest where the young pick it up. The parents also keep the nest clean. Many species remove the nestlings' droppings with their beaks and either throw them out or swallow them. The young of other birds drop their faeces over the edge of the nest or squirt it out, e. g. raptors. Only in some species do the droppings remain in the nest, the young birds sitting on top of the pile as it grows.

The time spent in the nest varies greatly. In the case of smaller songbirds it is usually twelve to twenty days, in larger birds about a month. The young of some large raptors, e. g. vultures, remain in the nest about a hundred days and those of certain species of albatrosses as long as 240 days. In some species the period is very short. For instance, in the case of the herring gull and common gull as well as other gulls the young may leave the nest after a few hours, scattering in the neighbourhood and concealing themselves whenever danger threatens; they may also swim.

A special group includes those birds that might be termed semi-nidifugous. Their young are capable of independent activity and run about, make their way through reeds and swim within a few hours of hatching. For the first few days, however, the parents bring them food, which the young take from their beaks. Rails are one such example. In some species of rails the fledglings of the first brood bring food to the offspring of the second brood. The young of these species begin to forage for food themselves — when only a few days old.

Birds nesting in colonies often place their nests very close to one another and there are a great number in a fairly small space. Such a colony, say of gulls, may have thousands. How, then, are the birds able to locate their own nest amidst so many? Experiments have proved that gulls and other birds find their nest according to its location, which they have firmly fixed in their memory. It was also discovered that as a rule the size and colouring of the eggs are of no importance. Gulls settled on their nests even when they contained pebbles or other, angular objects put there instead of their eggs. Most birds cannot tell the difference between their own eggs and artificial eggs placed in the nest.

How, then, are birds able to identify their offspring? Young gulls, for example, that scatter when danger threatens and stray into other gulls' territory are not only chased by the other gulls but also pecked on the head, sometimes even killed by them. The same is true of other species of colonial nesters. It was discovered, however, that for about five days following the hatching of

their own offspring gulls will also feed the young of other species, but after that no. The reason is that by that time the adult birds have learned to recognize the particular voices of their young even amongst the many similar nestlings in the area. Hearing plays an important role in a bird's life. Parents are able to distinguish almost perfectly the voices of their young, which can be heard while they are still inside the egg. Parents also react immediately to the voice of a strayed nestling, even though they do not see it, whereas when a hen, used in experiments for this purpose, saw that its chick was in danger but could not hear it she made no response whatsoever. Wild turkeys pecked their own offspring to death in experiments where they were deprived of their hearing and, on the other hand, unhesitatingly warmed a stuffed polecat, a known predator, in which a microphone emitting the cries of a turkey nestling had been installed. Other birds, too, respond to the voices of their progeny.

How the young recognize their parents is another question. Most nestlings do not learn to recognize their parents until some time after hatching. Ducklings, for example, learn to recognize their mother after eight to twenty hours. During this period the young birds impress the image and the voice of their parents on their memory and thereafter recognize them without fail. In some species of birds, for instance ducks, young drakes impress the likeness of the duck upon their memory not only as a mother but also as a female so that in the wild when the time comes, apart from the rare exception, they select a mate of their own kind. In captivity, on the other hand, where the young are often reared without parents, cross-breeding is quite common, even amongst non-related species.

Substituted Eggs

One unusual facet of the behaviour of birds is their habit of depositing their eggs in the nests of other species, a phenomenon known as social parasitism. After hatching the nestlings are raised by the foster parents often at the cost of their own young. In Europe the most typical example of the social parasite is the cuckoo. As a rule, the female cuckoo lays her eggs in the

30/   The cuckoo depositing its egg in a pipit's nest

nests of the species that she herself was reared by. The mere sight of a partially built nest arouses the laying instinct in the hen, but if there are few such nests in the territory, this instinct is suppressed. The female flies around looking for a suitable nest, preferably one which contains a clutch of eggs. As soon as she finds one she waits until the adult birds depart, then quickly lays her egg there, removing one or sometimes several of the foster parents' eggs. Frequently she lays her egg apart from the nest and puts it inside with her beak. The cuckoo generally lays from twelve to twenty-five eggs in one breeding season.

It has been found that cuckoos deposit their eggs in the nests of 162 different species of birds, though usually the choice is limited to some twenty species of small songsters. Cuckoo eggs are very small in proportion to the bird's body but have a much thicker shell than those of other birds. This is to prevent them from breaking when they are dropped from a fair height into the nest or cavity.

Birds that have been 'selected' by the cuckoo as foster parents for its young often cannot tolerate the cuckoo's presence in the vicinity of their nests and try to chase it away. If the cuckoo does manage to lay an egg in their nest many birds simply throw it out, while others abandon the nest and build a new one. Redstarts and some warblers simply cover the whole clutch, including the cuckoo's egg, with a new lining and lay a fresh batch of eggs. Not all birds behave like this; a full two-thirds hatch the eggs and rear the young cuckoos.

How some birds do and others do not recognize the danger posed to their species by the cuckoo's egg is something that still remains to be explained adequately.

The cuckoo nestling generally hatches sooner than or at the same time as the young of its foster parents since it has a very short incubation period. It is completely naked at birth and hatches with closed eyes. However, some ten to sixteen hours later it instinctively feels the need to remove from the nest anything which gets in its way. The skin of the young cuckoo's back is extremely sensitive to contact with foreign objects. It puts its head and neck under the object, spreads its feet wide and rests its head against the bottom of the nest. It then lifts the object onto its back, holding it in place with its stumpy wings, and pushes it towards the edge of the nest until the object tumbles out. The process continues until all the eggs or the young nestlings of the foster parents have been cast from the nest. This instinct remains active for three or four days. The young cuckoo thus remains the sole occupant of the nest and receives the foster parents' full attention. It consumes enough food for a whole family of small songbirds and grows very rapidly.

When it hatches the young cuckoo's cry resembles that of most songbird nestlings, and it is not till the fifth day that it changes to the typical cry of cuckoo nestlings demanding food. Because its gullet is a bright orange colour, its open beak stimulates the foster parents to hasten with the feeding. The cuckoo nestling remains in the nest for 20 to 23 days, after which it is fed by the foster parents for a further three to four weeks, in other words far longer than they would feed their own progeny.

What Food Birds Eat

Birds of various groups are excellently adapted for various means of obtaining food and many of them are food specialists.

Interesting is the way many woodpeckers obtain their food. With their strong beaks they chisel holes in the bark as well as wood of trees to get at the larvae of various beetles and other insects that live there. The woodpecker extricates its prey with its pointed, extensible tongue, supplied at the tip with tactile and taste buds in the form of recurved hooks, which make it easy for the bird to find its prey even deep inside a long corridor. Before boring a hole, however, it determines whether there is such a corridor in the wood by first drumming on the tree trunk; riddled wood apparently gives off a different sound than healthy wood. Some species, such as the green woodpecker, often drill deep tunnels in the ground to reach ants in their anthills, extricating them with their long tongue. When seeking food some woodpeckers proceed in a characteristic manner, climbing the tree in a spiral from the bottom up to a certain height and then flying to another tree.

Many insectivorous birds capture their prey, mostly flying insects, on the wing. These birds are generally the best fliers in the avian realm. One such is the common swift, which catches insects solely in the air. The house martin, common swallow and sand martin also feed on insects which they catch on the wing. Certain raptors, such as the red-footed falcon, and in many cases even some species of owls, capture flying insects in the air. As a rule the European bee-eater also captures insects in the air, overtaking even such rapid fliers as hornets, wasps and bees. Other birds that often catch insects in flight are the wagtails and flycatchers.

Thrushes seek their food mostly on the ground. A well-known example is the blackbird, which may be seen in parks and gardens waiting patiently for the appearance of an earthworm which it skilfully grasps and pulls out of the ground. The song thrush is noted for its habit of grasping the shells of various snails in its beak, taking them to a stone and striking them against it until they break. The common dipper, which is normally found along fast flowing rivers and streams, is interesting because of the manner in which it forages for food. It walks into the water and deliberately submerges or plunges straight in from the air or a stone, then expertly runs about on the bottom feeding on aquatic insects, often using its wings to help propel itself along. This species also has strong claws which enables it to hold on to the larger stones and prevent it from being carried away in the strong current.

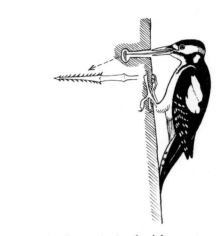

31/ *The great spotted woodpecker extricating food from a tree trunk*

During the winter season many insect-eating birds feed on various seeds and kernels which they must extract from hard pips. Examples are the hawfinch, which can split even cherry stones with its strong beak, and the nutcracker, which can crack tough hazelnuts.

Owls mostly hunt small rodents on the ground, but occasionally also bats, and some even capture small birds on the wing, though they generally take them unawares at night when they are roosting.

European raptors feed almost exclusively on animal food, apart from the few exceptions such as the honey buzzard, which also likes to eat soft fruits. The methods by which raptors obtain their food, however, are many and varied. Some members of the family Falconidae hunt their prey mainly in the air, e. g. the peregrine falcon

32/ *Pattern of the black woodpecker's movements as it forages for food*

29

33/ A snowy owl attacking its prey

and hobby. The buzzard hunts it on the ground. The goshawk as well as other species of raptors capture mostly birds on the wing. Vultures are partial to carrion from which they tear pieces of flesh and innards. A real specialist is the osprey, which hovers above the water in a single spot on sighting its prey, then plunges down after it, catching its prey with its long, curved opposite-facing claws, sinking them into the victim's flesh. It catches fish weighing as much as two kilograms, which it then carries to a tree or post to eat. The black kite, on the other hand, skilfully gathers dead fish floating on the water's surface, as well as other vertebrates and their remnants.

Many species of birds are fish-eaters. Fish form the mainstay of the auks' or murres' diet. Puffins hunt mostly small herrings, often carrying ten or twelve in their beaks at a time. People have long wondered how a puffin can hold so many fish without any slipping from its grasp as it takes up another. The explanation is simple — the fish's head is held fast between the tongue and edge of the bill thus enabling the bird to open its bill and catch further fish without any trouble. The puffin pursues its prey under water, propelling itself with both wings and feet at such speeds that few fish escape. It also eats various molluscs and crustaceans.

The black guillemot *(Cepphus grylle)* also propels itself under water with the aid of its wings. The razorbill, too, hunts mostly fish, especially herrings in search of which it flies as far as thirty kilometres from its nesting site. It can also hold several fish in its bill at a time.

Auks likewise hunt small fish, molluscs, crustaceans as well as sea worms underwater. Fish comprise fifty to eighty percent of their diet.

Albatrosses, shearwaters and petrels likewise feed in great part on fish, crustaceans, molluscs and other sea animals which they capture mostly on the surface. They often fly in the wake of ocean-going liners waiting for refuse to be thrown overboard. Some species also feed on dead animals cast up on the shore by the tide. Some species even capture various small birds.

Gannets feed almost solely on fish. With their wings pressed close to the body they plummet in a steep dive from heights of twenty to thirty metres into the water in pursuit of their prey. Sometimes they dive to remarkable depths, as great as thirty metres. Usually, however, they hunt fish only several metres below the surface.

Pelicans, too, feed mainly on fish and are very well equipped for fishing in strength. When fishing, a flock of pelicans forms a semi-circle and advances towards the shore, the birds beating the water with their wings and stabbing at it now and then with their long bills. The fish are thus driven into the shallows where the birds scoop them up with their beaks into their distensible pouches. Some species, such as the brown pelican *(Pelecanus occidentalis),* cruise in circles above the water seeking their prey. On sighting a fish near the surface they abruptly press their

34/ An osprey about to grasp a fish

35/ *The black guillemot swims underwater with outspread wings*

wings to the body and plunge downwards, often submerging completely for a few seconds.

Cormorants, too, are expert fishers, which can dive to great depths. It was found that they hunt at depths of as much as thirty metres. Having caught their prey they swim to the surface before swallowing it. The cormorants' insatiable appetite was put to good use by fishermen in China and Japan. A common technique was to tie around the base of the bird's neck a thong attached to a long tether which the fisherman held in his hand. When the cormorant surfaced after diving for fish the thong was pulled tight to prevent it from swallowing the catch and the fisherman then took the fish from it. The usual method was to fish from a boat with a team of about twelve trained birds, one man tending four cormorants.

Most terns likewise feed on small fish, which the birds catch primarily near the surface, though some may submerge for a few seconds. Some species of terns, mainly the ones known as marsh terns, capture insects on the wing.

Herons, too, feed largely on fish, standing in a single spot in the shallows or else wading slowly through the water while keeping a sharp lookout. As soon as a fish comes close the heron makes a swift thrust with its pointed beak and spears its prey. The swift thrust is aided by the S-shaped neck. The same method is also used to catch other small vertebrates and even insects. Storks are partial to frogs, which they hunt in shallows; they also catch small fish, and other small vertebrates and various insects.

Members of the Anatidae family, e. g. geese, have notches on the edges of the bills which are useful for nipping off grass and aquatic plants. Geese and swans, however, are not solely vegetarians and occasionally will also eat insects, swans even eat small vertebrates. Some geese, e. g. the emperor goose *(Anser canagicus)* eat mostly animal food — various molluscs which they find on the shore.

The kingfisher, too, feeds primarily on small fish. The bird frequently dives with such force that it disappears under water. Grasping the prey in its beak, it then flies up onto a branch to swallow it. The kingfisher often hovers motionless in a single spot above the water on sighting prey.

Skuas obtain their food in a striking manner. They harass gulls and terns until they regurgitate their catch, which the skuas skilfully retrieve in the air and then eat. However, they also feed on small vertebrates and insects as well as the eggs of other birds.

Large gulls eat mostly animal food. Some species often eat vegetable food as well, chiefly various soft fruits.

The methods whereby some waders obtain their food are quite interesting. The avocet wades in shallows, stamping its feet on the sandy or muddy bottom and stirring up countless aquatic invertebrates, which it collects with its upcurved bill.

Also specially adapted is the powerful bill of the oystercatcher, which is used to open mussels and clams or chisel limpets off rocks.

36/ *Terns fishing*

Rails gather food on the water's surface or in reeds, their diet consisting of insects, molluscs, spiders as well as small seeds and bits of green plants.

Why do We Protect Birds?

Many species of birds are becoming increasingly rare from year to year. In some cases man's greed has been responsible for their total extermination. One such example is the great auk. In the eighteenth and nineteenth centuries it still nested in fair abundance in Iceland, on the coasts of Ireland, Scotland and Newfoundland, in the Hebrides and Faroes, on the coasts of Denmark, southern Sweden, Norway, Greenland and the eastern coast of North America. In the eighteenth century its eggs were still being collected in large numbers so that by the end of the century it had completely disappeared in many places. Hunters took not only eggs but killed even adult birds for their feathers, meat and fat, which they sold. Nowadays this sea bird is a thing of the past and stuffed specimens may be seen only in a few museums; there are only seventy-four known specimens in museum collections throughout the world.

The great auk, however, was not the only bird that became extinct as a species. The same fate met the Labrador duck, which nested in Labrador and on rocky islands round the Gulf of St Lawrence and wintered in the area stretching from the coast of Nova Scotia to New Jersey. Its history is very brief. It was first discovered by scientists in the year 1788. Thirty years later the land was settled by man and the islands where the birds nested were visited by large numbers of hunters who shot the birds and took the eggs from the nests, selling them on the market in New York. The Labrador duck thus rapidly disappeared from its haunts, the last specimen being shot in the year 1875 near Long Island. Today there are only forty-two stuffed speci-

mens in museum collections and not one egg survived.

Several other birds have become extinct, including the spectacled cormorant, which at one time nested in large numbers in the Komandorski Islands, and many other species have survived only thanks to timely protective measures.

In the first half of the twentieth century the number of guillemots in Labrador, on the coasts of Norway, Sweden, Iceland, Greenland and other places declined alarmingly. Other auks, too, were killed for their meat and eggs, which were gathered in large numbers. In some breeding grounds, e. g. in Labrador and Heligoland, the puffin has disappeared altogether. In the past puffins were killed for their tasty meat, which according to experts was as good as that of the partridge. Even though in many places these birds are now protected, in others they continue to be hunted even to this day. They are caught in flight nets attached to long poles. Today, thanks to protective measures, the puffin breeds again in greater numbers on the coasts of Norway,

37/ *The great auk — now extinct*

Iceland, Greenland, Great Britain, the western coast of France and eastern coast of North America. It forms colonies containing several hundreds to thousands of paired birds. Some 50,000 pairs nest on Vedoy Island, whereas the colonies on the coast of Greenland number only several hundred birds. Largest are the colonies in Iceland and the Faroes, where some 2.5 million birds nest, as well as in Great Britain, where they number two million all told. The entire world population is now estimated at fifteen million and in view of the fact that many breeding grounds are now reserves you would think that its survival was assured, but it would be far from the truth. The accidental introduction of predators such as rats to its breeding islands and chemical or oil pollution at sea could soon reduce its numbers.

Guillemots and razorbills were also killed in large numbers in the past and thus in danger of becoming extinct. Greatest damage was caused through the gathering of their eggs. In Iceland, in the year 1913, more than 110,000 guillemots and razorbills were captured in addition to a quarter million puffins, in 1923 some 50,000 and in ensuing years, when their numbers had been greatly decimated, only 9,000. In Greenland some 20,000 Brunnich's guillemots were still captured yearly at the beginning of the twentieth century. In the Faroes half a million guillemots' eggs were gathered within a period of six weeks in the year 1945. In Novaya Zemlya no less than three million eggs and some half a million auks were captured from 1930 to 1950. In 1932 and 1933 the meat and eggs of auks comprised more than thirty percent of Novaya Zemlya's entire production. It is estimated that until recently some ten million eggs of the guillemot and one million eggs of Brunnich's guillemot were gathered yearly. The number of eggs of other European birds, e. g. gulls and terns, also totalled hundreds of thousands. Adult guillemots and razorbills were captured by hunters in snares (and still are in some places). Their meat was dried and, in Iceland, even fed to dogs. The meat does not smell of fish and is considered a delicacy by the natives. Their skins are used by Eskimoes for making outer garments. Fresh sea bird eggs are still considered an important food to this day. In some places it is still permitted to collect eggs, but only those of the

38/ *The Labrador duck — now extinct*

first clutch; the second clutch is protected by law. Birds will lay a second clutch within fifteen to twenty days. In northerly regions, however, conditions are not as conducive to rearing the young of the second clutch. Besides, eggs may be collected in this manner only in such nesting grounds as are not visited by foxes, which destroy not only the eggs but kill young nestlings as well. If provided with full protection a colony of birds has a potential increase of only about ten percent a year, but if only the second clutch is protected by law then at most the colony retains its status quo unless its numbers are depleted by other circumstances such as natural enemies, bad weather and the like.

One bright spot in the overall picture is that these endangered birds are rigidly protected in wildlife reserves and their populations are gradually increasing in number. Countries that provide protection for sea birds include first and foremost Sweden, Norway, Great Britain, the U.S.S.R., German Federal Republic and certain other European maritime nations.

Somewhat better off was the eider. Even though its eggs were gathered in some places it was protected in general. However, this was not primarily for conservationist but for mercenary reasons, because the soft down which the duck plucks from her breast to line the nest is a lucrative item of commerce. Fresh down that has not become soiled is the most valuable. When the down is taken from the nest the duck plucks out further down to replace it, usually after she has begun incubating. This down, however, is of lesser value for it is generally soiled. In order to provide eiders with more opportunities for nesting down collectors in many places construct hollows of stones or place tree trunks on the shore underneath which eiders are fond of building their nests. The eiders are disturbed by no one here apart from the collectors and they have therefore no fear of man. Eiders are very plentiful in some protected areas. Paired birds build their nests close beside each other thus forming whole colonies. A single nest generally contains about fifteen grams, occasionally as much as thirty to thirty-five grams, of eiderdown. Only the occasional nest is without any down lining. The incubating instinct in eiders is so strong that many young unpaired females seek out the clutches of other birds, often abandoned, and incubate them themselves. A single collector can gather about two kilograms of down a day. The greatest supply of eiderdown comes from Iceland where it was already harvested centuries ago and where, according to records, eiders were protected in some places from as early as 1281. Since 1702 eiders throughout the whole of Iceland have been protected by law and killing just a single bird was punished by a heavy jail sentence. In 1805 Iceland sold 1,072 kilograms of eiderdown and in 1916 even 4,355 kilograms, which is the equivalent of down from more than 220,000 nests. This number represents practically half of all the nests of the Iceland population, which is estimated at about half a million.

Eiderdown has also been gathered for almost a thousand years on the coast of Norway. The eider is now protected in that country. There are about 200,000 eiders in Norway, 100,000 in Finland, 10,000 on the coasts of Great Britain, and over 4,000 in Denmark. The total European population numbers about one million birds and the world population is an estimated two million.

Many other waterfowl, notably geese, are far

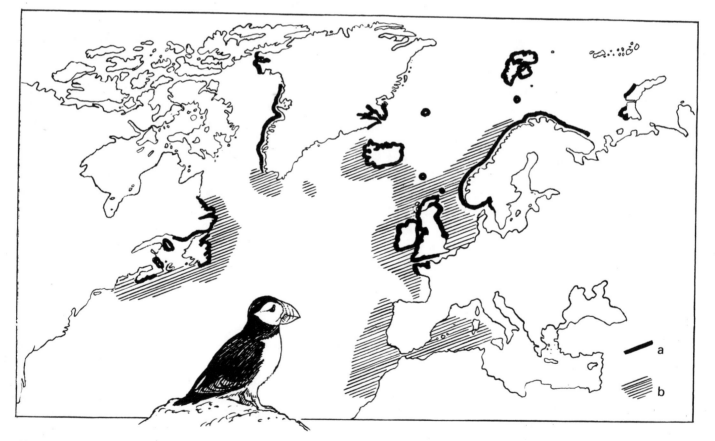

39/ *Distribution of the puffin*

worse off and some species have to be strictly protected not only during the breeding season but also in their wintering grounds, which are far from their nesting grounds in totally different countries. One such is the red-breasted goose *(Branta ruficollis)*, which breeds in the northern parts of central Siberia, flying off to the southern shores of the Caspian Sea for the winter. In the past this goose was greatly hunted but at present it is strictly protected by law, for the entire population numbers an estimated 40,000 birds. Stragglers occasionally go as far south as Egypt where they may once have been common as they are represented on ancient tombs.

The barnacle goose *(Branta leucopsis)* is not much better off. It is found in the northern part of the Atlantic and winters on the coasts of western Europe. From Greenland it also journeys to the eastern coast of North America. The number of all birds is an estimated 30,000.

The brent goose *(Branta bernicla)* breeds in the arctic tundras of Europe, Asia and North America. Its numbers, however, have also declined markedly during the past few decades. In 1931 an average of 10,000 birds wintered in Holland but in 1953 only 1,000. In Denmark their numbers declined from 7,000 to 2,000. At the beginning of this century some 350,000 of these birds wintered in Europe, whereas by the 1950s there were only 20,000. Although in Britain their numbers have risen again in recent years, the American populations comprise ninety percent of all existing brent geese, their estimated number being 175,000, which is not very much.

Other species of geese have also declined markedly in number compared with past years. The white-fronted goose *(Anser albifrons)* of northern Europe, Asia and North America, winters in western and southern Europe, Asia Minor, northern India, eastern China, Japan and on the Atlantic coast of North America. Holland is nowadays host to some 50,000 of these geese in winter, England to some 7,000. The estimated

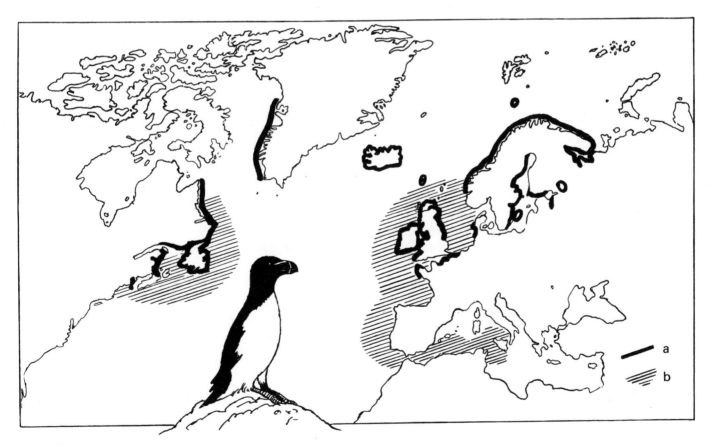

a

b

40/ Distribution of the razorbill

35

number of white-fronted geese in the whole world is half a million.

Much rarer is the lesser white-fronted goose *(Anser erythropus),* which has an estimated world population of 100,000. It breeds in the tundras of Europe and Asia and winters in western Europe, Asia Minor, south of the Caspian Sea as well as in the Nile region.

The bean goose *(Anser fabalis)* has likewise become less plentiful in recent years. Its breeding grounds are the arctic regions of Europe and Asia and the coasts of Greenland. In Europe it winters in the western and southern parts. In some places it is still quite plentiful, e. g. in Iceland there are an estimated 50,000 of these birds at present.

Today it seems that the large numbers of snow geese *(Anser caerulescens)* have increased somewhat even though they have not yet reached their previous levels. The snow goose breeds mainly on the arctic coasts of North America, to a lesser degree on the coasts of southwestern Greenland and on Wrangel Island. In the mid-eighteenth century it was still plentiful in the tundras of Siberia but by the beginning of the nineteenth century it disappeared, though no one knows exactly why. In former years it also wintered in great numbers in Japan, but by the middle of this century was also nonexistent there. Doubtlessly, one of the reasons was the shooting of these birds during the moulting period when they are unable to fly. The snow goose breeds mainly along the coast in places that are accessible. Eskimoes killed hundreds and even thousands of these birds during the moulting period besides also taking their eggs. The greater part of the Siberian population wintered in southwestern North America, where birds that breed on Wrangel Island still winter to this day. In the 1840s the wintering grounds were visited by many hunters from Europe and the eastern United States, a hundred geese being killed in one day by a single hunter. Nowadays, the snow goose is only found in greater numbers in Asia on Wrangel Island, but in recent years, thanks to the protection of birds in general, it is becoming more plentiful in its former breeding grounds in Siberia, where its numbers are increasing every year. The greatest number of snow geese breed in arctic Canada, where the population is estimated at 50,000 birds.

41/ *The rare barnacle goose*

One of the sea birds that has again become more plentiful thanks to conservation measures is the gannet *(Sula bassana).* Its numbers had been rapidly declining because the eggs, and also the young birds, were being taken from the nest. The number of gannets in 1834 was an estimated 330,000 whereas by the end of the century it was a mere 60,000. Most of the birds were killed in the years 1880 to 1910, when fishermen raided the nesting grounds of the gannet — their 'competitor' for the herring catch. Some gannet colonies were entirely destroyed. Not only were eggs and young birds taken from the nest but also the feathers lining the nest. The Iceland colonies numbered some 4,000 gannets. These were killed by fishermen also on the open sea. In Iceland they had been hunted since the thirteenth century. As of 1940, however, the gannet is strictly protected on certain islands off Iceland and Norway and so their numbers have increased somewhat in recent years, the same as in the protected colonies in the British Isles.

Birds of prey have also suffered a marked decline. Europe is the home of some forty species of raptors, but most of them are extremely rare species. Man is responsible for the almost total disappearance in Europe of the lammergeyer or bearded vulture *(Gypaetus barbatus).* At one time this handsome raptor was a regular nester in the German Alps; the last specimen living there was shot in 1855. Up to 1866 the bearded vulture also nested in the Swiss Alps, but it was not seen again until 1955, almost a hundred years later, when it showed up in the Salzkammergut in Austria. Records of its nesting in the Carpathians date from as late as 1935, but there have been none since.

Members of the falcon tribe, apart from the Eurasian kestrel and red-footed falcon which is widespread in southeastern Europe, are also increasingly rare birds nowadays. The peregrine falcon *(Falco peregrinus)*, though widespread throughout Europe, is a rare species. It was often hunted mercilessly to prevent it from killing off domestic pigeons and its former nesting grounds were greatly depleted. It is true that the peregrine hunts birds, but mostly pigeons, starlings, magpies, crows and rooks, which have greatly increased in number recently because of the absence of natural enemies. Furthermore, when falcons migrate they feast on pigeons which have reverted to the wild state and which are found in abundance in large cities. In view of the fact that in recent years the peregrine has not nested at all in many European countries where it formerly did so, it is most urgent that it should be protected by all possible means. The greatest threat at present is the removal of eggs and young birds from the nest by egg collectors and falconers.

Long past are the days when the saker falcon *(Falco cherrug)*, one of the largest of the family, used to nest in central Europe. Today it occurs only in eastern Europe with any regularity. The disappearance of the saker falcon from central Europe in the nineteenth century was caused primarily by collectors, who shot adult birds for ornithological exhibits, and by those who took eggs from their nests.

The gyrfalcon *(Falco rusticolus)*, one of the handsomest of the family, is likewise extremely rare nowadays and is strictly protected in its breeding grounds in the far north of Europe and in Greenland.

The hobby *(Falco subbuteo)*, though small and harmless to game birds as it feeds mostly on small birds and insects, was mercilessly killed by hunters and in many places exterminated completely. It, too, should be rigidly protected.

The treatment of some birds of prey like the goshawk is a subject of dispute between conservation groups and gamekeepers. It is true that the goshawk preys mostly on birds (they comprise about ninety percent of its diet), but these are mainly corvine birds which cause much damage to small songsters and game birds. Naturally, the goshawk's victims also include useful birds as well as game birds and domestic pigeons. However, it nevertheless deserves to be protected. Experience has shown that wherever it has been exterminated jays, crows and magpies have multiplied in such numbers that they have caused far greater damage to wildlife than that wreaked by several goshawk families. Furthermore, the goshawk in the main is a resident bird and its young remain in the vicinity of their home base, usually settling within sixty kilometres of the nest. This makes it possible to keep a check on the goshawk population in a given territory.

42/ *Family of lesser white-fronted geese afloat on the water taking a swim*

43/ *The lammergeyer (bearded vulture) — a fast disappearing species*

The sparrowhawk, one of the most common of small raptors, likewise catches many small birds; at the head of the list, however, is the house sparrow, a generally acknowledged pest. Although its victims also include many other birds, like the goshawk it plays an important role in the regulation of ecological balance.

Absolute protection throughout the year should be afforded to the common buzzard, still common throughout most of Europe, because it feeds chiefly on voles, mice and other harmful rodents, as well as on insects. Detailed analyses of the stomach contents of buzzards have revealed that mice and voles comprise a full ninety-six percent of their diet; four percent consisted of wild game, mostly birds that were weakened or diseased.

The rapid disappearance of eagles, harriers, kites, vultures and other kinds of European raptors indicate an indisputable need to protect and preserve the species.

Owls, too, of which there are fourteen species in Europe, should be given protection throughout the year. The Eurasian eagle owl *(Bubo bubo),* largest of the European species, is one of a number of owls that were almost on the brink of extinction in Europe and which now, thanks

to stricter rules governing their protection, have again increased in number. Even though its victims are sometimes a young hare, pheasant or wild duck, the greater part of the eagle owl's diet is made up of voles and mice, thus making it a useful bird.

Unlike raptors which first pluck their victims clean and then tear off pieces of flesh, owls swallow large pieces or entire small animals. The indigestible parts — feathers, hairs, and hard insect covers — are regurgitated in solid lumps that look as if they have been pressed. If these are carefully separated they will be found to contain entire skulls of voles and mice and the elytra of beetles. This makes it possible to determine not only the quantity but also the kind of food consumed by the owl. Analyses of these have revealed that the diet of the tawny owl, one of the most common of European owls, consists mainly of voles and mice. In the case of some individual owls, birds make up about fourteen percent of the diet; of this half are sparrows and the other half is made up of finches, warblers, starlings and blackbirds, in other words birds which are normally found in abundance. If cockchafers are in large supply a great part of the owls' food will be made up of these harmful beetles.

Another common species, the long-eared owl, feeds largely on small rodents, especially in years when there is an overpopulation of voles

44/ *The black kite — a rare bird in central Europe*

insects make up a large proportion, but the little owl also hunts to a lesser extent shrews and small birds, mainly starlings, followed by house sparrows, blackbirds and thrushes, i. e. birds that are very plentiful.

The above four species of owls are fairly common in Europe. Other types are rare and therefore should be afforded exceptional protection.

Mortal Threat to Birds — Oil!

A great threat to sea birds has loomed in recent years, one that threatens even strictly protected birds and entire colonies. Oil. Every year oil tankers are damaged at sea, mostly near the coast. In January 1953, for instance, an unknown tanker spilled five hundred tons of oil into the sea between Heiligenhafen and the island of Fehrmarne off the northeastern coast of Germany. Thousands of sea birds winter here at

45/ The little owl on the hunt

or mice. Otherwise, the chief food is again the house sparrow, almost sixty-seven percent of this more or less harmful bird, followed by the finches, tree sparrow and blackbird. Only in rare instances was the food consumed found to contain a partridge. When cockchafers are in abundance these also represent a major part of the long-eared owl's diet, being fed also to the young.

In the case of the barn owl voles and mice average about sixty-nine percent of the diet, shrews twenty-five percent, birds only three percent, and bats, reptiles and amphibians make up most of the remainder. In years of 'mouse' overpopulation their share in this owl's diet has been recorded as being as high as 95.7 percent. It is interesting to note that when mice are in great abundance the barn owl regularly has two broods a year.

The little owl also feeds mainly on voles and mice, which together comprise about twenty-six percent and occasionally as much as a hundred percent of the bird's diet. In the summer months

46/ The rare Eurasian eagle owl

this time of the year, mostly eiders, mergansers, other species of ducks as well as divers. The outcome was that thousands of these birds died.

In December 1955 a like catastrophe occurred in the same area causing the death of five thousand wintering eiders. A similar disaster occurred on 19 January 1955 near the North Frisian Islands when a Danish tanker spilled eight thousand tons of oil that spread over 1,600 square kilometres of water. The results were catastrophic. Some half a million various sea birds died in the oil slick, not to mention the countless fish. In January 1960 five thousand sea birds died off the coast of the Swedish island of Gotland after coming in contact with oil. In recent years there have been many more such disasters off the coasts of western Europe and Great Britain. Hundreds of thousands of sea birds lost their lives. In some places hundreds of conservationists have come to the aid of the afflicted birds but the results have been far from rewarding. Despite all their efforts they succeeded in saving only several hundred. The feathers of birds that come in contact with oil lose their compactness and water-shedding properties, the birds become chilled, lose the power of flight, are unable to hunt for food and the oil furthermore enters their digestive tracts through preening, the result being slow but certain death. Spilled oil furthermore fouls shores and beaches.

Visitors complain that they cannot bathe and hotel managements are faced with a loss in income. The most terrible thing, however, is the slow death suffered by thousands of birds which are damaged by oil.

Problems Caused by Certain Sea Birds

On many islands where birds were strictly protected in wildlife reserves, certain species began to multiply rapidly. This was true particularly of various species of gulls. Thus, for example, on the island of Walney off the northwest coast of England, there were only 120 pairs of herring gulls in 1947 and today there are some 17,000 pairs. Another colony, on the Isle of May off Scotland's east coast, started with only several pairs of herring gulls in 1907, in 1936 455 pairs

of birds nested there, in 1954 3,000 pairs, in 1967 some 11,000 pairs and today more than 15,000 pairs. Until recently the herring gull was protected throughout the whole year also on the coasts of Germany and other European maritime countries. In the German Federal Republic and Denmark, however, it multiplied considerably. The same thing happened on the islands of Memmert, Mellum and Langeoog where about 3,000 pairs of birds nested in 1906 but by the 1930s this number had grown to 30,000 pairs. Herring gulls on these islands made it impossible for other species of birds to nest there. The same thing happened in the islands of the North Sea. Here the herring gull had practically no natural enemies, what with the decline in the number of raptors. However, even on the neighbouring islands, which were breeding grounds of terns, ducks and other birds, these species were unable to rear their young successfully for the herring gulls flew there and robbed their nests of eggs and nestlings as well. For this reason it is now permitted to kill this gull in the German Federal Republic between 1 August and 31 March and collect its eggs until 15 June. In recent years, however, the herring gull has also settled on the Baltic coast where it previously nested only rarely. Today the coast teems with thousands of pairs of these gulls. They have also begun to multiply in large numbers on the coast of southern Sweden, where they cause great damage to the nests of ducks and other birds. Thus, conservationists here are also considering regulating their number by collecting their eggs.

The great black-backed gull, which until recently was a rare nester on Europe's shores, has also begun to multiply rapidly as a result of protective measures. In England and Wales its numbers were very low, no more than 1,200 pairs nesting there in 1930. Today, however, the number has risen to more than 2,200 pairs. It has shown the same rapid increase on the eastern coast of the United States, where it nested for the first time in 1916. This large gull feeds mostly on the eggs and young of other sea birds and gulls, fish remnants, fish and mammal carrion, young and sick rabbits, also refuse and scraps. An overpopulation of these gulls on some offshore islands may entirely decimate the other sea bird populations. In places where terns nest they comprise as much as fifty percent of the gulls' diet. In one colony of avocets nesting on the English island of Havergate, a bird sanctuary belonging to the Royal Society for the Protection of Birds, great black-backed gulls were responsible for killing practically all the young one year.

In the Camargue in southern France, narcotics were added to bait used to control the gulls and in some places in Holland bait was poisoned with strychnine, but this is a very dangerous method because poison baits, alas, do not discriminate amongst the victims and thus many other species of birds have been killed by them as well. There is also the danger of other carrion feeders eating the dead gulls. Another method that has been tried is the use of a sterilization drug.

In recent years it has also become necessary to reduce the number of common gulls on certain offshore islands as they, too, have been causing much damage to other birds, primarily by robbing their nests of eggs and young nestlings.

Certain species of gulls that have settled in coastal towns, e. g. the black-legged kittiwake, are also proving troublesome because they nest on buildings and their droppings cause unsightly damage.

These problems caused by certain sea birds show how disastrous can be the results when the ecological balance is disturbed. First and foremost is the absence of raptors that serve to regulate the numbers of sea birds. Their protection (which is discussed elsewhere in this book) is therefore one of man's foremost obligations.

Practical Protection of Birds

Many useful birds, mainly insectivorous species, are declining in number every year. They build their nests in dense thickets where they forage for food. Their homes in the undergrowth of hedgerows, alongside paths and on the margins of woods are often destroyed and they are deprived of their habitat. Many are unable to adapt themselves to the new conditions and are abandoning their homes. The shrike has an inborn instinct to build its nest in thorny thickets in open country and cannot live, for instance, in a spruce wood, nor will it build its nest on the ground in a field, like the lark. Individual pairs of nesting birds cannot squeeze into the remaining suitable localities for each pair requires a specific space for nesting and this cannot be continually decreased.

The only remaining way to preserve birds in their original homes is to plant trees and thickets on such land as cannot be used for agricultural purposes — on slopes bordering roads, in abandoned quarries, alongside brooks and field boundaries. Not only will many birds build their nests here but these places will also provide shelter for hares, deer and other small wild game. Best suited for the purpose are shrubs that bear edible fruits or berries, especially in the autumn and winter, providing a source of food for birds at this time, e. g. hawthorn, snowberry, blackthorn, privet, cornel cherry, elderberry, sweetbriar and dogwood, and trees such as mountain ash, birch and alder. Field boundaries should also include several small oaks, lime trees, pines, and spruces in whose thick branches many birds build their nests. Naturally, the planting of field boundaries is not primarily an individual concern but the responsibility of nature conservationists and local authorities.

Nevertheless, even the individual can contribute to the protection of birds nesting in thickets, mainly by planting green hedges around the edges of gardens and parks. The best hedges are hawthorn, hornbeam, common maple, privet and dogwood. Green hedges may be planted even close to a house; small birds are generally not disturbed by the presence of man and can coexist. It is important, however, to trim the hedges every autumn, for this makes them thicker. Single trees and shrubs in gardens will also attract many birds. Particularly suitable for this purpose are ornamental spruce trees with close-set branches as well as various juniper trees. Warblers are often quite satisfied with thick gooseberry bushes. The small birds which are thus provided with a shelter will reward us by destroying troublesome and harmful insects.

Widely varied species of birds seek the sanctuary of parks and large gardens thickly set with ornamental shrubs and old shade trees as well as conifers. Even woodland birds sometimes make their homes there for the environment is similar to their native habitat and affords countless opportunities for nesting. Owls, too, may be found there as well as cuckoos. This is one of the principal reasons why such oases of greenery in the heart of large cities should be cherished.

Special note should be taken of birds nesting in cavities. Natural cavities are to be found chiefly in old trees, which are often cut down nowadays, thus depriving the birds of nesting opportunities. Some seek substitutes as a hole in a hollow tree stump or pile of stones, but the clutch is vulnerable to attacks by small predators and stray cats.

Tits are typical tree cavity nesters in parks and gardens. They play an important role in the biology of life in the wild, being among the best eradicators of harmful insects. Simple acts such as putting up a nest box and food out during the winter months can help increase their number to such an extent that they will help keep the insect population within reasonable limits. Nest boxes especially attract the great tit and blue tit to the garden. Any box will do, whether made by hollowing out a tree trunk or by nailing together a few boards. The former resembles a natural cavity for only the roof is made of wood and fashioned so that it can be opened by tilting up or sliding out to make cleaning easier. However, it requires a bit of work and it is liable to crack in the second year if the trunk does not happen to be sufficiently dry. On the other hand, nest boxes of wood are very easy to make and can be constructed of inferior wood. The boards should be placed close together without any cracks in between and the bottom should be fitted between the walls to prevent the entry of water during a downpour. Two or three small holes should be bored in the bottom, however, to allow any water that might have penetrated to run out. The roof should be either removable or fastened with hinges so that it can be opened.

The entrance hole should be located in the upper third of the box wall, best of all in the centre, though it may just as easily be made in the corner. A natural entrance hole is always circular, but many birds have no objection to a square one. A perch should not be put in front of the hole for it not only hampers the bird's entrance (it flies straight into the hole), but also makes it easier for pests to get in.

Nest boxes should not be nailed directly to a tree branch but onto a baseboard that may be attached front to back or even from the side. Some boxes may also be suspended from a branch.

The best kind of box for a blue tit or other small bird measures twelve centimetres square and twenty centimetres high with an entrance hole twenty-six millimetres in diameter, hung 1.5 to five metres above the ground. There is no danger of its being usurped by a house sparrow for the latter cannot squeeze through such a small opening.

For the great tit the nest box should be the same size, though it may be five centimetres higher, but with an entrance hole thirty-two to thirty-five millimetres across. Other tits, the collared flycatcher, pied flycatcher and sometimes even a European redstart or black redstart may nest there. In gardens sparrows will readily use such a comfortable refuge. The great tit, however, is not put off by such an intruder and will chase out the sparrow, throw out its nest and build one of its own.

Nest boxes fifteen centimetres square and twenty-eight to thirty-five centimetres high with an entrance hole fifty millimetres across are favoured by the starling, but may be used also by the nuthatch and sometimes even the great spotted woodpecker. Woodpeckers, however, often chip the opening with their strong bills and thus sometimes wreck the box. For that reason in neighbourhoods where woodpeckers are plentiful it is worth nailing a piece of plywood with a hole of the same size on the outside. These

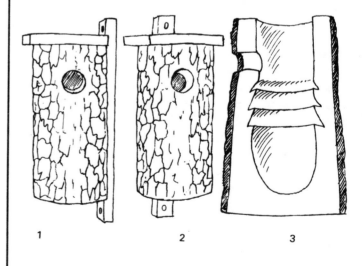

1   2   3

47/ 1, 2 Nest boxes, 3 section

boxes should be hung three to eight metres above the ground.

The largest nest boxes are twenty to thirty centimetres square and thirty-five to forty centimetres high with an entrance hole ninety to 130 millimetres across. The occupants of such boxes include the jackdaw, kestrel, tawny owl and other larger birds nesting in cavities. The boxes should be hung six metres or more above the ground. The entrance hole may be square and located in the upper corner of the front wall.

Slightly different are the open-fronted nest boxes sought out by birds nesting in open cavities, such as the spotted flycatcher and wagtail. Such a box is twelve centimetres square and twelve centimetres high and the front wall reaches only midway. It should be hung 1.5 to four metres above the ground under the eaves of low buildings, on the walls of cottages, woodsheds and the like. For redstarts and wagtails one can also make semi-cavities in walls.

The swallow and house martin can likewise be helped in finding a suitable place to build their nests of mud. For the swallow, which likes to nest inside buildings, in passageways and stables etc., one can attach a wooden board or ledge on which to build its nest. For the house martin, which normally nests only on the outside walls of buildings, some kind of bracket under the eaves or balcony is necessary to serve as a support for the nest, for being made of mud, the latter might dry out and, failing to adhere to a smooth wall, drop to the ground together with the eggs or nestlings.

Nest boxes should be hung in places not easily reached by cats, polecats and martens. If put up in a tree, the trunk can be encircled with a protective band of wire mesh or twigs over which such enemies cannot climb.

Furthermore, nest boxes should not be hung close to each other for, as has already been said, birds have their specific nesting territories. Boxes are generally spaced at least twenty to thirty metres apart. In woods this distance should be greater. An area of 0.25 hectares should be provided for one box.

The end of February is the best time to put up boxes in parks and gardens. At the same time old boxes should be repaired and cleaned, for birds will not nest, as a rule, in soiled boxes.

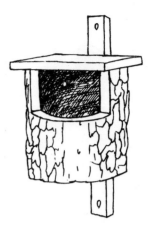

48/ Open-fronted nest box

Owls, too, can be helped during the nesting period. Boxes for owls, of the aforementioned size, should be fastened to a tree at the edge of a wood so that the owl can hunt in the surrounding fields. For the little owl and Tengmalm's owl the nest box should be about twenty centimetres square and thirty-five centimetres high and the entrance hole should be about ninety millimetres across. Small owls, such as the pygmy, will even make use of a sparrow's nest box. Boxes for this owl should be hung four to eight metres above the ground.

Certain water birds can also be effectively protected, chiefly during the breeding season.

It is essential that the greatest possible quiet be maintained on ponds, lakes and pools, particularly in reed beds, so that birds are not disturbed unnecessarily while incubating and so that they can care for their offspring as they should. Great harm can be caused by freely roaming dogs, which flush sitting ducks or other birds, some of which abandon their nests altogether if disturbed. Also important, however, is to provide sufficient places for concealment. Ducks, and naturally other birds, too, need to feel safe and this is possible only in thick stands of reeds, rushes and grass. That is why the continuous belt of the previous year's reeds should be preserved on the edges of all ponds, and on the lakes where reeds and rushes are harvested they should be left standing in some spots where ducks and other water birds can seek shelter, especially in spring before the new vegetation has grown in. Most important for ducks are open stretches of water, only partly covered with reeds and low clumps of grass. To

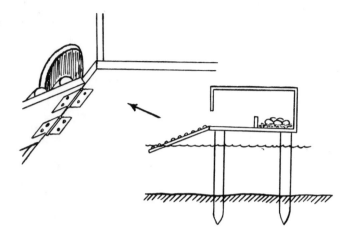

49/ *Nest box for ducks*

leave some of these untouched, therefore, is a must and need in no way be an obstacle to successful pond management. Old stands are a good shelter also for grebes, rails, gulls and many other species of birds. Reeds that are left standing, however, should be located alongside shallows where the offspring of various species of ducks forage for food. Another cardinal rule should be never to cut reeds during the nesting period for such harvesting is responsible for the death of many nestlings or the destruction of eggs.

A suitable spot for ducks to nest is an islet or several islets on a larger pond; these islets may also be at the edge of the pond. Overgrown islets have a great many advantages. Ducks are fond of building nests there close to water, and on such islets the nests are not in danger of being flooded if the water level rises. Furthermore, vermin find it difficult to reach such islets and in addition to that the birds are not as exposed to disturbance as on the shore. Also clumps of grass on the shore are a good place for ducks to build their nests. Wooden nest boxes can be placed to good advantage in reeds and rushes as well as on islets, where many species of ducks will lay eggs and rear young. The nest boxes should be located above the highest probable water line and a wooden ramp with cross-bars should be affixed to the opening. This makes it easy for the birds to enter no matter what the level of the water, which thus cannot affect the successful outcome of incubation. The nest boxes should be about seventy centimetres long, forty centimetres wide and forty centimetres high, with an entrance hole twelve to fifteen centimetres in diameter. They should be impregnated with a water-resistant substance so that they are impervious to damage from damp. The nesting hole itself, which should be separated by a low wooden partition, should be lined with some turf and soft, dry leaves and moss. For ducks that nest in tree cavities, e. g. goldeneyes, the nest box should be placed in a tree beside water. Such a box should be about seventy centimetres high, forty centimetres wide and the entrance hole ten to twelve centimetres across. These nest boxes should be lined similarly and a shallow depression made so that the eggs do not roll out.

On ponds we can also provide ducks with flat feeding boxes that either float on the water or else are attached to wooden piles about thirty centimetres above the surface and reached by means of slanting ramps. A roof above the box serves to keep the food dry when it rains.

With such fairly inexpensive constructions it is possible to increase the number of ducks and other water birds.

When bogs and swamps are being drained some spots should be left intact in certain areas so that water and marshland birds which nest there do not move away, thus impoverishing the local fauna and characteristic stamp of the given countryside.

Suitable nesting conditions can also be provided for certain sea birds, thus helping to increase their number. For the common merganser *(Mergus merganser)* wooden nest boxes may be put up in a tree 2.5 to eighteen metres above the ground. These should be about eighty-five centimetres high, twenty-three to twenty-eight centimetres wide, with an entry hole twelve centimetres across.

For the eider *(Somateria mollissima)* hollows of stones or tree trunks, placed so they can build their nests underneath, will also provide more opportunities for nesting.

Feeding Birds in Winter

Many birds remain in their nesting grounds throughout the winter, no matter how cold the weather. Others, whose diet consists of berries, remain as long as there is enough for them to feed on and then fly off to seek food elsewhere. Finally there are the birds that inhabit the far north, up to and beyond the Arctic Circle, and migrate south in flocks, remaining in central and southern Europe for the winter.

Among resident species are most tits, the nuthatch, woodpeckers and also many seed-eaters, such as the sparrow, greenfinch, chaffinch, siskin, goldfinch, and various buntings. All roam the countryside, usually in small flocks, throughout the winter, often visiting gardens. Their numbers are increased by such northern guests as the brambling.

As a rule birds have no difficulty obtaining food in winter as long as there is not too much snow and the ground and trees are not coated with ice. Tits and tree creepers pick concealed insects or their eggs and cocoons out of cracks in

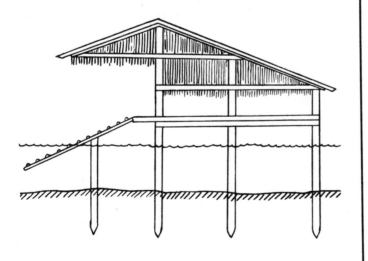

50/ Feeding box for ducks

the bark, but a coat of ice often blocks their access to food. Many seed-eaters are likewise deprived of nourishment when there is a deep layer of snow for they generally seek their food on the ground where many grass seeds are to be found.

When bad weather lasts a longer time the birds are hard put to find food and many of them die of hunger. At such a time city outskirts and houses are visited by large numbers of birds, even woodland birds, and the provision of food saves many from starving to death. Birds, however, cannot be fed only on bits of bread or rolls. For the majority crumbs make a totally unsuitable diet. Natural food is by far the best, especially seeds, provided, of course, that they are not mouldy or rancid. Oil seeds in particular provide birds with ample calories in winter. Seeds are eaten in winter also by birds that at other times feed mostly on insects, e. g. tits, nuthatches, and woodpeckers. Sunflower seeds are best for these species. A tit will take one at a time from the bird table and fly off with it to a nearby tree where, supporting itself on its feet, it cracks the hard shell with its bill and eats the sweet, oily kernel. The nuthatch, on the other hand, places the seed in cracks or holes in the bark and then proceeds to crack the seed. Hemp seed is also suitable, but as this has a hard shell it should be slightly crushed, e. g. with a small rolling pin, before being served to the birds. Birds may be fed millet, canary seed, flax seed, rape seed, hulled oats and poppy seed. The collared dove also eats wheat and maize. In addition one can provide them with the seeds of grass, thistles and conifers as well as rowan, hawthorn, elderberries and the like, dried during the late summer months. Tits also appreciate bits of suet and an occasional mealworm.

Some birds, like the goldfinch, will only rarely visit bird tables. For these it is possible to cut off whole thistle branches in the autumn and store them until the winter months. Then in winter they can simply be stuck upright into the snow.

Food is usually put out for birds in a feeder made of wood, which should be covered with glass. Small feeders may be put outside windows, larger ones in gardens or parks. The feeder should be topped with a small roof to protect the contents from rain and snow. Some-

51/ Garden feeding tray

times feeders are constructed with an entrance at the bottom, the birds flying in from below, and the feeding space proper enclosed with glass. Such a feeder also provides protection against the wind and birds can take shelter there in harsh weather. Equally suitable are automatic feeders with a larger supply of seeds in a reserve container from which they automatically drop as soon as those on the tray have been consumed. Such feeders must, of course, be replenished regularly.

The Spread
of Bird Species

The make-up of the bird population in a given region may change over the years. Some species may vanish from the area and other, new ones may establish themselves there.

Man is responsible for the disappearance of many species, either directly or indirectly, such as by draining wet areas, clearing land of under-growth, etc. Thus, for example, the common crane, which still nested in great numbers in England in medieval times, has been totally absent there since the eighteenth century.

On the other hand, birds that never nested there previously are extending their range and becoming established in new territories. Some have even launched large-scale 'invasions'. One such example is the collared turtle dove, originally a native of India and western and southern China. In the sixteenth century it was introduced to Asia Minor where it was kept in semi-captivity at the courts of various sultans. Later, in the eighteenth century, the collared turtle dove began to spread farther across Asia Minor and at the same time eastwards as far as Japan. Subsequently it spread throughout the entire Balkan peninsula and appeared in Bucharest, Budapest, Prague, Hannover, Munich and in 1951 even as far north as Rostock. In 1952 it appeared in England for the first time, in 1954 it made its way to Norway and later to Scotland, and in 1964 it showed up in Iceland. It is rapidly becoming established everywhere, multiplying at an amazing rate and seemingly impervious to long, hard winters. To this day no one is able to explain what prompted the dove to leave its home in the warm climate of India and later to spread west and north at such an astonishing speed from southeastern Europe. Within the space of a few years it has colonized the whole of Europe, settling chiefly in built-up areas.

Also of interest is the spread of the serin throughout Europe, where it is now a common inhabitant of parks and gardens. In the seventeenth century the serin's European range was restricted to the Mediterranean countries but around 1800 it began spreading rapidly northward across the Alps and even further. It returned as a migrant to its original home in the south every winter but with the arrival of spring again moved to new places, its range expanding year by year. In 1922 it began to nest in Holland, in 1942 it made its first appearance in southern Sweden and in 1949 it showed up in Denmark. Today it is settling further new territories, making its way even into mountain areas and nesting at altitudes as high as 1,350 metres above sea level.

Certain species of birds, however, were intentionally introduced by man to new environments, where they soon became acclimatized and since that time rank as members of the local avifauna. One such example is the pheasant, introduced as early as medieval times to central and western Europe, where it acclimatized itself to the new conditions and is now a common bird on the Continent. One reason for the pheasant's excellent acclimatization, of course, is the fact that it is a poor flier and thus is a resident species.

However, in the past few decades many marshland and water birds that are migrants and known to be excellent fliers have settled in entirely new territories and established new populations there, sometimes with and sometimes without man's intervention. One example of the latter instance is the tufted duck, originally indigenous to northeastern Europe. In the late nineteenth century it spread as far as Iceland, having previously settled also in Scandinavia and Great Britain. In the twentieth century it began to spread south, becoming established near the Baltic coast. Its southward spread continued, however, and in 1948 it appeared in southern Moravia, in 1950 in southern Bohemia, as of 1960 it also nests in large numbers in the German Federal Republic and is now one of the commonest of ducks in central Europe. However, it has not as yet become established in Austria or Hungary, but has been observed nesting irregularly in Switzerland, France, Yugoslavia, Bulgaria, Romania and also in Cyprus. Whereas previously it merely passed through central Europe on its migratory flight to its winter quarters in western and southern or southwestern Europe, in recent years individuals from the north have been wintering regularly in large flocks on the rivers of central Europe.

Another bird that is spreading its range, in this case northward, is the red-crested pochard, otherwise native to the islands of the Mediterranean, southeastern Spain and the northern parts of the Baltic and Caspian Seas. It is appearing in ever increasing numbers in central Europe and today it regularly nests locally in Germany and Czechoslovakia and has also established nesting grounds in Holland, Denmark and Belgium.

One of the latest settlers in central Europe is the goldeneye, a typical duck of northern Europe. It had already become established previously in some parts of northern Poland and the northern part of the German Democratic Republic but in 1960 it extended its range as far as southern Bohemia, where its numbers have since shown a steady increase. It furthermore nests regularly in Switzerland.

Of the water birds that have become established in Europe through man's efforts the Canada goose heads the list. This large goose, a native of North America, was raised in England as a semi-domesticated species from about the seventeenth century. Later it spread into the wild, where it now numbers more than ten thousand birds, according to the experts' estimate. The Canada goose was also introduced into Sweden, where it has likewise formed populations. These, however, unlike their English brethren, are migrant and fly for the winter to Holland and the German Federal Republic. In recent years the Canada goose has also appeared in other parts of central Europe, even during the breeding season; these individuals, however, were probably birds that had escaped from zoos. Even they, of course, may lay the foundation for further European populations.

During the past few years another increasingly frequent nester in certain parts of Europe has been the ruddy shelduck, which is indigenous to the western Mediterranean, Asia Minor and the desert lakes around the Aral Sea. Birds found nesting here and there in central and western Europe, however, are individuals that escaped from zoos or else were released voluntarily from captivity, and thus we cannot speak of populations as yet.

52/ Distribution of the collared turtle dove

53/ Canada geese on the wing

Another increasingly frequent nester in central Europe is the mute swan. Originally kept as semi-domesticated birds on the small lakes of chateaux and parks for ornament, many swans settled on lakes and ponds in the wild and began to nest there regularly. In some places, such as in the northern lake country of the German Democratic Republic and Poland, however, the mute swan populations are indigenous.

Also certain birds of the heron tribe are beginning to extend their range to new places, though not to such an extent as birds of the Anatidae family. The purple heron, for instance, nests commonly in southern, southeastern and southwestern Europe. In the past few decades it has been occurring with increasing frequency in central Europe, where, though still rare, it is already beginning to form regular populations.

The night heron is another bird that is becoming established in new areas in Europe with increasing frequency. In recent years new colonies have become established in some parts of central and western Europe. This spread of wetland birds may be due to many of their former breeding grounds being drained.

Certain species of waders are likewise spreading to new places. One such example is the black-tailed godwit, originally an inhabitant of northern Europe. During the past few decades it has become established in many parts of central Europe and is now fairly plentiful there. The avocet also nests occasionally in certain parts of central Europe nowadays.

Man's Associates

Countless species of birds congregate in built-up areas. Many have found suitable nesting sites on buildings, others have been attracted by the availability of food. Some species have even taken advantage of the favourable conditions man unknowingly has prepared for them and have multiplied at a fantastic rate, sometimes nearing catastrophic proportions. A typical example is the house sparrow, which has associated itself with man probably from the time grain was first cultivated and thus became the first species to settle in man's neighbourhood.

The house sparrow has become a pest because throughout the year eighty percent of its diet consists of grain kernels; furthermore, it snips off the buds of fruit trees and shrubs and also feeds on young lettuce plants. Even though it feeds its young on insects and their larvae during the nesting season this nowhere near balances its harmful activities. In large cities it is an especially unwelcome visitor to markets, exhibition halls and other similar places where it may soil food and also foul stalls and equipment. Experts have still not been able to solve the long-standing problem of the sparrow. There are records from the eighteenth century revealing that the killing of sparrows was mandatory in many European countries at that time and that farmers had to deliver a specified number of sparrow heads to the authorities as proof of their obeying this order. The house sparrow is furthermore very quarrelsome, chasing away other birds and often usurping nest boxes. Nowadays the house sparrow is found even in the heart of large cities, on bustling main streets and squares, where other birds would be quite incapable of existing. It adapted itself to this new environment with amazing rapidity and began to feed on all kinds of food remnants of both animal and plant origin. It has even learned to 'deal' with man, seeming to gauge instinctively how close it can safely approach in safety. In a park, for example, it will hop up to accept food from the hand knowing that there is no danger. However, not even lengthy association with man has made it lose its cautiousness. In many instances the need to reduce the numbers of house sparrows cannot be avoided, but this should be done expertly and without causing unnecessary suffering.

The blackbird, too, is regularly found in the company of man, but its 'domestication' occurred much later than that of the house sparrow. In the mid-eighteenth century ornithologists were still describing the blackbird as a very shy woodland bird. After that it gradually began to set up home in parks and gardens with increasing frequency, but only quite recently did it begin to invade the outskirts of towns and penetrate parks in city centres, making its home even in small backyards with a few shrubs or trees. Living close to man also markedly affected the blackbird's migratory habits. Originally it migrated southwest and wintered in the countries bordering the Mediterranean. Only a certain number of males remained in their nesting grounds during the winter months. Now, however, not only older males but also a number of younger individuals as well as females remain throughout the year because they find sufficient food for their needs. Nowadays blackbirds in urban areas build their nests not only in thickets and trees but also directly on roofs, windowsills, balconies, rafters in sheds, open letter boxes, and the like. The comings and goings of passers-by do not deter them and a sitting bird is sometimes so unafraid that it will allow itself to be stroked. In winter blackbirds often visit window feeders and they have even learned to eat various food scraps from the dinner table. This unnatural fare is obviously to their liking and causes no problems of digestion. Blackbirds have even been observed visiting window feeders in spring, filching titbits for their young.

Many blackbirds' nests in city parks are destroyed by roaming cats. The birds, however, ensure the preservation of the species by building a new nest and raising a brood. It is interesting to note that blackbirds in cities multiply more rapidly, have more nestlings and more broods in a year than do those that make their home in woodlands for they have ample food and a warmer environment. Blackbird populations in cities are continually increasing in number, and one may often see pure white or more often partially albino individuals.

During the past few decades the song thrush is also becoming a city bird, even though the ma-

54/ *The white stork*

jority are still woodland inhabitants. Every year, however, this bird is becoming a more frequent visitor to parks and gardens, building its nest in the immediate vicinity of man's dwellings or directly on buildings.

The swallow, a native of rocky localities, which used to build its nest under rock overhangs or at the entrance of caves, has almost entirely abandoned its original habitat. In Europe it is very seldom found in such places, having become increasingly accustomed to man's presence. Swallows have in fact invaded his homes and out-buildings, constructing nests in cowsheds, barns, corridors — even bathrooms and living rooms! It is not disturbed by the presence of human beings, requiring only a partially open window through which it can fly in and out. It is, of course, far safer indoors, espe-

55/ *Starling*

cially at night, for there it is virtually immune from attacks by vermin or an owl. The swallow has won the heart of man with its grace and beauty and is viewed by him as a 'bit of nature' in his home. In the centre of big cities, however, particularly in modern housing developments, this beautiful bird is no longer to be seen, the main reason being the lack of nesting opportunities and absence of insects. It is most abundant in rural areas where it can find not only suitable nesting sites but also an abundance of the insects on which it feeds. It returns regularly to the same nest and nesting site every year.

The house martin has also invaded man's domain. Whole colonies often build their nests on the walls of houses, under the eaves, below balconies.

Another bird that has settled in built-up areas is the swift. Originally an inhabitant of rocky regions it selects only high places for its nest, which it builds under the eaves of tall buildings, granaries, towers, as well as in cracks in high walls, but seeks no closer ties with man.

Another regular spring visitor to parks, gardens and backyards is the starling. Originally a woodland bird, nesting in the cavities of tree trunks or holes in tree branches, the starling, too, has become accustomed to the presence of man, who began putting up nest boxes in his gardens thus providing it with suitable nesting sites. One may say that it was virtually 'enticed' to settle in built-up areas. Many starlings, however, have remained faithful to their original habitat and may be seen in open woods where there are plenty of tree cavities.

Two other birds, the black redstart and Euro-

pean redstart, which both fly south for the winter, are seen with increasing frequency in built-up areas. The black redstart, in particular, may often be seen in the backyards of village houses and also in large cities, where it is content to occupy a hole in the wall left by a dislodged brick or better still a semi-nest box hung up for its use. Originally the black redstart inhabited only high mountain slopes, where it is still found even today, but many birds nowadays seem to prefer the vicinity of human habitations. In parts of Europe the redstart is also increasingly availing itself of the advantages afforded by built-up areas, being found chiefly in parks and established gardens.

One of the best known and commonest inhabitants of parks and gardens is the chaffinch. In parks it will hop up to people and even take food from the hand, especially in winter. It is, however, found just as often in woods. The reason for its frequenting built-up areas is probably to be found in a sudden increase in population. This explanation is borne out also by the fact that in recent years the chaffinch has been settling in northern areas where it was previously non-existent, even extending its range as far as the Arctic Circle.

The serin, too, often lives in the neighbourhood of man's dwellings. Likewise the collared turtle dove, as has already been stated, is found throughout the year in built-up areas, even on busy streets in large cities. All it needs are a few trees on which it builds its simple nest.

Certain corvine birds are likewise common inhabitants of today's European cities. First and foremost is the jackdaw, which nests on church steeples and castle turrets. Sometimes even whole colonies of rooks establish themselves in old parks and large gardens in big cities.

Other small birds that have moved in with man are the tits, mainly the great tit and the blue tit, which nest not only in nest boxes but also in cracks in walls, etc.

In the country and on the outskirts of large cities one will often find also the pied and grey wagtails nesting near houses as well as many other songbirds which build their nests in parks and gardens, likewise in some European cities certain members of the woodpecker family such as the wryneck and grey-headed woodpecker are found.

56/ *Sparrows*

Another bird that has been moving into large cities with increasing frequency is the kestrel. This small raptor often raises its brood on the high towers of churches or castles, often also in niches in tall buildings.

Some owls have likewise taken to nesting in the vicinity of human dwellings. The barn owl, for example, often nests in attics and dovecotes, and in cities even in church towers.

Mention should also be made of the white stork, which is fond of building its large nest on the roofs of houses or on tall chimneys, sometimes also in tall trees, both in rural areas and in small towns.

Each year further species of birds are moving in with man because they find better nesting opportunities there as well as ample food for their offspring. In western Europe, in recent years, such species have included the carrion crow, mistle thrush, wood pigeon and moorhen.

The world of birds found in the neighbourhood of man is slowly but constantly changing. Some species should be strictly protected, whereas in the case of others their numbers should be regulated in accordance with the given circumstances. To be able to state whether certain species are harmful or useful often requires in-depth studies and detailed investigation, based, of course, on the best possible knowledge of the entire avian realm in all its aspects. Only thus will birds remain a permanent part of the world of nature, which brings both joy and benefit to man.

1. Osprey
2. White-tailed Eagle
3. Red Kite
4. Black Kite
5. Sparrowhawk
6. Goshawk
7. Buzzard
8. Rough-legged Buzzard
9. Honey Buzzard
10. Golden Eagle

11. Black Vulture
12. Griffon Vulture
13. Marsh Harrier
14. Hen Harrier
15. Montagu's Harrier

16. Gyrfalcon
17. Peregrine Falcon
18. Hobby
19. Merlin
20. Red-footed Falcon
21. Kestrel

Plates

The plates depict 256 species of birds. In those cases where the coloration of the male (♂) differs markedly from that of the female (♀) — sexual dimorphism — both are shown. The birds are grouped according to the zoological system of classification.

The text below the line gives items of particular interest; e. g. the average length of the bird in centimetres, measured from the tip of the bill to the tip of the tail, a verbal description of the song, shapes and dimensions of the eggs; these egg dimensions are given in millimetres, the first figure denoting the minimum length of the egg, the second the maximum length, the third the minimum width and the fourth the maximum width. In many instances the reader will also find here the flight drawing of the bird.

Each species is described as resident, migratory or dispersive depending on its stability in relation to its breeding range outside the reproductive season.

The family to which each species belongs is given in the form of a running headline.

Black-throated Diver

Gavia arctica

The black-throated diver inhabits northern Europe and northwestern Asia, but also breeds in Scotland and, in rare instances, in Pomerania, northern Germany and Poland. During the breeding season it is found on lakes, generally near the coast. The nest is placed on islets near deep water, and is simply a shallow depression in grass, usually without any lining, generally sited right on the water's edge so that the birds can slip straight in. One, two, but sometimes three eggs are laid in April or May. The partners take turns incubating for 28 to 32 days. On hatching, the chicks take to the water with their parents, who supervise them for a further two months. When the young are fully grown, the divers form small groups. Birds from the extreme north leave their nesting grounds as early as mid-August, often while the young are still unable to fly, swimming with them down the rivers to the sea and on along the coast. The main southerly migration is usually in November, the return journey taking place between early March and late April. Wintering grounds are the Baltic, North Sea, and Mediterranean, as well as northern parts of the Black and Caspian Seas. During the migratory season, single individuals may be seen quite regularly inland on ice-free water. Black-throated divers feed mainly on fish, but crustaceans, molluscs and occasionally frogs, worms or aquatic insects also feature in the diet.

Voice:
A deep, barking 'kwow'; in flight, 'ga-ga-ga', like a goose.

Length:
58 to 69 cm.

Male and female have similar plumage.

Size of egg:
75.7–95.7 × 45.5–56.0 mm.

Migratory bird

Red-throated Diver

Gavia stellata

Iceland, northern Scotland, Ireland, Scandinavia, the Hebrides, Orkneys, Shetlands and the Murmansk region are all home to the red-throated diver. It is also found in Greenland and in the arctic regions of North America. Breeding grounds are the edges of small but deep pools, coastal lagoons and lakes. The nest is made of mosses like sphagnum and of plant stems and is always placed near water, sometimes even right on the water. Paired birds often return to the same spot every year. In May or June the female lays usually two eggs, which both partners take turns incubating for about 28 but sometimes as long as 36 days. Incubation starts as soon as the first egg appears. If the clutch is lost, the female lays again. Red-throated divers are migratory, although in the southern parts of their range they are dispersive. European populations winter on the Atlantic coast as far south as southern Spain, as well as on the North and Baltic, Mediterranean and Black Seas. On migration, the birds occur as vagrants on inland waters, where, however, they usually remain only a few days. The mainstay of the diet is sea fish, such as herring, sprats and cod, but the species does take amphibians, crustaceans, molluscs, aquatic insects and worms.

Migratory or dispersive bird

Size of egg:
62.5–86.0
× 41.0–51.0 mm.

Length:
53 to 61 cm.

Male and female have
similar plumage.

Voice:
A repeated, quacking
'kwuck'; also a high, thin
wail.

Great Crested Grebe

Podiceps cristatus

The great crested grebe is widespread through-out most of Europe except the north, inhabiting lakes or large ponds with large beds of reeds and rushes. In northern and eastern parts of the range, birds are migratory, elsewhere resident. They sometimes return to their breeding grounds as early as February, but more usually in March or April. An interesting courtship ceremonial takes place: the partners, separated by several yards, first greet one another by stretching their necks out along the water's sur-face. Then they swim towards each other, spreading their crests, nodding their heads and finally embracing each other by rubbing necks. The birds call to each other throughout. Some-times they dive, surfacing with a piece of green-ery in their bills and treading water face to face with heads erect. The nest is made of various aquatic plants brought up from the depths. The female lays three to six eggs which are white at first, but then gradually acquire a brownish hue. Both partners take turns incubating for 25 to 27 days, though the female takes the major share. After the nestlings have dried, they climb onto their parents' backs and partially conceal them-selves under the wings, so to be carried about even though capable of swimming and diving by themselves. The parents feed the young small insects and molluscs; adult birds take mostly insect larvae and fish.

Voice:
A deep 'har-arr' or 'er-wick', mainly during the courtship period.

Length:
48 cm.

Male and female have similar plumage.

Size of egg:
46.5—62.7 × 33.0—39.7 mm.

Migratory, dispersive or resident bird

Black-necked Grebe

Podiceps nigricollis

The black-necked grebe was originally a native of southeastern Europe, but during the past 80 years has become widespread throughout western and central Europe, in Italy, England, Holland, eastern France and southern Spain. Eastern European populations are migratory. This species is partial to shallow but large ponds and lakes with extensive vegetation for cover. Pairs of birds return to the nesting grounds in March and April and begin their courtship display shortly after their arrival: partners swim rapidly towards each other, raise heads erect and shake them. This is a gregarious bird which stays in groups even when nesting, forming colonies with a great number of nests spaced several yards apart, though they may be more densely clustered. The nest, of rotting vegetation, is located on water among reeds, though it may float freely at the edge of a reed bed. It is the female who builds while the male brings material. The clutch, consisting of three, four or sometimes as many as six eggs, is laid from April to June and both partners share the duties of incubation for 19 to 23 days. The nestlings are carried about on their parents' backs, being cared for by them for a number of weeks. Diet consists of insects and their larvae, small molluscs and crustaceans as well as tadpoles and small fish. The black-necked grebe hunts under water, usually at depths of no more than two metres.

Size of egg:
39.0—48.5
× 27.1—34.0 mm.

Length:
30 cm.

Male and female have similar plumage.

Voice:
Whistling notes that sound like 'poo-eep'.

Migratory or resident bird

Little Grebe

Podiceps ruficollis

The little grebe inhabits the whole of Europe except the north; individuals inhabiting eastern Europe are migrant and the populations of central, western and southern Europe are resident. The species is found on lakes, ponds and slow-moving water courses with overgrown banks. It will also be encountered on very small pools with banks thickly bordered by reeds. A remarkably shy bird, it remains concealed in thickets most of the time, venturing onto the open water only rarely. The birds arrive at the breeding grounds already paired, partners often remaining together throughout the winter. Courtship display begins shortly after arrival: the male puts his head back, ruffles his feathers, pecks at the water and often kicks up spray with his feet. He is very tenacious in defending his nesting territory. There is a first brood in April and second in June or July. The nest, consisting of a pile of rotting water plants, floats on the water among or near reeds, although in shallow water it rests on the bottom and in deeper water is firmly anchored. As a rule, the female lays four to six eggs. Both partners share the duties of incubation for 20 to 21 days, and both tend the young for eight to ten weeks. The little grebe's diet consists of insects and their larvae, small molluscs, worms, crustaceans, tadpoles, as well as small fish, which it hunts mostly underwater.

Voice:
A trilling 'whit, whit'.

Length:
27 cm.

Male and female have similar plumage.

Size of egg:
32.8—43.0
× 23.0—28.3 mm.

Migratory or resident bird

Storm Petrel

Hydrobates pelagicus

Storm petrels are found over the eastern North Atlantic and western Mediterranean. Except in the breeding season, they inhabit the open seas. In winter, storm petrels journey as far as the western and southern coasts of Africa, but individuals remain in the areas of their breeding grounds throughout the year. On occasions they occur as vagrants as far inland as central Europe. Storm petrels generally arrive at the small rocky islands where they breed in late April, but even before that they often occur at sea in the same vicinity. The storm petrel nests in ground burrows, rock crevices, rabbit holes and below rock ledges, only rarely digging its own hole. The female lays a single egg in late May or early June, though sometimes as late as the end of August. If the egg is lost, a new one may be laid as late as September. Both partners take turns incubating. The young hatch after 38 to 41 days and are fed by the parents every night. These birds are most active between 10.30 p. m. and 3.30 a. m., even outside the breeding season. One of the parents remains in constant attendance on the chick until it is 30 days old; then it is left to fend for itself. The young bird leaves the nest after 54 to 68 days. A storm petrel's diet consists of small cephalopods, crustaceans, molluscs, small fish and insects.

Migratory bird

Size of egg:
25.0–30.7
× 19.0–23.0 mm.

Length:
15 cm.

Male and female have similar plumage.

Voice:
At the breeding grounds, rasping, buzzing and grunting sounds such as 'hikav', 'ti-ti-tihk-ti-ti-tihk', 'arrr-r-r-r'.

Manx Shearwater

Puffinus puffinus

Manx shearwaters are widespread in Iceland, the Faroes, Shetlands and Orkneys, the west coasts of Britain and Ireland, in Brittany and on the smaller islands of the Mediterranean. The species is both dispersive and migratory, and while on migration it often occurs on the coasts of the North and Baltic Seas and on the Portuguese coast. Single birds sometimes occur as inland vagrants. Outside the breeding season, Manx shearwaters spend their time on the open sea. Birds arrive in flocks at their breeding grounds in February and March, settling in large colonies on cliffs and rocky islands. Courting takes place at night to an accompaniment of ghastly screams and cackles. The nest is a burrow, dug often by the birds themselves, sometimes in very hard ground. The nest chamber is lined with feathers, leaves and grass. A single, white egg is laid in April or May, or sometimes, though rarely, in early June. The partners take turns incubating for stretches of three to five days, the bird on the nest going without food or water throughout its shift, while the other flies out to sea in search of food, on occasions covering distances of more than a thousand kilometres. The young hatch after 51 to 61 days and leave the nest at ten weeks, clumsily making their way to the water. At this stage, the flight feathers are not fully grown. Diet consists of small fish, crustaceans and molluscs.

Voice:
Various crooning and crowing notes.

Length:
36 cm.

Male and female have similar plumage.

Size of egg:
54.5–65.7
× 39.2–45.1 mm.

Migratory or dispersive bird

Fulmar

Fulmarus glacialis

During the breeding season, the stocky but brilliantly aerobatic fulmar is distributed through Iceland, Ireland, Great Britain, Brittany, Greenland, Novaya Zemlya in the Arctic Ocean and the western coast of Norway. At other times, it keeps to the high seas. Both dispersive as well as migratory, it arrives at its nesting grounds any time from December to April, assembling offshore in huge 'rafts'. Not until the end of April (more often in May or early June) does it move ashore to cliffs or rocky islands. There it breeds in a colony sometimes numbering hundreds or even thousands of birds. The nests are unlined, spaced between 1 and 5 metres apart, and placed on rocky ledges. The female lays one egg (occasionally two), which the partners take turns incubating for about 52 days. The young are fed only once a day and during the first two weeks are kept warm by one or other of the parents. They leave the nest after 48 to 57 days already capable of flight, but do not attain maturity until the age of seven years. The fulmar feeds on pelagic molluscs, crustaceans and fish, generally gathered from the surface. Only rarely does it dive and then to a depth of 1 metre at the most.

Size of egg:
67.0−81.5
× 43.2−54.8 mm.

Length:
47 cm.

Male and female have
similar plumage.

Voice:
A hoarse, chuckling
'ag-ag-ag-arrr'.

Migratory or dispersive bird

Gannet

Sula bassana

In Europe, gannets breed on the coasts of Ireland, England, Scotland, Brittany, Norway, Iceland, Faroes and other small islands in the area. This is a truly pelagic species which spends most of its life on the open sea, although young birds occasionally stray inland. The birds arrive at their breeding grounds between February and early April, forming enormous breeding colonies (one, in the Outer Hebrides, is 70,000 strong), generally on rocky islands, on an open, elevated spot. The nest is made of seaweed, grass and pieces of wood and there may be as many as two or three to a square metre. The female lays a single, thick-shelled egg, which both partners incubate in turns for 39 to 46 days. Sometimes the chick takes more than a day to peck its way out, and up to another three days before opening its eyes. Covered with a thin coat of down and having a fantastic appetite, it is fed by the adult birds day and night, taking food by thrusting its head right into gannet's throat. By 11 weeks the chick weighs a kilogram more than an adult. It abandons the nest at 75 days, as yet incapable of flight, but able to swim. Sometimes it travels as far as 70 kilometres from the colony before taking to the air, usually between 95 and 107 days. Having abandoned the colony, a young gannet must fend for itself, which it does by catching herring, mackerel and sardines. An excellent diver, it hunts by day and night.

Voice:
Usually a barking sound
'arrah' and similar noises.

Length:
91.5 cm.

Male and female have
similar plumage.

Size of egg:
62.0−87.5
× 41.0−54.0 mm.

Migratory bird

Cormorant

Phalacrocorax carbo

Cormorants breed over Asia, Europe and North America. In Europe, the species is found in large numbers on coasts but also inland on rivers and lakes. Both a dispersive and a migratory bird, when migrating it keeps close to the shore. It nests colonially on rocky islands, often with gannets, as well as in trees, and the gatherings may number several thousand pairs of birds. Inland, cormorants can be found breeding in heronries. Nests on rock ledges are only sparingly lined, nests in trees are woven of twigs and grass stems. The bird may build a new nest using the foundation of an old one. Both partners take part in the construction, in tree colonies breaking twigs with their strong beaks. The female lays three to five eggs between April and June, both partners taking turns to incubate for 23 to 29 days. The chicks do not open their eyes until three days after hatching. Food is taken from the parents' throats. After 35 to 56 days in the nest, the juvenile birds form flocks and range widely together with the adult birds. Cormorants feed mostly on fish, occasionally on crustaceans, and especially crabs, which it may catch in great numbers. They hunt in small groups, say eight birds, harrying the fish into a compact shoal, pursuing their prey underwater. Undigested bones and scales are regurgitated. In parts of their range, cormorants will be found in company with pelicans.

Size of egg:
56.2−70.8
× 33.8−44.4 mm.

Length:
91.5 cm.

Male and female have
similar plumage.

Voice:
Various guttural groans.

Migratory or dispersive bird

Shag

Phalacrocorax aristotelis

The shag is widely distributed on the western coast of the Murmansk region, in Norway, Iceland, the British Isles, Ireland, the coast of western Europe as far as the islands of the Mediterranean and also on the coast of southeastern Europe. In some places it is resident, in others a dispersive bird. It is found exclusively on seacoasts, mainly ones with steep rocky cliffs. In winter it is also found on the coasts of the North and Baltic Seas. Only rarely does it stray inland. It nests in looser colonies than the common cormorant. The nest, made of seaweed, grass, leaves and small twigs, is placed on rock ledges. As a rule the female lays two to six eggs between the beginning of April and end of June, which the partners take turns incubating for thirty to thirty-two days. Within half an hour of hatching the young are already clamouring for food, which the parents give them three to four times daily. The young feed by thrusting their heads into the throats of the parent birds. They remain in the nest for 47 to 50 days and then take to the water, though they are as yet unable to fly. They begin to try their wings at the age of 55 to 58 days. The rate of mortality among the young is high — as many as eighty percent may die during the first year, whereas that of adult birds is around fourteen percent. The shag feeds exclusively on fish, for which it dives to depths of twenty metres.

Voice:
Usual note a loud,
rasping croak.

Length:
76 cm.

Male and female have
similar plumage.

Size of egg:
56.6—74.6
× 34.9—41.7 mm.

Resident or dispersive bird

Dalmatian Pelican

Pelecanus crispus

The Dalmatian pelican is widespread in south-eastern Europe, where it breeds in Bulgaria, Rumania, Yugoslavia and Greece. Greatest numbers occur on the Danube delta, where the birds pause on migration. In winter, the Dalmatian pelican travels mostly to the Nile, leaving its nesting grounds in late August and returning again in March. Nest building usually begins about a week after arrival. The male brings material in his beak, delivering it to the female on the water beside the nest. This is generally located on flattened reeds or other vegetation and always in shallows. In large colonies, the nests are often packed closely side by side. Between the end of March and beginning of May, the female lays as a rule two eggs, which both partners take turns to incubate, beginning as soon as the first is laid. The young generally hatch after 30 to 32 days. At first they are fed food regurgitated by the parents into the nest; later they thrust their heads into the parents' pouches. They are able to fly at 12 weeks but are not fully independent until 14 to 15 weeks. The diet consists solely of fish for which the birds forage in groups in coastal inlets or on the open sea.

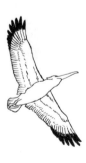

Migratory bird

Size of egg:
78.0−106.0
× 53.0−64.0 mm.

Length:
171 cm.

Male and female have
similar plumage.

Voice:
Bellowing notes such as
'wo-wo-wo', 'kh-kh-kh'.

Grey Heron

Ardea cinerea

Grey herons breed in most European countries, though only intermittently in Spain. Western populations are resident; those in northern and eastern regions migrate to the Mediterranean in September or October. In March the birds return to their breeding grounds — overgrown rivers with tree-lined banks, ponds, lakes, swamps, and woodland near water. Arrival is followed by an interesting courtship display. When the male has acquired a mate, the two build a nest of twigs, sticks and reeds, usually high in a deciduous or coniferous tree. Only rarely is the nest placed among reeds and rushes. There may be several nests on a single tree, often used by the birds several years in succession. In April or May, sometimes even in late March, the female lays four to five eggs which she and her mate take turns incubating for 25 to 28 days. The young hatch successively. At first the parents feed them by putting regurgitated food directly into their beaks, but later they deposit it in the nest. At eight to nine weeks the young are fully grown and capable of flight. The grey heron lives off small fish caught in shallow water, tadpoles, frogs, small mammals, small birds, reptiles, molluscs and insects.

Voice:
Numerous croaking and retching notes.

Length:
91 cm.

Male and female have similar plumage.

Size of egg:
52.4—69.5
× 38.5—49.7 mm.

Migratory, dispersive or resident bird

Purple Heron

Ardea purpurea

In Europe, the purple heron breeds in southern and central France, Spain, Portugal, Italy, the whole of the Balkan peninsula, Hungary, and on rare occasions in Austria, Czechoslovakia, Switzerland and Holland. European herons are migrant and generally fly to western or eastern Africa for the winter. They return in pairs during April and nest in colonies. Both partners share the task of building the nest in a dense reed bed or in bushes. It is usually made of broken reeds or rushes and is added on to and enlarged during the period of incubation. The clutch consists of four to six eggs, which the parents take turns to incubate for an average of 26 days. Because they begin sitting as soon as the first egg is laid, the young hatch one after the other. The adult birds bring food in their gular pouches and the nestlings take it direct from their parents' beaks. Later, the adults regurgitate food into the nest, leaving the young to feed themselves. The chicks leave the nest at six weeks and are fully independent by two months. The purple heron feeds on small fish, frogs, tadpoles, lizards, small mammals, and the occasional young bird, and also invertebrates. The typical hunting technique is to wait motionless until prey comes close, whereupon the kinked neck is straightened with startling speed and the sharp beak seizes its victim.

Size of egg:
50.0−61.2
× 36.5−44.7 mm.

Length:
79 cm.

Male and female have
similar plumage.

Voice:
Calls sound like 'rrank'.

Migratory bird

Little Egret

Egretta garzetta

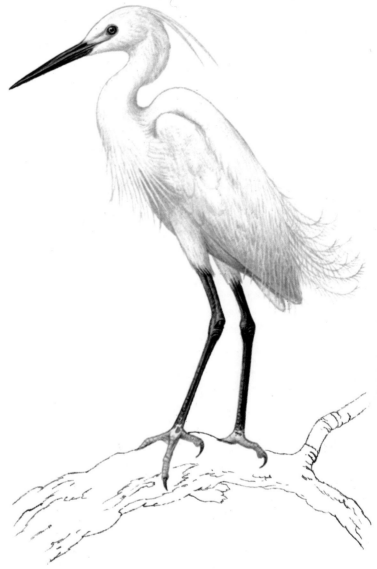

The little egret is widely distributed in Africa and Asia. It visits Europe to breed in Spain, southern Portugal, southern France and the Balkan peninsula, and it is found mostly on river deltas, lagoons and marshes, but also occurs inland. On migration it frequently strays into central and western Europe. Winter quarters for European birds are southern Africa and Asia. Departure from northernmost breeding grounds is in late August or September, and from areas farther south as late as November or December. It returns between mid-March and May, in southern France as early as February. The little egret breeds in colonies, often with other herons. The nest is placed in bushes or on trees, sometimes in dense forests. Over 20 may crowd a single tree, often only 75 centimetres apart. Made of sticks and reeds, the nest is built by both partners soon after the birds' arrival. The female usually lays three to six eggs in May or June, which both partners take turns to incubate for 21 to 25 days, beginning as soon as the first egg is laid, with the result that the young hatch in succession. The chicks are fed by both parents, who fly in search of food as far as 20 kilometres from the nest site. Diet consists of small fish, amphibians, worms, crustaceans and insects, and on rare occasions small songbirds.

Voice:
A croaking 'kark'.

Length:
56 cm.

Male and female have similar plumage.

Size of egg:
41.1–55.0
× 30.0–38.0 mm.

Migratory bird

Night Heron

Nycticorax nycticorax

The night heron inhabits southern, south-eastern and south-western Europe, has a discontinuous distribution in central Europe, and also occurs in Holland and the south of France. It departs for tropical Africa in autumn and returns during April. The habitats are rivers bordered with trees and thickets, swamps, lakes and ponds. The nest is a haphazard structure of twigs laid on top of each other, usually placed between one and five metres, but in trees sometimes more than twenty metres above the ground. Building is begun by the male, who then tries to attract a partner. She in turn continues the task while the male keeps her supplied with materials. The clutch consists of three to five eggs, which the female begins brooding as soon as the first is laid. Incubation is shared by both partners, the male relieving his mate every two to four hours. The young hatch successively in 20 to 23 days and are fed in the nest by the adult birds for 21 to 28 days. Then they climb out onto the surrounding branches and at six weeks begin to fly about, being fully fledged by the time they are seven to eight weeks old. The diet consists principally of various fish, insects and worms. Occasionally, the night heron will catch a newt or even a fieldmouse. It usually forages for food at twilight or before sunrise and spends the day resting in a tree.

Size of egg:
43.7—56.5
× 31.0—39.7 mm.

Length:
61 cm.

Male and female have similar plumage.

Voice:
A far-reaching cry that sounds like 'guark'.

Migratory bird

Little Bittern

Ixobrychus minutus

All of Europe, except Scandinavia and the British Isles has little bitterns, though the birds sometimes make their way to England, Iceland and Scandinavia in August or September while on passage to winter quarters in northwestern and eastern Africa. The return to the breeding grounds is sometimes as early as late March, but April or early May is more usual. The species inhabits lakes, ponds, river deltas and small pools whose shores are covered with thick vegetation. It makes its home in large beds of reeds where it is well concealed, flying up only when disturbed and then quickly hiding again in the vegetation. First to return from winter quarters is the male, who selects a suitable site and begins building the nest. A few days later he is joined by the female, who finishes the task with materials brought to her by the male. The structure, made of reed stalks, is very well concealed. A clutch consists of five to six eggs and the female often starts incubating as soon as the first is laid, relieved by her mate at regular intervals. The young usually hatch after 16 to 19 days, remaining in the nest a further ten to 12 days, after which they climb out. The parents bring food which is regurgitated into the nest during the first few days, but later put directly into the nestlings' beaks. The little bittern feeds on insects, small fish, tadpoles, molluscs and crustaceans.

Voice:
A variety of short, croaking notes.

Length:
36 cm.

Sexually dimorphic.

Size of egg:
30.0–39.0
× 23.3–27.7 mm.

Migratory bird

Bittern

Botaurus stellaris

On warm, spring nights, one can hear a frightening, booming note sounding from swamps, marshes or reed beds on the edges of lakes. This is the bittern, announcing that it has taken up residence. The range of this robust bird covers all Europe except the north. In Scandinavia it occurs only in the extreme south and in England only in the southwest. Birds from the west and south are usually resident, those from other parts may winter in western and southwestern Europe and also in North Africa, leaving in September to October and returning again in March or April. The nest, a flat pile of reed stalks, is usually located among dense vegetation in the shallows and probably built by the female alone. She lays five to six eggs in late April or early May, sitting on them as soon as the first appears. The male, who may sometimes have several mates, does not help in incubating. Hatching is after 25 to 27 days and the female also cares exclusively for the young, feeding them regurgitated food. At eight weeks they are fully fledged. The bittern can camouflage itself perfectly against its reedy surroundings by freezing into an upright posture. The mainstay of the diet is insects and their larvae; the species also feeds on tadpoles, frogs, small fish and occasionally small mammals.

Migratory or resident bird

Size of egg:
47.5—58.2
× 33.5—41.0 mm.

Length:
76 cm.

Male and female have
similar plumage.

Voice:
A deep 'woomp',
sometimes also 'aark'.

White Stork

Ciconia ciconia

The white stork lives close to human habitations and is extremely conspicuous. It breeds in central, northwestern and southeastern Europe and also in Spain. A migrant bird, it leaves its nesting territory any time from early August to late September, flying southwest or southeast to eastern and southern Africa. In March or early April it is back again, often settling in the very heart of a village, where it builds a large nest, more often than not on a chimney. The nest itself, made of twigs and sticks, is often used for several years and added to every breeding season. A new one takes about eight days to complete. First to arrive at the nesting grounds is the male, the female joining him several days later. Four to five eggs are laid in April to May and both partners share the duties of incubation; however, only the female sits at night. The young usually hatch after 30 to 34 days, feeding themselves on food regurgitated into the nest by their parents. When they are about three weeks old, the young storks begin to stand on their feet and at the age of 54 to 63 days are capable of flight. Storks are carnivorous birds, hunting their prey in shallow waters as well as in fields and meadows. They usually feed on small rodents, frogs, lizards, small fish and various invertebrates.

Voice:
Clapping of the bill; the young make mewing sounds.

Length:
102 cm.

Male and female have similar plumage.

Size of egg:
65.0−81.5
× 46.0−57.0 mm.

Migratory bird

Black Stork

Ciconia nigra

The black stork inhabits damp coniferous and mixed woodland in northeastern, eastern and central Europe as well as in Spain. It prefers lowlands, but may be found also in mountains near ponds, larger brooks, streams and rivers. European populations depart for eastern and southern Africa in August and September, sometimes visiting England en route, and return again at the end of March or in April. The black stork usually starts building its nest in late April or early May. A large, flat structure, it is made of twigs and lined with smaller twigs, moss and grass and located about fifteen metres above the ground on the branches of a tree, usually close to the trunk. Sometimes an abandoned raptor's nest is used as a foundation for its own and in mountain habitats, the bird will even build it on the ledge of a cliff. The three to five eggs are incubated by both partners for 30 to 34 days and both bring the nestlings food, in quest of which they fly great distances, often several kilometres from the nest. The young leave the nest after 54 to 63 days. The diet consists mainly of fish, which are caught in streams, ponds and small rivers, but amphibians, small mammals, larger insects and other invertebrates are also taken. The black stork is a far shyer bird than the closely related white stork. Unlike the latter, it never places its head on its back and does not clap its bill. Hybrids of black and white storks have been bred in captivity.

Size of egg:
60.0—74.3
× 44.0—54.7 mm.

Length:
96 cm.

Male and female have similar plumage.

Voice:
Hissing sounds resembling 'feeoo'.

Migratory bird

Spoonbill

Platalea leucorodia

Spoonbills breed in southern Spain, Holland, on the Neusidler Sea, in Hungary and southeastern Europe, departing in August to September for winter quarters in tropical Africa, and returning in March and April. After the young have fledged, the birds regularly visit the North Sea coast. The habitats are lakes with overgrown shores, river deltas and marshes. The spoonbill breeds in colonies, often with other species. The nest is made of reeds and rushes placed on broken and bent reeds, sometimes also of twigs and sited in bushes or trees. It is built by both partners and is often used by the pair for a number of years. The female lays the eggs in May or June. A clutch consists of three to five eggs covered with spots that disappear during incubation. Both partners incubate for 24 to 25 days and both tend the young, which shove their bills down their parents' throats to obtain food. When they are six to eight weeks old, the young birds leave the nest, fledging a short while later. The spoonbill flies fairly rapidly with neck stretched straight out in front, now and then gliding through the air on motionless wings. Diet includes various water insects and their larvae, frogs' eggs, crustaceans, and small fish. This is caught in the huge, spatulate bill, which is swept from side to side in the water.

Voice:
Deep, hoarse notes and also bill- clapping.

Length:
86 cm.

Male and female have similar plumage.

Size of egg:
52.7–74.6 × 36.8–49.5 mm.

Migratory bird

Greater Flamingo

Phoenicopterus ruber

In Europe, the greater flamingo breeds in the Camargue area of the Rhône delta and in southern Spain. It usually migrates to northern Africa and the Mediterranean, but some birds remain in the countryside near the breeding area. Single individuals may occasionally be encountered in Great Britain, central Europe and as far north as Norway and Finland. The greater flamingo inhabits coastal lagoons, shallow lakes and inland salt lakes. Birds nesting in Russia fly regularly to the Danube delta where they may be found in shallow lagoons near the shore. This flamingo nests in colonies, often in large numbers, with an average of two nests to a square metre, placed either on shallow water or on the shore near water. Shaped like a chimney, they are made of mud or sand reinforced with small twigs and feathers. The birds use their bills to build the structure which they then tread down with their feet, hollowing out a shallow depression in the top where the female lays her single egg, or, occasionally, two or three. As a rule, she incubates by herself for a period of 30 to 32 days. On hatching, the chicks remain in the nest for four days, after which they form small groups and wade in the shallows. The adult birds feed their offspring a thick soup of regurgitated food for three weeks, after which the young birds can forage for themselves. A greater flamingo's diet consists mainly of small crustaceans, molluscs, worms, aquatic insects and some plant food.

Size of egg:
77.0–103.5
× 47.7–60.1 mm.

Length:
127 cm.

Male and female have similar plumage.

Voice:
Resembles the cackling of geese. In flight, 'ar-honk'.

Dispersive or migratory bird

Mute Swan

Cygnus olor

This is the common swan of Europe, and its range covers England, northwestern and central Europe, southern Sweden and southeastern Europe. In most places the birds are resident, though they roam the countryside in winter, seeking larger rivers and unfrozen bodies of water. Northerly populations are migrant and winter on the shores of the Baltic or Belgium and Holland. Mute swans usually return to their nesting grounds in late March or in April, seeking out lakes and large ponds bordered with reeds and other vegetation; they will also settle on a river delta. The birds arrive already paired, usually remaining with one partner for life. However, if one of them dies, the other soon finds a new mate. A large nest is built by the female in beds of reeds or rushes. She is aided in her task by the male, who brings her material from the neighbourhood. The four to seven eggs are incubated mostly by the female. Occasionally, she is briefly relieved by the male but otherwise he remains in the immediate vicinity keeping guard and attacking all intruders. The young generally hatch after 35 days and are cared for by both parents. They do not fledge until they are four-and-a half months old and attain full maturity at the age of four years. The diet consists mostly of vegetable matter, though the mute swan also takes animal food — insects, crustaceans, newts, tadpoles and small fish.

Voice:
A hissing sound.

Lenght:
Male 169 cm,
female 155 cm.

Male and female have
similar plumage.

Size of egg:
98.8−122.0
× 68.0−80.0 mm.

Resident or dispersive bird

Whooper Swan

Cygnus cygnus

The whooper swan is found in northern Scotland, northern Scandinavia, Finland, northern Russia, Iceland and also northern Asia. Its wintering grounds embrace practically the whole of Europe, but outside the breeding season it is in practice found mostly along the coasts of Iceland, Great Britain, Ireland, southern Scandinavia, Germany, Holland and the coasts of the Black and Caspian Seas. As a rule, it is seen inland only during severe winters, and then only in small flocks on ice-free rivers. Breeding grounds are coastal waters, river deltas, lakes and large rivers in the arctic tundra, with a preferance shown for well-reeded bodies of water. The nest, placed on islands or in swamps, is usually a large mass of reeds and other vegetation, the hollow being lined with down. Three to six eggs are laid, and incubation does not begin until three days after the last appears. The female broods alone while the male stands guard near by. Hatching is after 35 to 40 days and as soon as the chicks are dry, their parents lead them out onto the water. At first, they are covered with an attractive, pinkish down, but by two months this is replaced by dingy grey feathers, thus making it easy to dinstinguish young from adult birds, which are white. The whooper swan feeds almost exclusively on vegetable matter; the young, however, also eat animal food such as aquatic insects and their larvae.

Size of egg:
104.5–126.3
× 68.0–77.4 mm.

Length:
152 cm.

Male and female have
similar plumage.

Voice:
Loud, whooping sounds,
reminiscent of bugles.

Migratory bird

Bewick's Swan

Cygnus bewickii

Bewick's swan is found in the northern European and Asiatic tundras. Besides being smaller than the whooper swan, it also differs in the extent of yellow colouring on the bill, which is restricted only to the area above the nostrils. Its regular wintering grounds are the North Sea region, England and Ireland, where in some places it occurs in flocks numbering thousands of birds. Smaller numbers winter along the coasts of the Baltic Sea and a few make their way as far as the Black and Caspian Seas. The Bewick's swan leaves its northern breeding grounds at the beginning of October, returning again in early April. It nests in swampy tundra near the coast, preferring country with shallow lakes and streams. The nest is placed on an elevated spot near water. Built solely by the female, it is made of moss, lichens and other vegetation growing in the vicinity, and is lined with fine down. The eggs, usually three or four, are laid in the second half of June and are incubated by the female for 34 to 38 days while the male stands guard close by. Bewick's swan eats mostly plant food and, in small quantities, aquatic insects and their larvae, with the occasional small fish or tadpole.

Voice:
Musical notes reminiscent of bugles.

Length:
122 cm.

Male and female have similar plumage.

Size of egg:
96.0–114.0
× 64.3–71.7 mm.

Migratory bird

Bean Goose

Anser fabalis

Bean geese breed mostly in the tundra of the low arctic in Iceland, northern Scandinavia, Finland and northern Russia. These populations winter in the coastal regions of southern and central Scandinavia, western and southern Europe and the Black Sea. Birds also winter inland on pasture near fresh water. Like other grey geese, the bean goose associates in large flocks outside the breeding season. While a flock is grazing, birds take turns to act as sentinels, watching for danger. Bean geese arrive at their summer quarters in May, choosing as nest sites the edges of lakes or rivers, the banks of mountain streams and also moorland. The female starts building her nest in shallow depression under a bush or low tree soon after arrival, lining it with vegetation and down. The three to seven eggs are laid usually in June, and incubated by the female alone for 27 to 30 days while her mate stands guard. When danger threatens, both birds crouch on the ground with necks outstretched. Far northerly breeders depart southwards at the end of August or in early September, but birds from more southerly regions leave as late as October. Diet consists of grass, plant shoots and berries, and, in the autumn, a predominance of seeds. The goslings eat insects, as do adult birds in moult.

Size of egg:
74.0−91.0
× 42.0−59.0 mm.

Length:
71 to 89 cm.

Male and female have
similar plumage.

Voice:
Low, honking notes such
as 'ung-unk'.

Migratory bird

White-fronted Goose

Anser albifrons

In Europe the white-fronted goose breeds only in the northern part of Russia bordering the sea; it is also found in northern Asia, northern North America and on the eastern coast of Greenland. It winters on the coasts of western Europe, Great Britain and Ireland as well as in eastern Scandinavia and on the Black Sea. It occasionally occurs as vagrant deep inside central Europe. It returns to its breeding grounds from mid-May onwards, but if they are located in mountain areas then not until mid-June. It frequently nests in small colonies. It inhabits treeless tundras and open moorland near the sea, also islands in river deltas and slopes on the edges of rivers and lakes. The nest is placed in an elevated spot, often on terraced hillsides. The hollow is lined with various kinds of vegetation and from the start of incubation also with a thick layer of down. It is not unusual for the nest to be located near that of a peregrine falcon, because the raptor provides protection against attack by the arctic fox. In late May, or more usually in June, the female lays three to seven eggs, which she incubates by herself for 26 to 30 days. The male remains beside the nest or nearby throughout the entire period. When the young are grown families join to form flocks that may be found on wet pastures with rich vegetation alongside rivers and lakes. The white-fronted goose feeds on grass, shoots, various berries and also seeds.

Voice:
High-pitched notes such as 'lyo-lyok', 'kow-lyow' and the like.

Length:
66 to 76 cm.

Male and female have similar plumage.

Size of egg:
72.0−89.6
× 46.7−59.0 mm.

Migratory bird

Lesser White-fronted Goose

Anser erythropus

The lesser white-fronted goose lives in the coastal tundras of Europe and Asia. In Europe it breeds in northern Scandinavia, Finland and northern Russia. Winter is spent in south-eastern Europe on the coasts of the Black and Caspian Seas, and occasionally on the coasts of the Baltic and North Seas. Individuals may occur as vagrants inland, usually during migration. In central Europe it may be seen from September to November and again from March to early May. Arrival at the breeding grounds is at the end of May or beginning of June. The geese roam the countryside in flocks until all traces of snow have disappeared, after which they break up into pairs and establish their separate nests in concealed spots under bushes. The four to five eggs are laid in late June or the beginning of July and are incubated by the female alone for 26 to 27 days, while the male remains near by to warn her of approaching danger. When the young are grown, the geese form large flocks. In July, during the moult, they are often to be seen on land and when danger threatens they make their escape by running away at great speed. The lesser white-fronted goose forages for food only on land; it eats grass, leaves, shoots and berries.

Migratory bird

Size of egg:
69.0−84.5
× 43.0−52.0 mm.

Length:
53 to 66 cm.

Male and female have similar plumage.

Voice:
Male: a high-pitched 'kyn-yn' or 'kyn-yn-yn'.
Female: only 'kow-yow'.

Greylag Goose

Anser anser

Greylag, the ancestors of all domestic geese, breed in Iceland, western Scotland, Norway, Denmark and southeastern Europe. The main wintering grounds are northeastern Scotland and England and stretches of the western European coast in Holland, Belgium, France and Spain. Sites selected for nesting are large, still expanses of water, lakes and ponds with old reed beds, swamps, small islets by the seashore, flooded riverine woodlands but above all places with extensive meadows nearby. Greylag geese pair for life. On their return from their winter quarters they usually establish themselves in the same nesting territory as the year before. The nest, built by the female alone, may be located on dry as well as marshy ground or even in a willow. Nests on islets may be in quite open situations. Material for the nest is gathered in the immediate vicinity, and there is a thick lining made from down. As a rule, the goose lays four to nine eggs, which she incubates alone for 27 to 30 days while the gander keeps guard close by. Both parents care for the newly hatched goslings, which are capable of flight at 57 days but remain in the company of their parents, individual families then joining to form large flocks. The diet consists mostly of the green parts of plants and various seeds. Goslings feed themselves, starting with the tenderest leaves.

Voice:
The familiar
'aahng-ung-ung'.

Length:
Male 82.5 cm, female
70.5 cm.

Male and female have
similar plumage.

Size of egg:
74.0−99.0
× 51.4−62.0 mm.

Migratory or resident bird

Canada Goose

Branta canadensis

The original home of the Canada goose is North America. Since the seventeenth century, however, it has been raised in a semi-wild state in England and also in Sweden, where it was later let loose and went wild, thus giving rise to the European populations. British birds are resident, whereas birds nesting in southern Sweden depart in winter for the coasts of Germany and Holland, occurring at times as vagrants even in other European countries, though these may be escapes from zoos. In winter the Canada goose is found mostly by the coast. It breeds in coastal marshes as well as inland on pastures beside water and sometimes also in open woodlands with lakes and ponds. The nest is located on small islands or in swamps. The hollow is lined with dry leaves, grass and other vegetation and the eggs are covered with down. The five to six eggs are laid in early April and are incubated by the female alone for 28 to 29 days, while the male keeps careful watch close by. When the young are grown, families join to form flocks that roam the countryside. As a rule they forage for food on dry land, mostly in the early morning or at dusk. The diet consists of grass, grain, shoots, berries and seeds, occasionally also insects, their larvae, and molluscs.

Dispersive or migratory bird

Size of egg:
79.0—99.0
× 53.5—64.5 mm.

Length:
Male 99 cm, female
93.5 cm.

Male and female have
similar plumage.

Voice:
A hoarse honking that
sounds like 'aa-honk'.

Barnacle Goose

Branta leucopsis

The range of the barnacle goose extends over the north Atlantic from the eastern coast of Greenland and through Spitsbergen to south of Novaya Zemlya. Migration begins in late August or early September, the birds wintering on the coasts of Ireland, England, northern France, Holland, West Germany and Denmark, but individual flocks wander as far as Mediterranean, to the Azores and the eastern coast of North America. Barnacle geese from Spitsbergen migrate across the open sea and down the coast of Scandinavia; Greenland populations fly across Iceland and Novaya Zemlya populations fly across the Baltic Sea. The species nests in coastal colonies and alongside rivers, often near raptors, which protect them from the arctic fox. Arrival at the breeding grounds is in the second half of May. The nest is located as high as 50 metres above the sea, on steep cliffs, often in a colony of guillemots, kittiwakes or other seabirds. The female lays three to five, sometimes as many as seven eggs, usually in the second half of June, incubating them by herself for 24 to 26 days. When they have dried out, the goslings leap from the cliffs into the water. During the nesting season the barnacle goose feeds mainly on coastal vegetation and in winter on grass, aquatic plants, seaweeds and occasionally crustaceans, mollusc and aquatic insects.

Voice:
Usually rapid, repeated barks.

Length:
58 to 69 cm.

Male and female have similar plumage.

Size of egg:
68.0−82.7
× 46.0−54.0 mm.

Migratory bird

Brent Goose

Branta bernicla

The brent goose inhabits the tundras of northern Asia and North America; in Europe it breeds only on islands off the north coast of Russia. It is a sea and coastal bird. In Europe it winters chiefly on the coast of Denmark and West Germany, Holland, Belgium, France, England and Ireland. It returns to its breeding grounds in the first half of June, whereupon it immediately sets about preparing its nest — a hollow, not very deep, lined with vegetation and down. The brent goose nests in small colonies in dry, elevated places. In June the female lays three to six, sometimes eight eggs, which she incubates by herself for 24 to 26 days. It is interesting to note that the males abandon their families very early to form small flocks of their own sex. The complete summer moult begins in mid-July, the new flight feathers being fully grown-in between about the 10th and 15th of August. At this time the young are also already able to fly but have not as yet acquired their full plumage. In winter the brent goose feeds on marine vegetation, in summer on grass, lichens, moss and the like, as well as crustaceans, molluscs, aquatic insects and their larvae, and other invertebrates. The brent goose is now becoming increasingly scarce. Up to about 1930 some ten thousand of these birds wintered in Holland alone, whereas since 1953 their number has barely totalled one thousand, the same being true in other wintering grounds.

Migratory bird

Size of egg:
51.0—81.1
× 36.5—66.0 mm.

Length:
56 to 61 cm.

Male and female have similar plumage.

Voice:
Guttural sounds such as 'rronk' or 'rruk'.

Shelduck

Tadorna tadorna

In Europe, shelduck inhabit the coasts of Ireland, England, Scandinavia, Denmark, Germany, Holland, France and the Black Sea. World distribution extends as far as central China and Afghanistan, Asian birds being encountered also inland on salt lakes. The birds winter throughout western and southern Europe and in northern Africa, and on migration occasionally occur as vagrants on inland ponds and large rivers. In southerly parts of its range, the species is resident, favourite habitats being sandy shores, mudflats or islands, often near colonies of gulls and terns. The shelduck likes to nest in burrows, but will also lay on a pile of stones or in a rock cavity. The hollow is sparingly lined, either with leaves or pieces of wood, or more often with down. Between May and June, the female lays seven to 12, but sometimes as many as 20 eggs, which she incubates by herself for 27 to 29 days. During this period, the male remains close by looking out for danger. The newly hatched ducklings are led on to the water by their mother as soon as they have dried out. Shelduck feed on marine molluscs, crustaceans, worms, aquatic insects, their larvae, also on plant food and fish spawn or tadpoles.

Voice:
A characteristic, rapid call: 'ak-ak-ak' or 'ark, ark'.

Length:
61 cm.

Female not as brightly coloured as male.

Size of egg:
61.1−71.0
× 42.0−51.0 mm.

Migratory or resident bird

Wigeon

Anas penelope

Wigeon inhabit northern and northeastern Europe, also nesting in Scotland and on the shores of the Baltic Sea. In Scotland, Iceland and on Scandinavia's southwestern coast the species is resident or else roams the countryside in winter. Birds inhabiting other parts of Europe migrate southwest to the North Sea coast, the southern shore of the Baltic Sea, the west European coast, the Mediterranean countries and sometimes even to Africa. Occasionally, it winters on the rivers of central Europe. The southward migration starts at the end of August or in September, returning again in March or early April, arriving already paired. Wigeon are found on inland stretches of stagnant water bordered by thick vegetation. The nest, made of dry plant parts lined with a layer of grey down, is built by the female on the ground, generally close to the water and concealed by tall plants or a bush. The seven to ten eggs are incubated by the female alone for 22 to 23 days, on rare occasions as long as 25 days. When the newly hatched ducklings have dried, their mother leads them to the water, where they are joined by the drake. The diet consists mainly of eel-grass, green seaweeds or salting grass, though wigeon also graze on grass, and take animal food such as insects and their larvae, spiders, molluscs, and worms. Young ducklings feed mainly on small invertebrates.

Size of egg:
49.2—59.9
× 34.7—42.1 mm.

Length:
Male 49 cm, female 44 cm.

Sexually dimorphic.

Voice:
The male utters whistling notes that sound like 'whee-ooh'; the female a low, purring note.

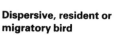

Dispersive, resident or migratory bird

Gadwall

Anas strepera

The gadwall is common in eastern Europe and the eastern part of central Europe; it is also found in northwestern Europe, Great Britain and the south of Sweden, and in rare instances southern Spain and France. Western European populations are resident, others are migrant, wintering mostly in southwestern Europe as well as in Africa as far south as Ethiopia. Gadwall leave their breeding grounds in September to November, returning in late March or April. The breeding grounds are mostly inland bodies of stagnant water bordered with thick vegetation. The birds are already paired when they arrive, but it is interesting to note that during the courtship display one female is surrounded by several males. The nest is placed on the ground, usually on a small islet, or bank near water. It is generally well concealed in grass and lined with bits of dry vegetation. In May or June there is a clutch of seven to 12 eggs, which the female incubates alone for 26 to 27 days. As soon as the newly hatched ducklings have dried, she leads them to the water. The young fledge at seven weeks, after which they roam the countryside until the time comes to leave for their winter quarters. The gadwall's diet consists of plant parts and seeds; only occasionally does the bird feed on molluscs and water insects. The young, however, consume animal food in plenty.

Voice:	**Length:**	**Size of egg:**
The male utters whistling notes; the female's cry sounds like 'kaaak-kaaak-kak-kak-kak'.	Male 51 cm, female 48 cm. Sexually dimorphic.	50.3–59.9 × 34.5–43.5 mm.

Migratory or resident bird

Teal

Anas crecca

The teal, weighing only about 300 grams, is the smallest of the European ducks. Its range includes all of Europe, the only places where it does not breed being Spain, Portugal, Italy and the Balkans, though in the latter it occurs in plenty during the winter months. Western European populations are resident. Some birds migrate to Africa — as far as the Sudan. The teal returns to its breeding grounds in March or early April, seeking out inland stretches of water bordered with thick vegetation and with meadows nearby. Pairs have been previously formed in the winter quarters during February and March. The nest is built by the female in tall grass, clumps of grass or beneath a thick willow or alder bush, and may be some distance from water. It is lined with dry vegetation such as stalks and leaves, and edged with down. Between mid-April and the beginning of June, the female begins incubating the eight to ten eggs, sitting on them alone for 22 to 25 days. During this time the male swims about nearby. The ducklings are small but very agile, able to dive and gather food for themselves. They begin to fly at one month. A teal's diet consists of vegetable matter and animal food, the latter being the mainstay in spring and summer; in autumn it feeds on seeds and plant parts. The young feed additionally on small invertebrates. When their young have fledged, teal form large flocks.

Size of egg:
41.0—50.0
× 30.0—35.5 mm.

Length:
Male 36 cm, female 34 cm.

Sexually dimorphic.

Voice:
The male's note is a ringing 'krrit', the female utters a rapid, harsh quack.

Migratory bird

Garganey

Anas querquedula

The garganey inhabits western, central, eastern and northeastern Europe. In England it occurs only in the southeast and in Scandinavia only on the eastern coast. Birds from central and eastern Europe migrate between August and November to Africa, wintering mostly in tropical areas. Western European populations also winter in Spain. The garganey inhabits marshy and swampy sites, lakes and ponds bordered with thick vegetation and is generally partial to places with meadows nearby. The birds arrive at their nesting grounds in late March or April, usually already in pairs; as a rule, several participate in the courtship antics, swimming in a circle, the males close behind their partners with ruffled feathers, heads bent and bills immersed in the water. The males also nod their heads up and down, occasionally bending them backwards, and complete the display by flying rapidly in small groups close above the surface. In late April, May or June the female builds the nest in shallow depression in the ground, lining it with pieces of fine greenery. She incubates the eight to eleven eggs alone for 21 to 25 days and also attends the young unaided by her mate. The diet of these ducks consists of seeds, green plant parts, insects and their larvae, worms, molluscs, spiders and occasionally small fish and tadpoles. Garganey are among the fastest fliers, attaining speeds of more than 60 miles per hour.

Voice:
The male utters a rattling noise, the female quacks.

Length:
Male 40 cm, female 36 cm.

Sexually dimorphic.

Size of egg:
39.3−50.1
× 29.7−35.5 mm.

Migratory bird

Mallard

Anas platyrhynchos

The mallard is one of the commonest and most widely distributed species of duck. It nests throughout Europe, where it is either resident or dispersive, or in northernmost areas a migrant to winter quarters in central and western Europe or the Mediterranean. Birds return to their nesting grounds in pairs at the end of February or in early March. The mallard inhabits still waters and sometimes rivers — even in towns. In courtship, the partners swim around each other, the male lowers his bill and ruffles his feathers, twitches his tail, nods his head, then plunges his bill into the water. The nesting site is selected by the drake but the nest itself is built by the duck. It is usually located on the ground, often some distance inland; also in trees, in nests abandoned by other birds and in holes. It is lined with leaves, plant stalks and small twigs and covered with a layer of down. Before leaving the nest, the duck carefully covers the eggs with down. There are usually nine to 13 eggs, which the female incubates alone for 22 to 26 days. When the ducklings' feathers have dried, she takes them out to the water. Mallard forage for food after dusk, feeding on various seeds, plant shoots and grass. They also collect food on the water's surface. The ducklings' diet consists largely of insects, but also crustaceans, molluscs and green plant parts.

Size of egg:
50.0—65.0
× 37.0—45.8 mm.

Length:
Male 57 cm, female 49 cm.

Sexually dimorphic.

Voice:
The male's note is a whistling 'yeeb'; the female quacks loudly.

Resident or dispersive bird

Pintail

Anas acuta

The pintail's range is mostly confined to northern and northeastern Europe, though the bird is
also found in the eastern and northern parts of
central Europe, in northwestern Europe and in
England. In England and northwestern Europe
it is partly resident, whereas birds inhabiting
other parts of the continent are migrant, wintering in western Europe, the Mediterranean and
Africa as far as the Sudan, but mostly on the
upper reaches of the Nile. The pintail leaves for
winter quarters in August to September, returning to its breeding grounds at the end of March
and in April. It favours large expanses of still
water, chiefly lakes, and in the north is found in
abundance in tundra, though it also occurs in
marshy areas and often near the sea. In Scandinavia it is one of the commonest of ducks. The
birds arrive at their nesting grounds in spring
already in pairs. The nest is fashioned by the
female in a depression in the ground lined with
dry plant parts gathered in the immediate vicinity. It is concealed in a clump of grass or in
thickets by the waterside, though it may also be
located in a meadow or even in woodland, often
several hundred yards from water. The seven to
eleven eggs are incubated 22 to 23 days by the
female alone while the male keeps guard close
by. The pintail feeds on various seeds, shoots
and green plant parts, as well as on insects and
their larvae, spiders, molluscs, worms and occasionally a tadpole or small frog.

Voice:
The male utters a low
whistle, the female a low
quack.

Length:
Male 70.5 cm, female
57.5 cm.

Sexually dimorphic.

Size of egg:
44.1—61.9
× 33.9—43.0 mm.

Migratory or resident bird

Shoveler

Anas clypeata

The shoveler breeds in eastern, northeastern, central and western Europe. In Scandinavia it occurs only in the southern parts of Sweden and Finland and on the eastern coast of Iceland. In western Europe it is resident or else roams the countryside, whereas birds inhabiting other parts of the continent are migrant, wintering sometimes in western Europe but mostly in the Mediterranean or in Africa as far south as Uganda and Ghana. The shoveler departs for its winter quarters in late August and September, returning at the end of March or in April. It nests on inland lakes and ponds, including quite small ones, whether open or bordered with thick vegetation. In May to June the female prepares the nest in a depression among grass, often in a meadow some distance from the water. It is lined with dry vegetation. When the clutch is complete (7 to 12 eggs), she lines and borders the nest with greyish down and then incubates alone for 23 to 25 days though this period may be as short as 21 and as long as 27 days. After the ducklings have hatched, she takes them to shallow water where they easily find food. At six weeks the ducklings are able to fly. The diet consists of various crustaceans, insect larvae, molluscs, worms, planktons and fragments of aquatic plants, which the bird sieves with its bill. In the autumn it also gathers various seeds.

Migratory, dispersive or resident bird

Size of egg:
47.1−58.0
× 34.5−40.0 mm.

Length:
Male 51.5 cm, female 47.5 cm.

Sexually dimorphic.

Voice:
The male's note is a deep 'tuk-tuk'; the female's sounds like 'woak'; neither is heard frequently.

Wood Duck

Aix sponsa

The wood duck breeds throughout the eastern half and northwestern parts of the USA and in southern Canada where it is resident. In autumn it moves southwards to spend the winter, some birds reaching southern California in the west and as far south as Florida and Cuba in the east. It inhabits lakes and rivers bordered by forests and nests in tree cavities, usually ones abandoned by woodpeckers, sometimes even quite far from water. The nest is generally located six to 18 metres above the ground but if suitable cavities are scarce then it may be located even in a mere depression as little as 1.5 metres above the ground. The female lays eight to 14 eggs but a nest may contain eggs laid by more than one bird. Young ducks nesting for the first time lay only five to seven eggs. These are incubated for 28 to 32 days by the female alone. As soon as they have dried the newly hatched ducklings leap from the nest to the ground in response to their mother's call. The impact of their fall is cushioned by their soft down and usually also by grass. The duck then leads her brood to water where they are joined by the drake. The ducklings are able to fly at the age of nine weeks. Wood ducks visit forests, where they gather seeds, berries and other fruit. In spring and summer the wood duck also eats animal food, chiefly insects, insect larvae, molluscs and worms, but plant food is the mainstay of the diet throughout the year.

Voice:
A loud 'whooo-eek' (female); a wheezy rising 'jeeee' (male).

Length:
50 cm.

Size of egg:
48.0–58.0 × 36.0–42.2 mm.

Migratory bird

Red-crested Pochard

Netta rufina

The range of this diving duck covers southeastern Spain, southeastern France, the Mediterranean islands, part of northwestern Europe, Holland and Belgium; the species also has an interrupted distribution in central Europe, where it has become more widespread during recent years. It is also found in parts of southeastern Europe and occasionally occurs as a vagrant in England and Sweden. Birds inhabiting the Mediterranean region are resident, those from other areas migrate to the Mediterranean in October to December. During late March or April the birds return to their nesting grounds on deep, still stretches of water or slow-flowing water courses with ample vegetation. On steppes, the red-crested pochard also inhabits salt lakes. In May and June, the female builds the nest among vegetation or in thickets on the ground, but sometimes also in reed-beds. It is generally lined with dry vegetation, small twigs and sometimes green leaves; it also contains a large quantity of buff-grey down. As a rule, the clutch consists of six to ten eggs, which the female incubates alone for 26 to 28 days. Although these are diving ducks, they will forage for food at the surface. Dives are to depths between 2 and 4 metres. The diet consists of various water plants and seeds, small crustaceans, molluscs, worms and insects.

Size of egg:
51.7—62.3
× 38.2—45.1 mm.

Length:
Male 57 cm, female 51 cm.

Sexually dimorphic.

Voice:
The male's call is a thin, hoarse note, the female makes a quacking or rasping sound.

Migratory or resident bird

Pochard

Aythya ferina

This is a very common diving duck with a widespread distribution embracing all of eastern, central and northwestern Europe including England. In Scandinavia it occurs only in the eastern parts of Sweden and Finland and in southernmost Norway. Where the climate is mild, pochard are resident or dispersive, whereas birds inhabiting northern and eastern Europe winter in the Mediterranean, and sometimes central Europe, where they form flocks on large, unfrozen rivers and lakes. Departure for winter quarters is in September to mid-November, the return from mid-March to early April. Favourite haunts are inland lakes and ponds bordered by thick vegetation. Although birds pair in their winter quarters they arrive at the breeding grounds in flocks. The nest is built by the female on the ground among vegetation near the water. The hollow is fairly deep and lined with bits of vegetation and thick, dark-coloured down. A clutch consists of five to 11 eggs, which the duck incubates alone for 23 to 26 days. The ducklings are led out on the water by the duck the day they hatch. Diet consists of the green parts of aquatic plants as well as seeds; plant food predominates but the young, and occasionally the adults, also take crustaceans, molluscs, insects and their larvae, other invertebrates and sometimes tadpoles.

Voice:
The male's call consists of whistling notes; the female makes a harsh, growling noise.

Length:
Male 46 cm, female 42 cm.

Sexually dimorphic.

Size of egg:
55.8–68.5
× 39.0–46.9 mm.

Resident, dispersive or migratory bird

Tufted Duck

Aythya fuligula

The tufted duck was originally a native of northern and northeastern Europe, whence it spread to western and central Europe and where it is now in many places one of the commonest ducks. The populations of western and northwestern Europe are resident, those of other parts are migrant. Scandinavian populations often winter in central Europe on large rivers that do not freeze over, even in large cities, but the tufted duck's main winter quarters are the shores of western Europe, particularly England but also the Mediterranean area. The birds return to their breeding grounds from mid-March to April, settling on stagnant water as well as slow-flowing water courses bordered with thick vegetation. They are partial to stretches of water with small islets, on which they like to build their nests. This task is performed by the female from May to July. The nest itself is a small hollow in the ground. Six to 12 eggs are incubated by the female alone, usually for 24 to 26 days. About 12 hours after they have hatched, the black ducklings are led out onto the water by the duck. At seven weeks they are already capable of flight. The diet consists mostly of animal food — crustaceans, molluscs, insects, their larvae and other invertebrates. It also feeds on vegetable matter, such as seeds, and pieces of aquatic plants. The tufted duck usually dives to depths of 2 to 3 metres.

Size of egg:
53.0—67.1
× 37.7—47.2 mm.

Length:
Male 42 cm, female 38 cm.

Sexually dimorphic.

Voice:
The male utters short, whistling courtship notes; the female has a hoarse 'arrr'.

Migratory or dispersive bird

Scaup

Aythya marila

The scaup, a small diving duck, inhabits the extreme northern parts of Europe, northern Asia, Canada and Alaska. In Europe it breeds in northern Scandinavia, Murmansk and Iceland. Outside the breeding season it spends practically all its time on the sea or river deltas, wintering in flocks sometimes numbering thousands of birds, along the coasts of western Europe, Great Britain, southern Scandinavia, Germany, Denmark, Poland, Italy and around the Black and Caspian Seas. It returns to its breeding grounds – still bodies of water on tundra or moor – in late April, showing a preference for sites near gull or tern colonies. The nest is generally built on dry land close to the water's edge and lined with a thick layer of down. Scaup often nest in colonies. From May to June the female lays between six and nine, sometimes as many as 12 eggs, which she incubates alone for 24 to 28 days, leading the newly-hatched ducklings out onto the water as soon as they are dry. At first the ducklings feed on insects, which they collect among vegetation or on the water. Adult birds feed mostly on molluscs, small crustaceans, worms and insects, and will sometimes also eat small fish. Seeds and aquatic vegetation form only a minor part of the diet.

Voice:
The male makes
a whistling note, the
female's call is a low
'karr-karr'.

Length:
48 cm.

Sexually dimorphic.

Size of egg:
54.5−68.3
× 39.0−48.0 mm.

Migratory bird

Eider

Somateria mollissima

In Europe the eider is found along the coast of Iceland, in all of Scandinavia, Finland, the Murmansk region, Scotland, Ireland, Denmark and the islands of West Germany and Holland. It also makes its home in northern Asia and northern North America. Birds inhabiting the extreme northern parts of the range are migrant, but otherwise the eider is either a partial migrant or resident. In winter it occurs in large flocks along the coast of western Europe and the North and Baltic Seas. Single young individuals may occur as vagrants in the heart of central Europe. The eider nests in colonies often numbering a hundred or even a thousand pairs. It is protected by law in practically all parts of its range and therefore exhibits no fear of man. The nest is located among rocks, under pieces of wood, under bushes and such like and is lined with small twigs, leaves, seaweed or only small pebbles. After the eggs are laid a great quantity of eiderdown is added to the nest. The female lays three to nine eggs, young females, however, only two or three. She incubates by herself for 25 to 28 days and within five to ten hours after the ducklings have hatched she leads them to water. The young birds are already capable of flight at the age of sixty to seventy-five days and are fully grown by the time they are 80 to 90 days old. The mainstay of the diet is molluscs, but the eider also eats crustaceans, worms, starfish and fish. It usually dives to depths of about six metres in pursuit of its prey.

Size of egg:
68.0—88.0
× 46.7—56.5 mm.

Length:
58 cm.

Sexually dimorphic.

Voice:
The male's call is a ringing 'coo-roo-uh'; the female's a quacking 'korr-r'.

Migratory, dipersive or resident bird

Common Scoter

Melanitta nigra

The common scoter is distributed across northern Europe, northern Asia and western Alaska. European populations breed in Iceland, central and northern Scandinavia, northern Finland, the coastal regions of Russia, in Scotland and in Ireland. Quite large migrant groups may be found along the coasts of western Europe, Great Britain, the North and Baltic Seas and, to some extent, the coast of northwestern Africa. The birds return to their breeding grounds on lakes, moors and tundra in May. The nest is located near water in tall grass, under bushes or among rocks, and is lined sparingly by the female with moss, lichens or dry grass. The clutch usually consists of five to eight eggs which the female begins incubating in June, shortly after which the male abandons her. Hatching is after 27 to 31 days and the chicks are led to water by their mother as soon as they have dried. They stay in her company for six to seven weeks after which they fend for themselves, though remaining in flocks. The scoter obtains food exclusively by diving, usually to depths of about six metres, taking molluscs, crustaceans, worms, and in the breeding grounds, aquatic insects and their larvae. The diet also includes vegetable matter. When pursued by a bird of prey, the common scoter makes its escape by diving into the water in mid-flight.

Voice:
Male, a ringing call.
Female, various rasping
sounds.

Length:
48 cm.

Sexually dimorphic.

Size of egg:
59.0−72.0
× 41.3−47.7 mm.

Resident or migratory bird

Velvet Scoter

Melanitta fusca

In Europe the velvet scoter is found in Scandinavia, Finland, northwest Russia and Scotland, also in northern Asia eastward as far as Kamchatka as well as in North America. Mostly a migratory bird, it winters mainly along the coasts of western Europe, the North Sea and Baltic Sea and also in the southern part of the Black Sea. In winter it may be encountered fairly regularly on inland lakes, ponds, and rivers. The birds arrive at their breeding grounds, already paired, in late April or early May. They nest along seashores and on islands, as well as on inland bodies of water in the tundra and taiga and in Scandinavia also in mountain areas. The nest is located in tall grass, under bushes, among rocks, usually near water. It is merely a depression lined sparingly with bits of leaves, grass, pine needles and such like but with a thick layer of down. Between the end of May and beginning of June the female lays six to ten, sometimes even as many as fourteen eggs, which she incubates by herself for 28 to 30 days. After the ducklings have hatched she remains together with them on the water. The diet consists of small crustaceans, molluscs, the larvae of aquatic insects and also small bits of green aquatic vegetation. Adult birds obtain food solely by diving for it to depths of two to five metres.

Migratory bird

Size of egg:
64.3—77.5
× 42.6—51.5 mm.

Length:
56 cm.

Sexually dimorphic.

Voice:
The male's call is a whistling note 'kiu' or 'whur-er'; the female makes harsh, rasping sounds.

Goldeneye

Bucephala clangula

The goldeneye is found throughout northern Europe and in central Europe in the Bohemian part of Czechoslovakia and Switzerland. It winters in western, central, southern and southeastern Europe on lakes, ponds and rivers, even in cities. The nest is generally located right by the water. The birds begin pairing in their wintering grounds and continue courting in their breeding territories, where they return as soon as the ice thaws. The female seeks out the nesting cavity, followed then by the male. The cavity is often one used the previous year but it may be a new one as well. Tree holes chosen for a nesting site are usually 2.5 to 5 metres above the ground. Often the nest is sited in an old nest hole of the black woodpecker. In April to May the female lays six to eleven eggs in the bottom of the cavity, which she only rarely lines with bits of moss. However, the eggs are surrounded with soft down. The female incubates by herself for 27 to 32 days. When the newly hatched ducklings have dried out they jump out of the nest, usually landing in soft grass or water unharmed. Food is obtained mostly in the water and consists of insects and their larvae, worms, molluscs, crustaceans as well as small fish and to a lesser extent green vegetation and seeds. The goldeneye dives to depths of as much as nine metres.

Voice:
The male utters sounds like 'qui-rrik', when courting 'rrrr'; the female usually makes a low-pitched 'grarr grarr'.

Length:
46 cm.

Sexually dimorphic.

Size of egg:
52.0—68.0
× 39.4—47.0 mm.

Migratory bird

Red-breasted Merganser

Mergus serrator

In Europe the red-breasted merganser is distributed over Iceland, Scotland, northwestern England, Scandinavia, Finland and Russia. In central Europe it breeds regularly along the coasts of Germany, Poland and Denmark and, in rare instances, Holland. It is also found in northern Asia, North America and Greenland. Outside the breeding season the bird spends most of its time at sea, being seen inland only on passage. In southern parts of its range, the red-breasted merganser is resident or a partial migrant; in northern parts, a full migrant. In early May, about two to three weeks before laying, the female begins seeking a suitable site for the nest. The male may accompany her, or he may wait on the water. Nests are built by females alone in dense clumps of grass or other vegetation, under bushes, among rocks, between the roots of trees, in holes in the ground, but always on dry land. The location is usually near water, but may be as much as 100 metres from its edge. The lining is of dry as well as green vegetation from the vicinity. At the end of May and in June, occasionally as late as July, the female lays five to 12 eggs which she incubates by herself for 28 to 32 days. On day two, the newly hatched young are taken out on to the water by their mother; they can fly at 59 days. Diet consists of small fish, molluscs, crustaceans, aquatic insects and worms.

Resident, dispersive or migratory bird

Size of egg:
56.5—70.7
× 40.3—47.6 mm.

Length:
Male 59.5 cm, female
52 cm.

Sexually dimorphic.

Voice:
Male has a rasping, disyllabic courtship note; the female's is generally 'rock-rock-rock'.

Goosander

Mergus merganser

Goosanders inhabit a large territory ranging from Iceland and the British Isles eastwards through northern Europe and the northern part of central Asia as far as northern China and Sakhalin. On rare occasions they also breed in the Swiss Alps. The species is either resident or, in the north of its range, fully migratory. In winter the goosander is often encountered inland on rivers. It nests chiefly on inland waters which must be unpolluted, sufficiently deep and bordered by old trees. In spring, the female seeks a suitable nesting cavity in old, usually broad-leaved trees, though the nest may also be located in rock cavities. A tree nest site is some 2.5 to 18 metres above the ground, a cliff site as high as 50 metres above the water. When a cavity is used, the eggs are laid on the bare surface, whereas in open nests the hollow is usually lined with grass, leaves and moss. Between mid-March and May, when the clutch of seven to 12 eggs is complete, the female begins incubating. Hatching is after 28 to 32 days, whereupon the chicks jump out of the nest into the water, and start swimming about with their mother. The goosander feeds mainly on fish, but also eats crustaceans and other small animal life it finds in water. It can dive into water from the air. Eels, salmon and fish are among its favourite prey.

Voice:
The male makes low-pitched, croaking sounds; the female's call sounds like 'karr'.

Length:
Male 75.5 cm, female 57.5 cm.

Sexually dimorphic.

Size of egg:
55.4—74.5 × 37.0—50.0 mm.

Resident or dispersive bird

107

Turkey Vulture

Cathartes aura

The turkey vulture is widely distributed throughout America from southern Canada across the USA and Central America to South America and the Falklands, and is plentiful in all parts of its range. It generally inhabits open plains in the vicinity of steep cliffs but also occurs in deserts and open woodlands. In the autumn it leaves its northern breeding grounds for its winter quarters in the south, often travelling in large flocks. It congregates in large numbers even outside migration times; such flocks often visit cities in quest of meat remnants and rubbish. The turkey vulture's chief food is fresh carrion; sometimes, however, it hunts small vertebrates including snakes, frogs and rodents, as well as small birds; occasionally it takes even birds' eggs from the nest. It is also fond of soft fruits and the fruit of the oil palm. It nests in caves on high cliffs, preferably ones with two entrances. It does not build a nest but merely lines the cavity with bits of cloth, etc. The female lays one to three eggs in the darkest part of the cave and she and her mate take turns incubating. The young hatch after 38 to 41 days and are fed partially digested food from the crop by both parents. They remain in the nest some 70 to 80 days before fledging. In Florida the nesting period begins in March but in more northerly parts not until May or even June.

Migratory or resident bird

Size of eggs:
62.0—84.0
× 43.0—53.0 mm.

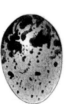

Length:
75 cm.

Wing span:
180 cm.

Male and female have similar plumage.

Voice:
A hoarse, wheezing sound.

California Condor

Gymnogyps californianus

Today the rare California condor inhabits only a small area inland and on the coast of southern California. Previously its range included also the state of Washington. The California condor is a bird of the high mountains. It lives on cliffs from which it flies over mountain or river valleys in search of large dead animals or remnants left by bears and other beasts of prey. The flesh of dead animals forms the mainstay of its diet. Only occasionally, when food is scarce, does it hunt live prey for itself — small vertebrates such as ground squirrels, for instance. It consumes about one kilogram of meat a day. The breeding period lasts from January to May. The nest is built in caves on cliffs or occasionally in an old tree cavity. It is usually located at a height of 500 to 1,500 metres above sea level, sometimes only several kilometres from the coast. In January or February the female lays one, very occasionally two eggs which both partners take turns incubating for 42 to 50 days. The young nestling is tended by the parents for a long time. At first they bring food to the nest twice a day, in the morning and evening, later only once a day. Not until it is 5 1/2 to 6 months old is the young California condor capable of flight and full maturity is not attained until the age of three years; the bird's life span, however, is up to 50 years.

Voice:
Usually only a hissing
sound, sometimes also
a wheezing sound.

Length:
125 cm.

Wing span:
300 cm.

Male and female have
similar plumage.

Size of egg:
102.0–120.0
× 62.9–71.0 mm.

Resident or dispersive bird

109

Griffon Vulture

Gyps fulvus

Dry, open, rocky sites on mountain slopes and cliffs, less frequently in lowland regions, are the griffon vulture's habitats. In Europe it occurs in Spain, southwestern France, northern Italy, Switzerland and the southeast. It may also be seen in England, Denmark, Finland and central Europe, but these populations are usually young fledglings. By January, adult birds have reached the nesting grounds, where the male courts his partner. A nest of sticks and branches, which the vulture often tears from trees with his beak, is built on an inaccessible cliff ledge in February or March. The nesting hollow is lined with the hair and skin of mammals, and the single egg is usually white, but sometimes spotted brown. It is incubated for 48 to 52 days by both partners. The young bird remains in the nest for about 80 days, during which time the parents feed it half-digested food from the crop. The diet consists chiefly of carcasses of larger mammals; the vultures first rip out the entrails, and then devour also the muscular tissue and skin. Sometimes they gorge themselves to the extent that they cannot fly, and must then rest for a number of hours to digest the food. If sudden danger threatens, they have to regurgitate before flying away. Luckily the birds can go without food for several days without harm. The griffon vulture attacks small live animals only in rare instances.

Size of egg:
82.0–106.0
× 64.0–75.0 mm.

Length:
100 cm.

Wing span:
About 240 cm.

Male and female have
similar plumage.

Voice:
A hissing or croaking
sound.

Dispersive bird

Black Vulture

Aegypius monachus

The black vulture inhabits the mountainous areas of Spain, Sicily and southeastern Europe, but outside the breeding season it may also be seen in Germany, France, Denmark, Poland, Czechoslovakia, and other European countries, although visitors to the latter countries are usually young birds. In eastern areas this huge bird of prey may be found also in lowland country. The large nest of branches, lined with pieces of animal skin and hair, is built in a tree in the middle of February. Branches used in its construction are broken off trees by the bird's strong beak. Both parents take turns incubating the single egg for 55 days. The nestling has a large head, can see as soon as it is born, but its legs are not fully developed, the toes being incapable of grasping. Contour feathers do not begin to grow in until 'he age of one month, and the plumage is not complete until a further month has passed. Both parents feed the young bird, providing half-digested food from the crop. The nestling remains in the nest for a long time, usually about three months, before it is capable of flight. The vulture's diet consists primarily of carrion, especially the carcasses of larger mammals. The bird consumes flesh, skin and even bone and regurgitates the undigested parts. Only rarely does it hunt live animals, primarily reptiles and amphibians. Conspicuous in flight are its long, broad wings with quills spread wide apart.

Voice:
Hoarse croaking or wheezing sounds.

Length:
103 cm.

Wing span:
265 to 287 cm.

Male and female have similar plumage.

Size of egg:
83.2—107.0 × 56.0—76.0 mm.

Resident or dispersive bird

Golden Eagle

Aquila chrysaetos

Golden eagles are birds of high, rocky places in Scotland, Scandinavia, Spain, the Alps, the Carpathians and sometimes other parts of Europe. This huge bird of prey is generally resident, though young individuals roam far afield at the onset of autumn and can often be found in lowland areas and even in the vicinity of cities. At the end of March or in April, the golden eagle builds its large nest resembling a huge basket composed of sticks and branches. It is usually sited on an inaccessible cliff face or very occasionally in a tree, and is often used for several years. However, within the confines of its territory, to which it remains faithful, it often builds several nests over a period, occupying them successively. The usual clutch of two eggs is incubated by the female for 44 to 45 days, the male occasionally relieving her so that she can stretch her wings. Food is hunted by the male, who passes it to the female to distribute among the nestlings, though when they are older he feeds them himself. The young take to the wing when they are between 71 and 81 days old, but remain in the company of their parents for a short time after. When fully grown, they leave their home territory, often travelling great distances. The golden eagle hunts marmots, hares, and small beasts of prey; sometimes it will kill a young chamois, stray lamb or kid. Young eagles also eat amphibians, reptiles and large insects, and welcome fresh carrion.

Size of egg:
70.1—88.9
× 51.0—66.0 mm.

Length:
82 cm.

Wing span:
188 to 196 cm.

Male and female
have similar plumage.

Voice:
A noisy 'kya', and a few whistling notes.

Resident or dispersive bird

Buzzard

Buteo buteo

At the end of February the buzzard may be seen circling above a wood, suddenly plummeting to the ground and the next instant soaring up again. This large bird of prey is one of the most common raptors of Europe, where it is absent only in the northernmost regions. It frequents forests of all kinds, from lowland to mountain altitudes, preferring country where woods alternate with fields and meadows. It usually remains in its nesting territory throughout the year, which extends from three to four kilometres in diameter, or roams the countryside far and wide after fledging. Many inhabitants of northern Europe migrate southwest in winter. In April the buzzard builds its nest high in the treetops, though in England it will also build on cliffs. The structure is made of twigs and lined with leaves, moss and hair; the edge is often decorated with leaves or seaweed. Both partners share the duties of brooding the two to four eggs for 28 to 49 days, though the female bears the brunt of the task. The nestlings are fed at first by the female, who first receives the prey from the male, but later he also feeds them. Fledging is after 41 to 49 days, but the chicks continue to be fed a further four weeks by the parent birds. The mainstays of the diet are fieldmice and other small rodents. A buzzard will often wait on the ground outside the hole of a fieldmouse, sometimes without moving for hours, in order to outwit its wary prey.

Voice:
A long, plaintive 'pee-o'.

Length:
53 cm.

Wing span:
117 to 137 cm.

Plumage is very variable.

Size of egg:
49.8−63.8
× 39.1−49.0 mm.

Resident or dispersive bird

Sparrowhawk

Accipiter nisus

The sparrowhawk — in effect Europe's common hawk — is found throughout Europe, frequenting woods and groves. After the young have fledged, the birds roam the countryside, though many fly southwest at the end of August or September, returning in March or April to their breeding grounds which are selected by the males; the females return somewhat later. The nest of dry twigs, lined with hair, is built in a spruce tree, with another tree selected nearby for use as a resting place. On the ground below this tree one will find regurgitated, undigested food pellets. The four to six eggs are incubated by the hen for 33 days, but the male brings her food, which she takes from him at a particular spot near to the nest. Incubation, by the female alone, begins as soon as the first, second or third egg is laid. Thus the young hatch successively, the last ones often being eaten by the elder and larger nestlings, especially when there is a lack of food. Initially the male hunts for prey, mostly small birds, which he plucks clean at a selected spot before passing them to the female. When the nestlings are a week old, the female also forages for food, which she shares out between the young. After the first two weeks, when the young are able to tear their own food, the male brings it to them directly instead of first passing it to the hen. The sparrowhawk hunts prey within a territory measuring some two to five kilometres in diameter. The young leave the nest at 26 to 31 days.

Dispersive bird

Size of egg:
34.2–46.7
× 27.5–36.0 mm.

Length:
28 to 38 cm.
The female is larger than the male.

Wing span:
Male 60 cm, female up to 80 cm.

Sexually dimorphic.

Voice:
Beside the nest, a repeated 'liik-leek-leek'; when alarmed, 'kew kew', also a soft, 'keeow'.

Goshawk

Accipiter gentilis

This magnificent predator inhabits woods near fields and meadows, in both lowland or mountainous country. It is distributed throughout Europe, but does not nest in England (except very occasionally), Ireland and Iceland. A resident bird, it remains in its breeding grounds all year, roaming the adjacent countryside; inhabitants of northern and eastern Europe, however, often fly to central Europe in winter. The large nest, of sticks and twigs, is built high in a pine or spruce tree from April to May, but the courtship displays may be observed as early as March. The female lays three to four eggs which she incubates 35 to 38 days, mostly by herself, being relieved only occasionally by the male. She stays with the nestlings for the first ten days, when the male supplies food, which the hen divides before passing to the young, eating the remnants herself. The male is unable to feed the nestlings, and should the hen die during this period they meet the same fate. The young leave the nest 41 to 43 days and, when fully independent, scatter throughout the countryside, usually settling within 100 kilometres of the nest. Occasionally, young birds from northern Europe fly as far as 1,500 kilometres from where they were born. The goshawk preys mostly on birds, some as large as the heron and, mainly during the winter months, will take owls such as the long-eared or barn owls.

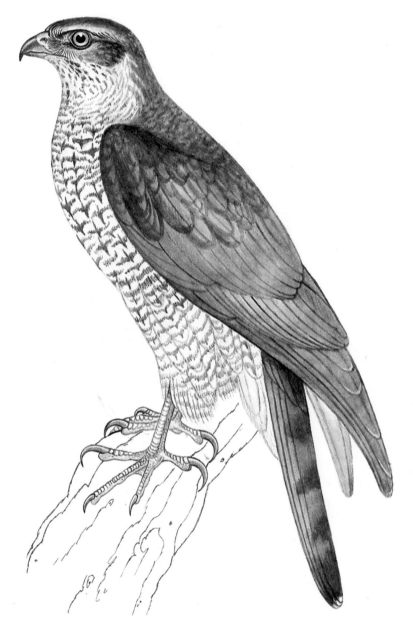

Voice:
A lengthy 'gig-gig-gig'; the young utter a piping 'kee'.

Length:
48 to 58 cm.
The female is larger than the male.

Wing span:
Male 100 to 105 cm; female 130 to 140 cm.

Male and female have similar plumage.

Size of egg:
51.0−65.0
× 40.6−51.0 mm.

Resident or dispersive bird

Red Kite

Milvus milvus

This handsome predator is widespread in the warmer parts of the continent: Spain, Italy, France, central Europe, the western parts of eastern Europe, southeastern Europe, Wales and southern Sweden. In the fifteenth and sixteenth centuries it was still one of the commonest London birds, but has since become extinct in the British Isles except for Wales. In southern regions it is locally quite plentiful, in more northerly parts, however, it is a rare bird. In Wales and the Mediterranean it is resident, but birds inhabiting other parts of Europe leave at the end of August or in September to winter in southern Europe and northern Africa. Migrants form flocks of 50 to 200 birds which hunt jointly and roost together in woodland. The nest is built in April or May, usually in the highest trees on a woodland edge close to meadows. The structure, measuring 1 metre across, is made of sticks and twigs, and lined with straw, rags and pieces of paper. Often, however, the bird will settle in an abandoned nest of some other raptor or even a heron. The female lays two to four eggs, which she incubates mostly alone for 28 to 30 days. The young remain in the nest for 40 to 54 days, during which time the parents keep them constantly supplied with food. The red kite feeds on various invertebrates and smaller vertebrates, such as frogs, lizards, rodents, small, weak-flying birds, occasional fish and bits of carrion.

Migratory or resident bird

Size of egg:
51.5−63.0
× 40.2−49.0 mm.

Length:
62 cm.

Wing span:
145 to 155 cm.

Male and female have
similar plumage.

Voice:
A trilling 'hi-hi-heea'.

Black Kite

Milvus migrans

Rising and falling in graceful undulations, the black kite may be seen winging its way over the surface of a pond, lake or river in almost any part of Europe except the west coast, England and Scandinavia. Only rarely does it nest in central Europe, birds seen there usually being on passage southwards. In southerly areas, however, the species is quite plentiful. August and September are the months for departure to winter quarters in Africa, March for the return to the breeding grounds. Black kites inhabit lowland, broadleaved, coniferous as well as mixed woodland, usually nesting in sites close to still or flowing water. They are often found in colonies of herons, cormorants and other fish-eating birds where there is access to ample fish remnants. In spring, paired birds perform spectacular courtship flights. The nest, built five to 25 metres high in a tree, is a haphazard structure of sticks and twigs. Frequently, the black kite will take over the abandoned nest of a stork or heron. Sometimes it nests in colonies. The two to three eggs are incubated for 28 days by the female, relieved now and then by the male. The young fledge at 42 to 45 days. The diet consists mainly of carrion and fish remnants: while prospecting the bird may be seen hovering above water. It also hunts frogs and small mammals, which are fed to the offspring. After fledging, the birds form large flocks.

Voice:
A trilling 'hihihihee'.

Length:
57 cm.

Wing span:
114 to 118 cm.

Male and female have similar plumage.

Size of egg:
46.0—61.0
× 37.0—46.5 mm.

Migratory bird

White-tailed Eagle

Haliaeetus albicilla

The white-tailed eagle inhabits the northern and eastern coasts of Scandinavia and Iceland, the eastern part of central Europe, northeastern and southeastern Europe, northern and central Asia and southwestern Greenland. In autumn and winter it is regularly encountered in central Europe. It nests on rocky coasts or large inland bodies of water as well as on water courses. As early as January or February it shows up at its central European breeding grounds and immediately sets about building the nest — a huge structure placed in a tall tree or on a cliff ledge, in rare instances even on the ground. It is made of a mass of sticks and branches, and despite the overall size, the actual nesting hollow is small. A nest is used for years in succession, being added to every year and sometimes growing as large as two metres across one and a half metres high. In February to April the female lays two to three eggs, or occasionally one, which both partners take turns incubating for 31 to 46 days. The young are fed fish and small waterfowl, and abandon the nest after 50 to 77 days. The mainstay of the diet is fish and birds, mainly coots. An experienced eagle will capture even a goose or heron, but young birds are not as skilled and often eat dead fish that have been washed ashore. The white-tailed eagle plucks its prey out of the water with its talons; only rarely does it plunge into the water in a steep dive.

Size of egg:
66.0—84.8
× 53.0—63.5 mm.

Length:
69 to 91 cm.
The female is somewhat
larger than the male.

Wing span:
Up to 240 cm.

Male and female have
similar plumage.

Voice:
A clear 'kri, kri, kri', also
a low-pitched 'kra'.

Dispersive or migratory bird

Bald Eagle

Haliaeetus leucocephalus

The bald eagle, national bird of the United States, is distributed from Alaska to the Gulf of Mexico, chiefly round large lakes and rivers but also in coastal regions. In former days it was very plentiful but it has been greatly persecuted by fishermen who regard it as a competitor. Furthermore this majestic eagle has little resistance to pesticides which cause infertility in the bird. It was found that only three out of 50 nests produced eagle fledglings. Today the total bald eagle population in North America numbers only 5000 birds and that is why it is now rigidly protected by law. The bald eagle pairs for life, changing to a new mate only if its partner dies. The nest is usually built on a high treetop or upon a rocky cliff but on islands it may be on the ground. It is made of branches and lined with pine needles, grass, roots, and the like. The birds continue to enlarge the nest adding green leaves on to the outside even during incubation and it can reach up to 3 metres in diameter. The female lays two or three eggs in February/March (in northern regions) or in December/January (in the south). The young hatch after 35 days and are fed by both parents. The baby eagles remain in the nest for ten to eleven weeks, after which they roam the countryside with their parents. When fully grown they often congregate in large groups that fly to the western coast of Alaska where food is plentiful. They hunt chiefly fish.

Voice:
Clear call that sounds like 'cac-cac-cac'.

Length:
Male 80 cm, female 110 cm.

Wing span:
Up to 220 cm.

Male and female have similar plumage.

Size of egg:
58.1—84.3
× 47.0—63.4 mm.

Resident or dispersive bird

Honey Buzzard

Pernis apivorus

This predator is a common inhabitant of all woodland, especially lowland forest. It is distributed throughout Europe, but does not nest in Ireland, Iceland and England and northern and western Scandinavia. A migratory bird, it spends the winter in tropical and southern Africa, journeying from its breeding grounds in August or early September and returning again in April or May. Soon after arrival in spring, it performs its courtship flight above the wood selected as its territory. The large nest of twigs, lined with fresh green twigs and leaves, is built by both partners high in a tree, usually 15 to 22 metres above the ground, though the female performs the greater part of the task. Sometimes the honey buzzard takes over an abandoned goshawk's or common buzzard's nest. Even after the young have hatched, the adult birds continue to cover the nest with fresh green twigs. The duties of incubating the two eggs are generally shared by the partners for 30 to 35 days. Instances have been recorded of the male alone hatching the eggs following the death of the female. As the partners change places on the nest, they clap their bills and utter loud cries. The duties of feeding the chicks are also shared, the chicks' diet during the first few days consisting of wasps and wasp larvae. Honey buzzards also feed on other insects, occasionally on small vertebrates and even soft fruits. The young leave the nest after 35 to 45 days, but return to it at night for a further short period.

Size of egg:
44.9—66.0
× 37.0—44.4 mm.

Length:
55 cm

Wing span:
120 to 126 cm.

Male and female have similar colouring, but individuals vary enormously.

Voice:
A high-pitched 'kee-er' and also a fast-repeated 'kikiki'.

Migratory bird

Marsh Harrier

Circus aeruginosus

A marsh harrier may be distinguished by its habit of gliding on raised wings close (say 3 metres) above reeds. Its habitats are reedbeds, marshes and, in southern Europe, fields close to water. Its range covers almost all of Europe; in Scandinavia, however, it is confined to southern Sweden and in England the southeast. It also occurs as an occasional vagrant in Ireland and Norway. Birds inhabiting central and eastern Europe leave in August or the beginning of September for Africa or the Middle East; those native to southern and western Europe are resident, roaming the countryside in winter. In late March to mid-April the birds return to their nesting grounds and in May or June build a nest generally of twigs or water plants among reeds. The female generally lays three to six eggs, which she incubates alone for 30 to 33 and sometimes as long as 37 days. During this period the male brings her food to the nest. When the young have hatched, he also brings food for them, passing it to the female, who then distributes it among the chicks. Not until they are older does the female join in foraging. The young are capable of flight at 40 to 50 days, though they often venture from the nest before that. Marsh harrier diet consists of small mammals and birds, occasionally fish and frogs, sometimes even birds' eggs and insects. As a rule, the bird does not molest ducks, which take practically no notice of it.

Voice:
During courtship the male's call is a ringing 'quee-a'; the female makes a whistling 'hieeeh'.

Length:
52 cm.

Wing span:
116 to 125 cm.

Sexually dimorphic.

Size of egg:
43.0—56.0
× 34.5—44.5 mm.

Migratory, dispersive or resident bird

♀

♂

Hen Harrier

Circus cyaneus

The hen harrier inhabits almost all of Europe, though it is locally absent. It nests, for example, only in northern England and southwestern Ireland, in Sweden only in the northeast and in Spain and Italy only in the north. Northern and eastern European populations are migratory, leaving at the end of August for winter quarters on the Mediterranean and in North Africa. Birds inhabiting other parts of Europe are resident, though some migrate south. The hen harrier inhabits open country with spreading meadows, bogs and swamps and also steppes. In Europe it favours vast marshes. During April it returns to the breeding territory, commencing its striking courtship aerobatics soon after arrival. In April to May the two partners build a nest on the ground, usually by a swamp, in heather, in stands of grain or maize, or the grass of a clearing. It is fairly small and made of twigs, reeds and grass. The female lays three to five, sometimes, though rarely, as many as eight eggs, which she incubates alone for 29 to 30 days. The male brings her food during this period and later also for the young nestlings, passing it to the female who divides it up amongst her offspring. At 35−42 days the young begin to try their wings. The hen harrier's diet consists mostly of small mammals. As a rule it hunts on the ground and never perches in trees.

Size of egg:
39.3−52.1
× 34.0−40.0 mm.

Length:
47 cm.

Wing span:
103 to 108 cm.

Sexually dimorphic.

Voice:
During the courtship flight the male's note sounds like 'ke-ke-ke'; the female's call is a high-pitched 'pee-e'.

Resident or migratory bird

Montagu's Harrier

Circus pygargus

♀

♂

Montagu's harrier is widespread but not very plentiful in western, southern, central and eastern Europe. It is not found in Ireland, and in Sweden occurs only rarely in the south. A migrant, it leaves its nesting grounds in August or September for tropical and South Africa, returning again at the end of April or beginning of May. It usually inhabits marshy meadows, dry bogs and large reed-beds. The climbing and diving display flights begin shortly after the birds' arrival; shortly after that they set about building the nest. Located on the ground, often in a very damp spot on the edge of a reed bed, it is usually made of small twigs and reeds and lined with fine vegetation. The female incubates alone the four to five eggs for 28 to 29 days, beginning as soon as the first is laid. The young therefore show marked differences in size and the youngest often does not survive the competition of the elder and stronger brothers and sisters. The male brings food to both the female and young during the first weeks, cleaning it partially before passing it to her for distribution. When the young are three weeks old she, too, leaves the nest in search of food. Once the nestlings are capable of tearing prey themselves, the male gives it to them directly. The diet consists of small mammals, lizards and birds' eggs. Sometimes Montagu's harrier hunts smaller birds and large insects such as locusts.

Voice:
Like that of the hen harrier; in gliding flight, 'kek-kek-kek'.

Length:
42.5 cm.

Wing span:
109 cm.

Sexually dimorphic.

Size of egg:
36.0—47.2
× 29.5—35.7 mm.

Migratory bird

Osprey
Pandion haliaetus

This handsome raptor inhabits northern and eastern Europe, occasionally also the north-eastern parts of central Europe, and a few localities in Scotland and the southern coast of Spain. It is migrant, leaving its nesting grounds in August or September for winter quarters in tropical and southern Africa. Favourite haunts are large, freshwater lakes and ponds, though the species is also found on the seashore. On returning to its breeding grounds in April or early May, it sets about building a nest, usually in a tall tree. This is made of very thick, dry branches without bark. Two to four eggs are laid in April or May and incubated by the female alone for 35 to 36 days. Sometimes she is relieved by the male, who otherwise brings her food. He also brings food for the nestlings, for the first few weeks alone; later he is helped by the female. The young leave the nest after 51 to 70 days, but continue to be fed by the parents a whole month longer. Ospreys feed mainly on fish, being excellently equipped for grasping prey: their long-clawed toes are reversible, so that they can be positioned opposite each other − two in front and two behind. When searching for food, the osprey flies above the water's surface at a height of about 25 metres, often hovering a while. On sighting prey, it plunges into the water with such force that it often vanishes below the surface.

Migratory bird

Size of egg:
50.4−69.0
× 40.2−52.0 mm.

Length:
55 cm.

Wing span:
155 to 170 cm.

Male and female have
similar plumage.

Voice:
A short, cheeping whistle.

Hobby

Falco subbuteo

A swift predator, the hobby makes its home in light open woodland, field groves and at the edges of deeper forests throughout most of Europe, but is absent from Ireland, Iceland and northern Scandinavia. It is a migrant; young birds leave for winter quarters in eastern and southern Africa as early as the middle of August but older birds do not depart until September or October. At the end of April or beginning of May they return to their breeding grounds, taking over the abandoned nests of crows, buzzards and similar birds, making only small alterations. They follow their breathtaking courtship flights, during which the birds circle high in the air, plummet to the ground and immediately sweep up again. The partners generally take turns incubating the three eggs for a period of 28 days. For the first few days after the young are hatched, only the male hunts prey, passing it to the female, who waits for it at some distance from the nest. Later she also joins in the search for food. Larger prey, such as a small bird, is passed by the male to the hen, who then feeds it to the nestlings, but insects are fed by the male directly. Both parents are very conscientious in their care of the young, bringing them food every two or three hours; if the food source is insects, they are fed several times an hour. At 23 to 34 days the young leave the nest.

Voice:
A short 'keu' or 'ket' or lengthy 'kikiki'.

Length:
33 cm.

Wing span:
75 to 79 cm.

Male and female have similar plumage.

Size of egg:
36.5—46.5
× 29.6—35.7 mm.

Migratory bird

Peregrine Falcon

Falco peregrinus

Often, a falcon can be seen circling a church spire, snatching suddenly at one of the hundreds of wild pigeons that are the scourge of modern cities. Pigeons are the mainstay of the handsome peregrine's diet and their abundance gives the falcon a distribution throughout Europe. When capturing prey on the wing, it climbs above the intended victim, then plummets downwards at a speed of up to 280 kilometres an hour, suddenly slowing its flight before striking upwards to sink its long talons into the victim's flesh. Peregrines take other birds in addition to pigeons and also the occasional small mammal. Nests are built in open country in rocky, wooded spots which command a wide view, as well as on coastal cliffs and sometimes on tall city towers. The bird often makes use of an abandoned raptor's nest, especially in wooded regions. The thinly-lined structure holds three to four eggs, which are incubated by the hen, relieved now and then by the male. The nestlings, which emerge after 29 days, are covered with thick down. For the first few days the male forages for food, which he passes to the hen, who divides it before feeding the young. The male gives food directly to the young only when they are old enough to tear it up for themselves, usually in the third week after birth. After 35 to 40 days the chicks leave the nest, but remain within close range for some time.

Migratory or resident bird

Size of egg:
46.0−58.9
× 36.3−44.9 mm.

Length:
43 cm.

Wing span:
Male 86 to 106 cm, female 104 to 114 cm.

Voice:
A loud, clear sound resembling 'kek-kek-kek', uttered repeatedly and a short 'kiack'.

Gyrfalcon

Falco rusticolus

The gyrfalcon is a bird of the arctic tundras, and also inhabits the mountains of central Asia, the arctic region of North America and Greenland. In Europe it breeds in Iceland and along the coast of northern Scandinavia. It is found in open rocky locations, on the seacoast and on islands, locally also on the edges of coniferous forests. Some birds are resident, some migrate south or southeast, but not too far from their breeding grounds. Only very occasionally does the gyrfalcon stray into central or western Europe. It occurs in a number of colour phases. There are two basic colour forms — one white and the other greyish brown. The white form is found in Greenland. There is, of course, a great range of colour variations between the two extremes. The gyrfalcon builds its nest on rocky ledges, preferably near colonies of waterfowl, which provide it with a rich source of food. However, it also nests in tall trees at a height of more than five metres. The nest is constructed of birch or willow twigs or the twigs of the tree it happens to be located in, and the hollow is lined with dry grass, willow leaves as well as food remnants. The three to four eggs are laid between mid-April and the beginning of May and are incubated alternately by both parents for 28 days. After 47 days in the nest the young venture forth for the first time. The gyrfalcon hunts mostly waterfowl but also takes corvine birds and ptarmigan, and, rarely, even small mammals.

Voice:
High-pitched barking sounds.

Length:
51 to 56 cm.

Wing span:
About 130 cm.

Male and female have similar plumage.

Size of egg:
48.4—64.5
× 36.5—54.6 mm.

Resident or dispersive bird

Merlin

Falco columbarius

Northern Europe, England, Ireland and Iceland are the home of the merlin, smallest of the European falcons. Northern European merlins generally migrate south to winter in the Mediterranean area and northern Africa, but some years will remain in central Europe, where they will be seen from the end of September until February. Birds occurring in England are usually resident. April or early May sees them again in their nesting grounds: moorland, tundras, coastal areas or open woodland (usually conifer forest), but also empty scrub country. The merlin does not as a rule build a nest, but lays its eggs in a depression which may be on the ground or a rock ledge. Occasionally it takes over the abandoned nests of crows or other birds. The three to five eggs are incubated mostly by the hen for 28 to 32 days, the male generally remaining close by on a high perch, though he sometimes relieves the hen. Fledging is at four weeks. The merlin hunts small birds and, during the winter in central Europe, its diet consists mostly of sparrows, finches, chaffinches and other small, common birds. It also captures house martins if they have not already gone south. The diet also includes an abundance of insects and, in dire circumstances, the merlin is known to catch a mouse or other small mammal. It is very agile and can be identified by the conspicuously long, pointed wings, resembling those of the swallow. The merlin was a popular bird in falconry, being trained to hunt small birds.

Size of egg:
35.0—44.0
× 28.0—33.8 mm.

Length:
28 cm.

Wing span:
61 to 64 cm.

Sexually dimorphic.

Voice:
Resembles that of the kestrel and sounds like 'kikikiki'. The female utters a slow 'eep-eep'.

Migratory or resident bird

Red-footed Falcon

Falco vespertinus

The red-footed falcon, a handsome raptor, is widespread in eastern and southeastern Europe as well as in eastern central Europe. During the migratory period it visits England, France, Spain and the more southerly parts of central Europe. It sets out on its journey to winter quarters in tropical and southern Africa at the end of August or beginning of September, returning again to its nesting grounds in flat country near water in April or early May. Red-footed falcons are gregarious birds and usually breed in colonies. Often they seek out the nesting grounds of rooks and occupy their abandoned nests. In May or June, occasionally in July, the female lays four to five eggs, which she and her partner take turns incubating for some 28 days. The newly hatched nestlings are fed by the female with food brought by the male, though when they are larger he also feeds them himself. The young falcons leave the nest after 28 to 30 days but continue to be fed by the parents a short while longer. After fledging, whole families roam the countryside until the time for their southward journey, when they gather in large flocks. Groups numbering as many as several thousands of birds have been observed in some places during autumn. The mainstay of the diet is insects. Red-footed falcons are fond of banding together in large groups to capture such insects as beetles and butterflies on the surface of still or flowing water. They will also take swarming ants.

Voice:
A note that resembles the wryneck's and sounds like 'kikikiki'.

Length:
Male 28 cm, female 30 cm.

Wing span:
70 to 72 cm.

Sexually dimorphic.

Size of egg:
30.7—42.0
× 26.3—32.5 mm.

Migratory bird

Kestrel
Falco tinnunculus

High above a field, as if pinned to one spot in the sky, hovers a kestrel, its keen eyes searching the ground below for prey. The instant some careless fieldmouse emerges from its underground passage, the predator swoops down to catch it in its claws. Besides fieldmice, it hunts other rodents, as well as insects, including grasshoppers. Farmers consider the bird to be a natural ally. In late April or early May it builds its nest on a rocky ledge, in an abandoned crow's nest, a tree cavity or large nest box. The female lays five to seven eggs which she incubates for 28 to 30 days. The young, covered with a thick layer of down, are fed by the male for the first few days and later by both parents. At about one month, the young kestrels leave the nest, remaining in the company of the older birds until autumn. Birds from northern and northeastern Europe migrate to southern Europe and North Africa for the winter. Populations inhabiting other parts of Europe are either resident or roam far afield. Kestrels are also to be found in Asia and Africa.

Resident, dispersive or migratory bird

Size of egg:
31.9—47.2
× 22.1—36.3 mm.

Length:
Male 32 cm, female 35 cm.

Wing span:
68—74 cm.

Sexually dimorphic.

Voice:
A clear 'kee-kee-kee' and a more musical double note, 'kee-lee'.

Partridge

Perdix perdix

Over much of Europe the common partridge is a favoured game bird, and in some central European countries it is even trapped for live export. Resident throughout its European range, outside the breeding season the partridge is to be seen in small, usually family groups. Because it frequents snow-blanketed fields and meadows during the winter months, it relies to a considerable extent on food put out for it by humans. Early in spring, the family groups break up, young birds beginning their search for a mate, adults having already paired for life. In May or June the hen prepares the nest, lined with grass and leaves, in a deep hollow, concealed in a clump of grass or under a shrub. She incubates the eight to 24 eggs for 23 to 25 days while her mate stands guard close by. The nestlings, which feed themselves, are reared by both parents: if the hen dies then the male continues alone. At first the diet consists of insects and green leaves but later it is supplemented by seeds. The young birds fledge at 16 days. Adult birds feed on seeds, insects, worms, spiders and molluscs and also nibble greenery.

Voice:
A grating 'krrr-ic' or 'kar-wic'.

Length:
29 cm.

Sexually dimorphic.

Size of egg:
31.6−40.4
× 24.1−29.4 mm.

Resident bird

Quail

Coturnix coturnix

Until a short time ago the quail was found in large numbers throughout Europe, the Middle East and through Asia as far east as Japan. In southern Europe and northern Africa more than 20 million of these small fowl used to be shot every year. Such large-scale killing naturally took its toll and numbers rapidly diminished, even though in places they are still fairly abundant. The quail is the only gallinaceous bird of Europe that is a migrant, leaving for its winter quarters in northern Africa and Arabia in the autumn and returning at the end of April or beginning of May. Its favourite haunts are steppes and dry meadows. Quail do not pair for life and a male often has several hens. These incubate the six to eight eggs and rear the young themselves. The tiny nestlings, spotted goldenbrown, hatch after 17 to 20 days, fully capable of feeding themselves from birth. They catch small insects and larvae, snip off bits of green leaves and later gather seeds. At 19 days they are already capable of flight and congregate in small groups until the autumn migration. Populations inhabiting southern Europe and Africa are resident.

Size of egg:
25.0—33.9
× 20.0—25.0 mm.

Length:
17.5 cm.

Sexually dimorphic.

Voice:
Characteristic trisyllabic call of the male — 'whic-whic-ic' — is heard over long distances until late summer.

Migratory or resident bird

Pheasant

Phasianus colchicus

The pheasant was introduced to Europe in Roman times. It quickly became acclimatized and was soon a common game bird, autumn pheasant shoots remaining popular to this day. Subsequently introduced Chinese subspecies interbred with the main population, producing a number of plumage variations. The pheasant is generally found in light woods, field groves, thickets beside water, and also in large parks. It is particularly abundant in lowlands, but is common also in hill country and is resident throughout the year. During the spring courting season, the cock utters his characteristic harsh note with head held erect, usually completing the display with a bout of wing fluttering. He will also circle a chosen hen in a jerky hopping motion, or engage in battle with other cocks. After the courting season he pays no further attention to his mate or the young. The hen scrapes a simple hollow in the ground, which she lines with dry leaves or grass, and then lays eight to 15 eggs which she incubates alone, generally for a period of 24 to 25 days. The chicks begin to fly at the age of two weeks and roost in the treetops with the hen. The diet consists of various seeds, berries, green plant shoots, insects, worms and molluscs. In winter it may be necessary to put out food for pheasants where they are raised in large numbers. Large pheasant reserves are commonplace on the farmland of England and Europe.

Voice:
The male's courting call is a harsh 'korrk-kok'.

Length:
Male 79 cm, female 60 cm.

Sexually dimorphic.

Size of egg:
39.0–51.1 × 32.4–37.6 mm.

Resident bird

Red-legged Partridge

Alectoris rufa

This game bird inhabits mountain areas, but also lowlands and hills with fields and vineyards, in southwestern Europe and England. In recent years it has been introduced to many parts of central Europe, but without much success for it has many enemies in these new locations, a typical example being the fox. The red-legged partridge favours stony places covered with grass and sparsely dotted with shrubs, beneath which it builds its nest in a depression in the ground, only sparingly lined with leaves and grass stems. The eight to 15 eggs are incubated by the hen for 24 days, while the male roams the neighbourhood, returning when the young are born. The nestlings usually leave the hollow on the second day, following the hen and by the end of a week make their first attempts at flight. The parent birds guide them in search of food, which the chicks gather for themselves. Even after they are fully grown, the young remain in the company of their parents, families later forming groups of about 20 birds. After sunset they seek shelter in rock crevices or protected rocky ledges, but despite such precautions many red-legged partridge fall prey to predators. In spring, the male's loud cry may be heard before dawn. In winter, flocks of these partridges descend into the valleys to seek places free from snow. Their diet consists of seeds, berries, grass, insects, molluscs and worms.

Size of egg:
41.4 × 31.0 mm.

Length:
35 cm.

Male and female have
similar colouring.

Voice:
A 'chuck, chuck-er' call
note, and an explosive
'pitchi-i' alarm signal; also
a variable 'tschreck'.

Resident bird

Ptarmigan

Lagopus mutus

This game bird of no great consequence inhabits the Alps, Scotland, Iceland and northern Europe. In the mountains it occurs up to the snow line on rocky, shrub-grown sites. In the far north, where it is plentiful, it inhabits tundra. It remains faithful to its breeding grounds, descending from the mountain heights into sheltered valleys only during winter. The nest, sparsely lined with grass stems or leaves, is built in May or June in a hollow in the ground beneath a shrub, in heather or in similar places. The female lays eight to 12 eggs, which she incubates alone for 22 to 26 days. By October the young ptarmigans are fully grown, and families congregate in small groups of 15 to 20 birds. At night they take cover beneath a rock, but also build shelters in the snow. They seek places where larger mammals have cleared the snow, thus providing easier access to food. In winter the diet consists of seeds and the remains of plants; in spring the ptarmigan nibbles catkins, buds, and, in some places, the buds of rhododendrons. In summer it feeds on berries, insects, their larvae and other invertebrates; in autumn it relies mainly on berries. The ptarmigan's summer plumage is chestnut brown with white primaries; its winter dress all white with dark tail feathers obscured by white upper tail coverts. The legs and toes are heavily feathered to prevent the bird sinking into soft snow.

Voice:
The male utters a sound resembling 'kraar'.

Length:
34 cm.

Sexually dimorphic in breeding season.

Size of egg:
41.2 × 29.9 mm.

Resident bird

Capercaillie

Tetrao urogallus

Largest of the European grouse, the capercaillie frequents woodlands (mostly conifer forests) with dense undergrowth in mountains and hilly country. In the north it may also be found in lowland areas. Native to Scotland, the Pyrenees, northern and central Europe, it remains in its breeding grounds throughout the year. Except during the courting season it is a very shy bird, adept at concealing itself. The spring courtship display, however, is conspicuous and remarkable and well known to sportsmen. During one phase of the display, which takes place while it is still dark, the cock is 'deaf' and 'blind' for a few seconds. When dawn breaks, he flies down to the ground, often engaging in battle with a rival. While this takes place the hens sit waiting on nearby branches, and are then led off by the victors. The nest is a hollow in the ground which the hen digs, usually at the base of a tree trunk, and is lined with grass and leaves. She incubates the five to eight eggs alone for 26 to 29 days, then leads the young, who can feed by themselves, in search of food. She also shelters them under her wings and generally gives them protection. The chicks are yellow-russet in colour with dark spots, and by ten days are able to fly about. The diet consists chiefly of insects, berries, buds and shoots of conifers. Capercaillie flesh tastes resinous, and for this reason the species is not one of the most popular game birds.

Resident bird

Size of egg:
50.8–62.2
× 39.0–43.5 mm.

Length:
Male 94 cm, female 67 cm.

Sexually dimorphic.

Voice:
The male's courting call begins with a rapidly accelerating 'tik-up, tik-up tik-up', ending with a 'pop', followed by hissing and whispering; the hen's call is a 'kok-kok' resembling the pheasant's.

Black Grouse

Lyrurus tetrix

The black grouse inhabits northern, eastern and central Europe, nesting also in England. It is most abundant in the arctic tundra, but occurs in marshland with birch trees, light decidous and mixed woods, as well as in mountain areas and among peat bogs. It also visits meadows and fields near woods, or forest clearings, where it performs its courtship display in the spring. As many as 100 cocks will arrive at the courting grounds before sunrise, where they perform all sorts of antics, hopping about, dropping their wings and uttering burbling sounds. To conclude, they leap up and attack one another with their beaks, but only rarely inflict serious wounds. As dawn breaks, the hens arrive on the scene and then fly off with their chosen partners, one cock being accompanied by several hens. Between the middle of May and June the hen scrapes a simple hollow in the ground, which she lines with leaves or grass before laying seven to 12 eggs. These are incubated for 25 to 28 days by the hen, the cock showing no further interest in the fate of his family. When the young hatch, the hen guides them in search of food and also protects them. The chicks, spotted yellow-black, grow very fast and by the end of October are almost the size of adult birds. A black grouse's diet consists of insects, worms, molluscs, seeds, berries, plant shoots and grass. This is a game bird, cocks being shot during the courtship display. Their lyre-shaped tails are prized trophies.

Voice:
The male utters a sound resembling 'tchu-shwee' and a whistling sound when he takes to the air; the female's call is a loud 'kok-kok'

Length:
Male 61.5 cm, female 42 cm.

Sexually dimorphic.

Size of egg:
46.0–56.3 × 33.4–38.5 mm.

Resident bird

Turkey

Meleagris gallopavo

The wild turkey is native to the central, southern, northeastern and eastern parts of the USA and also Mexico, but its distribution is discontinuous. In many places, for instance in Georgia and Carolina, it has been exterminated by hunters. It is a bird of the forests but is fond of places with grassy or shrubby areas or fields nearby. The male usually has two to four hens as mates. The nest is a simple affair — merely a depression scraped by the hen in the ground under a fallen tree trunk or dense bush and lined with a few blades of grass and leaves. In it are deposited usually nine to 12 eggs but older hens may lay as many as 20. The hen does not begin incubating until the clutch is complete, remaining in the vicinity and covering the eggs with leaves until that time. The young hatch after 28 days and generally follow the hen to forage for food the second day after hatching. They feed on small insects and their larvae, spiders, young plant shoots and leaves. The female protects them at night and in bad weather by sheltering them under her wings. The chicks begin flying when they are about ten days old and roost on the branch of a tree with their mother at night. Adult birds also roost in trees. When the young are fully grown turkeys congregate in groups of ten to 40 to forage for food. Often they visit cultivated fields where they eat the grain. They also eat fruit, various berries, etc. and adult birds may even capture an occasional rodent.

Resident bird

Size of egg:
56.3—71.0
×42.0—51.0 mm.

Length:
Male 120 cm, female
100 cm.

Male and female have
similar plumage.

Voice:
Only the male makes the
typical gobbling noises.

Crane

Grus grus

This sizeable bird is today found only in northern and northeastern Europe and the northern parts of central Europe. At one time it was very plentiful throughout central and western Europe, but its numbers have been reduced by the advance of industrial society. Cranes migrate as far as the Sudan and Ethiopia, but some winter in the Mediterranean. They leave their breeding grounds in September to October, returning again between the middle of March and April. The habitats are marshy areas with lakes, extensive meadows near large ponds and lakes and swampy areas. Pairing takes place after the return to the nesting grounds. The courtship antics are striking and noisy: the birds utter loud trumpeting calls, leap high in the air and spread their wings, hop on one foot and run around in circles; in short, they do a sort of dance. The nest of reeds and twigs is built on small flat islets, on broken and bent reeds in swamps, or on clumps of grass. In dry locations the nest walls are low, in swamps, high and broad. In April or May, the female generally lays two, sometimes one or three eggs, which she and her partner take turns incubating for 28 to 31 days. On hatching, the young cranes, which have a short bill at first, scamper about the neighbourhood; they are also able to swim. The crane feeds on seeds, grain, green plant parts, insects and molluscs, occasionally taking small vertebrates.

Voice:
Loud trumpeting calls; in the vicinity of the nest, cries that sound like 'kr-r-r'.

Length:
Male 122 cm, female 112 cm.

Wing span:
About 220 cm.

Male and female have similar plumage.

Size of egg:
85.0—109.0
× 56.0—67.0 mm.

Migratory bird

Whooping Crane

Grus americana

The whooping crane was once widely distributed throughout North America, nesting from the northern Mackenzie south to Illinois and Iowa. It was severely persecuted until 1915 when ornithologists succeeded in obtaining strict protection for the species, but by that time it already nested only in Canada. In 1923 there existed only a single breeding territory in the Canadian province of Saskatchewan. By 1938 there were only 14 survivors. It was at this point, and just in time, that a society to protect this bird — the Cooperative Whooping Crane Project — was founded. As a result of its efforts cranes were protected also in their winter quarters on the Matagorda islands off Texas and thus by 1955 there were 28 individuals in the wild, and 57 by 1968 since when their numbers have continued to increase. The whooping crane builds a large nest of twigs and reed stalks on the ground in the dense reeds of swamps, usually on a small islet. The nesting territory staked out by a pair of birds is quite large. The female lays two eggs which the partners take turns incubating for one month. On hatching the young birds roam the nest surroundings; they are also able to swim. When the young are fully grown the cranes congregate in large flocks that travel south in the autumn for wintering on the gulf in Mexico. The whooping crane feeds mainly on frogs, small mammals and large insects, seeds, berries and green plant parts.

Size of egg:
87.0—108.0
× 59.0—67.5 mm.

Length:
125 cm.

Wing span:
225 cm.

Male and female have similar plumage.

Voice:
A loud, clear resonant whoop.

Migratory bird

Water Rail

Rallus aquaticus

Water rails inhabit all of Europe except the far north. In Scandinavia they occur only in the south, but do breed in Iceland. Birds inhabiting western and southern Europe are resident; those from other parts migrate in September and October and usually winter in the Mediterranean region: in mild winters, however, eastern populations may go no farther than central Europe. In March and April they appear in their breeding grounds — thick vegetation bordering lakes and ponds as well as bogs, marshes, and similar places. The nest of dry or green plant parts is built by the partners in a well concealed spot in a thick clump of grass or reeds. In April and May the female generally lays six to 12, sometimes 16 eggs, which she and her partner take turns incubating for 19 to 21 days. In June or July the two birds build a new nest and have a second brood. The newly hatched nestlings are black in colour and very agile; as soon as they have dried they scatter in the reeds. When they are hungry, they utter soft peeps to attract the notice of their parents who bring them food, which is taken direct from the adults' beaks. They eat insects and their larvae, molluscs, spiders, green plant parts and in the autumn, various small seeds. The water rail is on the move mostly at twilight and at night. When it walks, it holds its neck stretched forwards, jerking it as it goes along. It can swim and is even known to dive.

Voice:
'Krruih', and
a much-repeated 'pit';
during the courtship
display, 'gep-gep-gep'
followed by a ringing 'krui,
krui, krui' and 'kik, kik, kik'.

Length:
28 cm.

Male and female have
similar plumage.

Size of egg:
31.9–40.0
× 23.5 – 27.6 mm.

Migratory or resident bird

Spotted Crake

Porzana porzana

The spotted crake nests over practically all of Europe except the far north, but it is absent in Spain, Portugal and Ireland. In September to October it leaves its breeding grounds for wintering sites in southwestern Europe and the Mediterranean, and especially in northwestern and eastern Africa where thousands of birds stay in the Upper Nile region. When migrating, spotted crakes fly by night. They inhabit lakes and ponds bordered with thick vegetation, marshes, swamps and overgrown river deltas. Arrival at the breeding grounds is in mid-April to May or June; the well-concealed nest is made of both dry and green reed leaves. A second nest is built in June or July. The clutch usually comprises eight to 12 eggs, which the partners take turns incubating for 18 to 21 days. The young remain in the nest for one or two days, then run around in the thick vegetation, their parents bringing them food which usually consists of insects and their larvae, worms and spiders. However, the species also feeds on small molluscs, centipedes and other invertebrates as well as the green leaves of duckweed and, in the autumn, small seeds. The adult birds are sometimes still bringing the young food when the female is preparing to have the second brood. Even after these have hatched, young birds of the first brood remain near their parents.

Migratory bird

Size of egg:
29.1–37.5
× 21.7–26.8 mm.

Length:
23 cm.

Male and female have similar plumage.

Voice:
During the nesting period, a whistling 'whitt', especially in the evening and at night.

Corncrake

Crex crex

Late in the evening, walking along a path in a field, one may suddenly hear strange sounds resembling the scraping of a comb against the edge of a matchbox. This is in fact the call of the corncrake, returned from tropical Africa to its breeding grounds in Europe. It arrives about the middle of May seeking out dry nest sites in fields and meadows. The song is mostly heard on warm nights after dark or before dawn. The simple nest, lined with bits of leaves and grass stems, is placed in a well concealed depression in field or meadow. A clutch usually comprises six (but sometimes as many as 18) eggs which are incubated by both partners for 19 to 21 days. The nestlings are entirely black and leave the nest the day after hatching, running about close by. For the first few days, they are fed such items as caterpillars, beetle larvae and small spiders by both parents. Later they themselves hunt various insects and worms on the ground and sometimes gather seeds as well. Corncrakes can move rapidly through cornfields because the sides of their bodies are flattened.

Voice:
The song 'rerrp rerrp rerrp...', carries a great distance, especially at night.

Length:
26.5 cm.

Male and female have similar plumage.

Size of egg:
31.4–41.6
× 24.1–29.0 mm.

Migratory bird

Moorhen

Gallinula chloropus

The moorhen is widely distributed throughout the whole of Europe except northern Scandinavia. Inhabitants of eastern and northern regions are migratory, those from other parts remain in their nesting grounds for the winter, though sometimes they migrate partially, for example, to western Europe and the Mediterranean. The moorhen returns to its breeding grounds often as early as the middle of March. It inhabits ponds, lakes and slow-moving water courses bordered with thick vegetation. When swimming, it continually flicks its tail. The nest, located in rushes, reeds or clumps of grass, is made mostly of dry reeds by both partners. Each pair has its own nesting territory, which both birds fiercely defend. They have one brood in April or May, a second in June or July, and sometimes a third in August. The female usually lay six to eight, sometimes more, eggs, which both partners take turns incubating for 19 to 22 days. The young, coloured black with a reddish head, are fed by the parents in the nest for two to three days, after which they swim about, but keeping close to cover. The partners bring them insects and their larvae, spiders, small molluscs and the tenderest leaves of duckweed. In the autumn, adult birds add small seeds to their diet.

Size of egg:
36.2–54.0
× 26.0–34.2 mm.

Length:
33 cm.

Male and female have
similar plumage.

Voice:
'Kr-r-rk', or a note that
sounds like 'kittick'.

**Resident, dispersive or
migratory bird**

Coot

Fulica atra

The coot is the commonest member of the rail family and is found throughout all of Europe except the northernmost parts. Birds inhabiting eastern and northern Europe leave their nesting grounds in October to November and fly south-west, those from other parts of the continent are resident or dispersive. Coots arrive at their breeding grounds in March, and soon after the males wage fierce combats amongst themselves to win a mate. The paired birds then begin building a nest in reeds, rushes, grass or other vegetation. It is usually sited away from the water's edge, and leading to it from the water is a ramp of leaves. The structure itself is made of reeds and grasses and sometimes covered with a roof of broken plant stems. The female usually lays six to nine eggs, which she and her partner take turns incubating for about 22, sometimes as many as 24 days. The young hatch successively, the first being led out on the water by the male, who after a few hours swims back to the nest for the next. They are cared for by both parents. Their plumage is black but the head is orange-red. Adults place food directly inside their offspring's beaks. The diet consists mostly of green plant parts, but seeds are eaten in autumn, and during the nesting period includes insects and their larvae, molluscs, crustaceans, spiders and other small invertebrates.

Voice:
A clear 'tewk' or 'kt-kowk'; also a short, sharp 'skik'.

Length:
38 cm.

Male and female have similar plumage.

Size of egg:
40.0–61.0
× 31.2–40.6 mm.

Resident or dispersive bird

Great Bustard

Otis tarda

Today, northwestern Africa, the steppes of western Asia and Asia Minor as well as certain areas in the flat farmlands of central Europe, comprise the range of the great bustard. This huge grassland bird used to be far more widespread in Europe and in the eighteenth century was found in the British Isles. It generally stays the winter in its breeding grounds, congregating in small flocks that roam the fields and meadows. In spring, the male performs his distinctive courtship display on the ground, inflating his throat pouch and spreading his wing and tail feathers to form a fan, so that from a distance he looks like a large, black-and-white, dancing ball. Before pairing, the males fight fiercely among themselves to win the favour of the hen. Hers is the task, in April or May, of preparing a simple hollow in the corn or tall grass in which she generally lays two eggs, incubating them for 25 to 28 days. The spotted nestlings are very independent and their diet comprises chiefly insects and later plant food. Adult birds occasionally catch small vertebrates. Nowadays, the great bustard is protected in most of Europe, and an attempt is now being made to reintroduce the species to the British Isles.

Size of egg:
69.0–89.5
× 51.5–63.1 mm.

Length:
Male 102 cm, female
80 cm.

Wing span:
Up to 240 cm.

The female lacks
moustachial feathers.

Voice:
Low, bellowing sounds.

Resident or dispersive bird

Oystercatcher

Haematopus ostralegus

The oystercatcher is found practically through-out the whole world. In Europe it may be seen almost everywhere on the coast. Birds inhabiting the area south of the British Isles and Denmark are resident, those from more northern parts are usually migrant, wintering in southern Europe and along the coast of North Africa. North of the Black Sea and in central Asia it also breeds on shallow, inland salt lakes. Outside the breeding season it runs about in groups in shallows, on mudflats or sandy beaches seeking food. Spring is the time of the courtship display during which several birds run beside or behind one another, constantly uttering loud piping trills. Paired birds then stake out their nesting territories, which are not very big but which they courageously defend against all intruders. The nest is a shallow scrape in the ground, usually on the shore near water, lined with small shells or shell fragments, also leaves or grass. Both partners take turns incubating the two to four eggs. The young hatch after 26 to 28 days and remain in the hollow for 1 or 2 days after which they roam the neighbourhood with their parents. At first they are brought food by the adult birds but very soon they gather it themselves. The diet consists of molluscs, worms, insects and such like. The birds often probe deep in the mud and sand with their long bills to catch small invertebrates.

Voice:
A loud 'pic, pic, pic'; when courting, piping trills.

Length:
43 cm.

Male and female have similar plumage.

Size of egg:
47.7—70.1
× 32.8—48.9 mm.

Resident or migratory bird

Lapwing

Vanellus vanellus

The lapwing is widespread throughout most of Europe, the only countries where it does not breed being Portugal and Italy. Between August and October it migrates to southwestern Europe and northwestern Africa, but southern and western European populations are resident. The lapwing usually returns to its breeding grounds in March, but it may arrive by the end of February. Its favourite sites are damp meadows and fields near water. The male performs an exuberant, tumbling display flight; having attracted a mate, he then displays again, his movements being exaggerated versions of those by which a nest scrape is made. In late March or April, sometimes also in May, the birds start building the nest in a shallow depression in the ground in a meadow, field, or perhaps on a raised spot in a swamp. It is lined sparsely with leaves, plant stalks or small twigs. Like all shore birds, the female usually lays four eggs, which she and her partner take turns incubating for 24 to 28 days. The speckled nestlings remain in the nest for a day or two and then scatter in the neighbourhood, concealing themselves in clumps of grass when danger threatens. They begin flying at five weeks. The diet consists of insects and their larvae, spiders, molluscs and the like as well as small pieces of green vegetable matter and various seeds.

Size of egg:
37.8—60.4
× 27.8—36.1 mm.

Length:
32 cm.

Male and female have
similar plumage.

Voice:
A ringing 'peese-weet';
during courtship display,
'pee-r-weet'.

Migratory or resident bird

Ringed Plover

Charadrius hiaticula

This is a bird of sandy and muddy shores. In Europe it breeds in Scandinavia, Finland, Russia, Iceland, Great Britain, Germany, Denmark, Holland, Belgium and France. Occasionally it also nests on the shores of inland lakes and ponds in central Europe. British birds are mostly resident, but those from other areas migrate south, wintering chiefly in southeastern Europe and northern Africa. During migrations the species may often be encountered on inland waters. Flocks arrive at the nesting grounds in April or May, forming pairs shortly after. It is interesting to note that the females are the first to arrive; the males follow and their advent in followed by courtship display. Paired birds then establish nesting teritories, often the same ones as the previous year. The male makes several nests (shallow scrapes in the ground) from which the female chooses. They are usually located close to water, in sand or among rocks, and are lined with small stones or shell fragments. In May and June, sometimes also in July, the female lays four eggs which both partners take turns incubating for 23 to 26 days. The newly-hatched young abandon the nest as soon as they have dried and are tended by their parents. When they are able to fly they roam the countryside in small flocks. The females are the first to depart for winter quarters. Ringed plovers feed mainly on insects and their larvae, but also take worms, small crustaceans and molluscs.

Voice:
A mellow call that sounds like 'too-li'; when courting, a repeated 'quitu-weeoo'.

Length:
19 cm.

Male and female have similar plumage.

Size of egg:
32.0—39.6 × 22.8—28.5 mm.

Migratory or resident bird

Little Ringed Plover

Charadrius dubius

The diminutive and delightful little ringed plover inhabits all of Europe except the northernmost parts, being partial to sandy river banks and dry muddy situations near lakes and ponds. It also favours the area around a dried-out pond with a sandy bottom, even though the nest is often flooded out by the rising water when the pond fills. The species also makes its home in disused sand pits where large pools or a reservoir have formed at the bottom. Birds leave in August and September for winter quarters in Africa, returning again between the middle of April and beginning of May. The nest is a simple scrape in the ground, but in muddy places the depression is lined with small pebbles, small shells or pieces of twigs and plant stalks. In open situations the nest is hollowed out near a large stone or other conspicuous object which makes it easier to find. The four eggs, laid in April or May and as a second brood in June or July, are incubated by both partners for 22 to 26 days, the one relieving the other at short intervals. The young leave the nest as soon as they are dry and follow in the wake of their parents. At 21 days they are capable of flight. The diet of the little ringed plover consists typically of insects and their larvae, worms, spiders, molluscs and small crustaceans. The bird seeks its prey on muddy ground, where it can often be seen rapidly running about.

Migratory bird

Size of egg:
25.5–35.5
× 20.9–24.9 mm.

Length:
15 cm.

Male and female have
similar plumage.

Voice:
A whistling 'tee-u'; when
alarmed, 'tree-a'.

Kentish Plover

Charadrius alexandrinus

The inappropriately named Kentish plover is found mainly on seashores from East Germany along the western, southern and southeastern coasts of Europe, the coasts of the Black and Caspian Seas and on the Danube delta. It also occurs in Africa, Asia, Australia and America, occasionally even on inland salt lakes. Birds inhabiting southern regions are resident, those in more northerly localities migrate to southern Europe and northern Africa. Most birds arrive at their breeding grounds in the first half of April. The nesting territory is selected and staked out by the male, who also prepares the nest, which is usually a shallow depression in the sand lined with small pebbles, bits of wood and grass. Often these birds nest in colonies, sometimes together with the little tern. The full clutch of three eggs may be found in May or June, occasionally as early as late April and sometimes as late as July. If the eggs are lost, the birds make a new nest and the female lays another clutch, often within a week. Both partners take turns incubating for 24 to 28 days. By 40 days the young are able to fly, and they then roam the coastline in small flocks looking for food. The diet consists of small crustaceans, molluscs, insects and their larvae. On wet sands and mudflats, Kentish plovers may be seen pattering about, their stamping feet stirring up the concealed invertebrates, which they then eat.

Voice:
Delicate sounds such as 'wit-wit-wit' and a flutey 'poo-eef'; when courting, trills such as 'tritritritritrirr'.

Length:
16 cm.

Male and female have similar plumage.

Size of egg:
30.1–35.4 × 22.1–25.2 mm.

Migratory or resident bird

151

Dotterel

Eudromias morinellus

Northern Europe, Scotland and the mountain regions of central Europe are the breeding grounds of the dotterel, where it frequents grass-covered, rocky slopes, or tundra in the far north. In mountains it is found above the tree line, where it will nest at altitudes above 2000 metres. Between the end of July and September it wings its way through Europe to winter quarters in northern Africa or the Middle East, returning by the same route in April and May. At the end of May or the beginning of June it prepares its nest in a fairly deep hollow in the ground about nine centimetres in diameter, sparsely lined with grass stems, leaves and lichens. The female generally lays three eggs, which are incubated by the male alone for 18 to 24 days. When sitting, he is so meek that he will often allow a human to pick him up, and when returned to the nest does not fly off. In northern countries the dotterel appears in legends as the reincarnation of the Good Spirit. The young remain in the nest for only one day, after which they follow their parents, nevertheless remaining hidden by day, and sheltering beneath the parents' wings at night. The dotterel is very skilful at moving about in rocky places. Its diet consists chiefly of beetles, flies, worms and small molluscs, and it will occasionally eat green leaflets or small fruits and seeds.

Size of egg:
36.0—46.7
× 26.6—31.5 mm.

Length:
21.5 cm.

Male and female have
similar plumage.

Voice:
Delicate, flutey notes that
sound like 'titi-ri-titi-ri'.

Migratory bird

Golden Plover

Pluvialis apricaria

These large plovers are found in Iceland, Scandinavia, Finland, Great Britain, Ireland and northern Russia. They breed locally in Denmark, West Germany and Holland. There are two subspieces − the northern and the southern. The latter differs from the former in that it lacks the black cheeks and also the broad black band on the flanks and belly. In eclipse plumage (i. e. in winter), the two forms are alike. British birds are resident, but birds from the north migrate across central Europe in large numbers in the autumn (and spring) on their way to (and back from) their wintering grounds in southern Europe, North Africa and the Middle East. At this time small flocks may be seen on fields. After their arrival at the breeding grounds (open marsh and moorland) in late March and April, the flocks disband to form pairs, which settle into territories. The nest is a hollow in the ground lined with plant stems, leaves and small twigs. As a rule the female lays four eggs, which she incubates alone, relieved now and then by the male. Her mate, however, remains on guard close by, warning of approaching danger by trying to distract the intruder and lead him away from the nest. The young usually hatch after twenty-seven days. Diet consists mostly of small invertebrates.

Voice:
A flutey 'tlu-i'; when courting, 'tirr-peeoo' and similar noises.

Length:
28 cm.

Male and female have similar plumage.

Size of egg:
45.5−56.3 × 33.2−38.3 mm.

Migratory bird

Turnstone

Arenaria interpres

Turnstones breed on the coasts of Scandinavia, Finland, northern Siberia, arctic North America and Greenland. During the migrating season they may be encountered practically throughout the whole of Europe, but the wintering grounds themselves are the coasts of western and south-western Europe and North Africa. Some individuals fly as far as Australia and South America. Turnstones leave their breeding grounds as early as the end of July, but more usually in August or September, returning again in April or May, though birds bound for the extreme north often do not arrive there until early June. The species inhabits rocky islands and shores in the arctic. Its nest, a shallow depression lined with dry vegetable matter, is located near water. In May or June, or in the far north as late as July, the female lays her clutch of four eggs. The partners take turns incubating, but towards the end of this period the female often leaves the task to the male, who also cares for the young when they hatch, which is after 23 to 24 days. It has been discovered, however, that the young are often in fact tended by both parents. When foraging for food, the turnstone has a characteristic habit of stooping to turn over small stones with its bill, thus uncovering prey. The diet consists of insects and their larvae, worms, small molluscs and spiders.

Size of egg:
36.0—44.6
× 26.0—31.3 mm.

Length:
23 cm.

Male and female have
similar plumage.

Voice:
Abruptly uttered notes:
'tuk-a-tuk' or 'khikhikikikiki'.

Migratory bird

Snipe

Gallinago gallinago

Snipe inhabit all of western, central, eastern and northern Europe, but do not breed in the south. They leave their breeding grounds from July to September making for Africa as far south as Uganda, though large numbers also winter in southwestern, southern and western Europe. In March and April it returns to its breeding grounds in marshy and damp meadows beside ponds and lakes. The nest is built during April, May or sometimes June in a hollow in a clump of grass. The structure consists of dry stalks and long leaves and is well concealed from above by drooping grass stems. The clutch consists of four prettily coloured eggs, which the female incubates alone for 19 to 21 days. While she sits on the nest, the male often flies high in the air, swooping down to the ground every now and then. When he plummets earthwards he makes a characteristic drumming sound caused by the vibration of the specially-shaped outer tail feathers. The nestlings scatter throughout the neighbourhood as soon as they are dry. They are brownish-black with white spots, which is excellent camouflage. Both parents care for the young. At 20 days they begin to fly, and in the autumn join other snipe to form flocks. The diet consists mainly of insects and their larvae, also small molluscs, worms, spiders and other invertebrates.

Voice:
On the ground makes sounds like 'chic-ka'.

Length:
26.5 cm.

Male and female have similar plumage.

Size of egg:
35.0−42.9
× 26.3−31.0 mm.

Migratory or resident bird

Woodcock

Scolopax rusticola

The woodcock is established throughout Europe, except for the most northerly regions. Inhabitants of western and southwestern Europe stay for the winter, those from other areas travel to countries bordering the Mediterranean — Spain and France being the chief winter quarters. From the middle of March to April the species returns to its breeding grounds in lowland woods, mostly deciduous or mixed forests. Pairing follows a courtship display, in which the hen sits on the ground and entices the male by spreading her tail, which has a conspicuous white patch, at the same time uttering a special cry. As soon as he sees or hears her, the male descends rapidly to the ground and hops around the hen in a sort of dance. Sometimes two males arrive at the same time, and soon become involved in combat. In April, and often for a second time in June, the female lays four eggs in a shallow scrape in the ground, lined with a few leaves and moss. The young hatch after 20 to 23 days, and as soon as their down has dried, leave the nest, keeping close to the hen. The woodcock gathers its food (insects, their larvae, molluscs and worms) on the ground, often probing among soft soil and leaves with its long beak, which can sense the presence of prey. Woodcocks are not among the main game birds, but their flesh is a great delicacy.

Size of egg:
40.1−49.0
× 31.6−36.4 mm.

Length:
34 cm.

Male and female have
similar plumage.

Voice:
During the courting season
the male utters a soft
croaking 'orrrt-orrrt' and
a sneezing 'tsiwick'.

Resident or migratory bird

Curlew

Numenius arquata

Curlews are widely distributed along the coast of Scandinavia, in Great Britain, Ireland, western France, central, eastern and northeastern Europe as well as in northern and central Asia. A great many winter in western Europe and along the coasts of the Mediterranean; some individuals, however, fly as far as eastern and southern Africa. Western European populations are usually resident. During migration the curlew is often encountered on inland ponds and lakes and in recent years it has even begun to settle and breed in such places. The birds' typical habitats are moors, wet meadows, marshlands and also steppe areas with water. Curlews return to their breeding grounds in late March. The nest is placed in tall grass or other vegetation; it is a hollow lined with dry grass, leaves or other vegetable matter, made by the male, who often prepares several such nests in the same area. In April or May the female usually lays four eggs which she and her partner take turns incubating for 26 to 30 days. The young birds are dry within twelve hours of hatching and then leave the nest, though they continue to be protected by the parents while foraging for food. When the young are grown, families join to form flocks. Curlew's diet consists of worms, molluscs, spiders, insects and occasionally small tadpoles; the birds also nibble parts of green plants, berries and seeds.

Voice:
A flutey call such as 'cour-li', which may be heard throughout the year.

Length:
53 to 58 cm.

Male and female have similar plumage.

Size of egg:
56.2−78.6 × 41.7−55.1 mm.

Migratory or resident bird

Whimbrel

Numenius phaeopus

The whimbrel is found in northern Scandinavia, northern Finland, northern Russia, the Faroes and Scotland. It is also widespread in Siberia and North America. Favoured habitats are the seashore as well as inland on tundra, moors and wet meadows. It is a migratory bird, which flies mainly along the coasts of Europe, and sometimes also across central Europe; eastern populations migrate across the Caspian Sea. Winter quarters are northwestern, eastern and southern Africa, southern Asia and occasionally the coast of Spain. The whimbrel leaves its breeding grounds often as early as late July, but more often in August or September, at which time it occurs as a chance visitor in central Europe on the mud bottoms of drained ponds, on meadows and on fields near water. It returns to its nesting site again after mid-April and in May. The nest is a shallow hollow in the ground, well concealed in a tussock of grass, heather or other vegetation and lined with grass, moss, lichens and the like. The female usually lays four eggs from mid-May, in June or sometimes in July. Both partners incubate for 21 to 25 days. The newly-hatched young leave the nest as soon as they are dry, remaining concealed in the surrounding vegetation where they are tended by the adult birds. Whimbrels feed on insects and their larvae, worms, molluscs, spiders and other invertebrates. They also eat vegetable matter such as berries and seeds.

Size of egg:
52.0—65.1
× 36.0—45.0 mm.

Length:
41 cm.

Male and female have
similar plumage.

Voice:
Flutey notes.

Migratory bird

Black-tailed Godwit

Limosa limosa

This robust shore bird is widespread in eastern Europe and is also found in the northern parts of Germany, Denmark, Holland, Belgium, the southern tip of Sweden, and, of recent years (in ever growing numbers) in central Europe. It also inhabits Iceland, southeastern England and western France. In late July and August it leaves its nesting grounds for winter quarters, mostly in the Mediterranean region but also on the western coast of Europe. March or April mark the return of the species to its breeding grounds, where it inhabits peat bogs, meadows near ponds and lakes as well as fields near water. After arrival in small flocks, pairs of birds stake out their own nesting territory. The courtship flight consists in the male flying in arcs above the nesting site, slowing every now and then, expanding his tail feathers and emitting a loud call. In April or May, the birds build a simple nest in shallow depression in grass. The female lays four speckled eggs which are cryptically coloured to blend almost perfectly with their surroundings. She and her mate take turns incubating for 24 days. Shortly after hatching, the young scatter in the immediate vicinity, concealing themselves in grass. The black-tailed godwit feeds on insects and their larvae, worms, molluscs, spiders and small crustaceans.

Voice:
A note that sounds like 'reeka-reeka-reeka', repeated several times in succession.

Length:
40.5 cm.

Male and female have similar plumage.

Size of egg:
45.3–63.9
× 32.4–41.3 mm.

Migratory bird

Spotted Redshank

Tringa erythropus

Spotted redshanks are encountered in northern Scandinavia, Finland, northern Russia and east as far as Kamchatka. Northern European populations winter mainly in the Mediterranean region and less extensively along the coast of western Europe. During migration (i. e. from August to October), small flocks may be regularly encountered inland in central Europe on the muddy shores of ponds and lakes. The return to breeding grounds is in April and May but sometimes non-nesting birds may be encountered in central Europe as late as June or July. The spotted redshank inhabits open places such as the edges of forests, moorland and meadows near water. Its nest is a shallow depression lined sparingly with vegetation. The female usually lays four eggs in May or June, which both partners take turns to incubate. The young hatch after three weeks and leave the nest as soon as they are dry, concealing themselves in clumps of grass, heather or similar vegetation in the vicinity. They are tended until able to fend for themselves, after which the birds join in flocks. Food is obtained in mud shallows, the birds often wading belly deep in the water. When a strong wind is blowing, they keep to the sheltered part of the shore, taking their prey from the incoming waves. The diet consists mainly of small molluscs and aquatic insects.

Size of egg:
42.0—51.5
× 30.0—34.0 mm.

Length:
30.5 cm.

Male and female have
similar plumage.

Voice:
A loud 'tuinit'; also
'chick-chick-chick';

Migratory bird

Redshank

Tringa totanus

Redshanks are distributed practically all over Europe; the range is disrupted only in some western and southern parts of the continent. They winter chiefly in the Mediterranean area and on Europe's west coast, leaving for these parts in July to September. Most of the British population is resident. The birds return to their breeding grounds in mid-March to April, to be found mainly on wet meadows (also drier meadows with short grass, near lakes), marshes, swamps, and generally near water. The nest, a shallow depression in the ground sparsely lined with dry vegetation, in carefully concealed, perhaps in a clump of grass; the male builds the base and the female contributes a lining. In April or May, sometimes in June, four eggs are laid, which both partners take turns incubating for 22 to 25 days. The young remain in the nest only one day, after which they scatter throughout the neighbourhood. They are watched over by both parents, but gather their food themselves. At 25 days they can fly, and at 40 days are fully mature, after which they roam the countryside, forming groups on the muddy shores of ponds and lakes. The redshank's diet consists of insects and their larvae, spiders, worms, small molluscs and other invertebrates.

Voice:
A flutey 'tleu-hu-hu'; when danger threatens, a note that sounds like 'teuk' repeated several times in succession.

Length:
28 cm.

Male and female have similar plumage.

Size of egg:
38.6–50.6 × 25.7–33.5 mm.

Migratory or resident bird

Greenshank

Tringa nebularia

The greenshank is found in Scotland, western and northern Scandinavia, northern Finland and northern Russia. It winters throughout Africa and in southern Asia, but populations from eastern Asia may fly as far as Australia. Less commonly it winters no farther than southwestern Europe. During migration, from the end of July till the end of September and sometimes occasionally as late as November, it may be met with throughout Europe, even inland. It occurs in groups, often of about ten, rarely as many as forty birds. The greenshank returns to its breeding grounds again in April or May. The breeding grounds are located in moors, heaths near water, treeless tundras and open woodlands. The nest is a shallow hollow lined with grass or other plant matter. In May or June the female usually lays four eggs, which she incubates mostly by herself, though the male occasionally relieves her. The young hatch after 23 to 25 days and, as soon as they are dry, scatter throughout the neighbourhood, concealing themselves in grass, heather, and the like. They are tended by the adult birds. The greenshank is one of the few waders to feed regularly on fish, which form about one-quarter of the bulk of its diet. When catching fish it immerses its entire head in the water. Besides fish it also feeds on aquatic molluscs and insects, especially water boatmen.

Migratory bird

Size of egg:
45.7—59.8
× 31.0—37.7 mm.

Length:
30.5 cm.

Male and female have
similar plumage.

Voice:
A loud 'tew-tew-tew';
when courting, a flute-like
'tew-i'.

Green Sandpiper

Tringa ochropus

The green sandpiper is a common wader in the southern and central parts of Scandinavia and northeastern and eastern Europe. In late July or in August it leaves its breeding grounds for winter quarters, some birds stopping in western Europe and on the Mediterranean, but most flying on to Africa as far south as the equator, occasionally even farther south. During the autumn, migratory flocks may be seen in plenty in central and western Europe. The return to the nesting grounds is between the end of March and the beginning of May, the latest arrivals being those that nest in the northernmost regions. Soon after arrival, the birds prepare for nesting. During this period they occur in marshland, or on lakes and rivers with wooded banks. Unlike other sandpipers, this species nests in trees, taking over the abandoned nests of other birds. Like other waders, the female lays four eggs which she and her partner take turns incubating for 20 to 23 days, hers being the more frequent stint. After they have hatched, the young remain in the nest for one or two days and then tumble over the edge to the ground, usually falling unharmed on soft grass or moss. They are led to food and watched over by the parents until they reach maturity, after which the birds fly to marshland, ponds or lakes in open country. Diet consists mostly of small invertebrates.

Voice:
A flutey 'weet-tluitt'.

Length:
23 cm.

Male and female have
similar plumage.

Size of egg:
34.6–43.1
× 25.5–30.5 mm.

Migratory bird

Common Sandpiper

Tringa hypoleucos

The small and agile sandpiper inhabits all of Europe except Iceland. In July to September it migrates to winter quarters in the Mediterranean, sometimes in western Europe, but mainly in Africa as far south as Madagascar, returning again in mid-April to May. The species is found in swampy places and on the shores of lakes, ponds and rivers. As a rule, the birds arrive at their nesting grounds in pairs. The nest is a shallow depression in the ground, usually under overhanging plants near water, sometimes even on a substantial floating raft of vegetation, and possibly near a colony of gulls. The depression is lined with plant stalks and leaves. In May, (sometimes also in June or July if the first clutch has been accidentally destroyed), the female lays four eggs which are incubated mostly by the male, relieved occasionally by the hen. The young hatch after 21 to 23 days and leave the nest as soon as they are dry. Caring for the young devolves mainly on the male, who leads them to food and provides them with protection; the female is in attendance for only a few days. When they are a month old, the young begin to fly, after which they form small groups that may be seen in marshy locations near water or in shallows, where they gather food. The diet consists of various worms and crustaceans as well as insects and their larvae, spiders, centipedes and other small invertebrates.

Migratory bird

Size of egg:
32.2—40.2
× 22.5—28.0 mm.

Length:
19.5 cm.

Male and female have similar plumage.

Voice:
In flight, 'twee-see-see'; during the courtship display a trilling 'titti-weeti, titti-weeti'.

Wood Sandpiper

Tringa glareola

Wood sandpipers are widespread throughout Scandinavia, Finland, Scotland, northern Russia and in central Europe along the coasts of Poland and Germany. They migrate regularly through central Europe from late July to September and winter throughout practically all of Africa; eastern populations, however, fly to southern Asia and even as far as Australia. The birds return to their breeding grounds in April and May, though single, non-nesting individuals may be met with in central and western Europe even in summer. The wood sandpiper is a small, active bird the size of a skylark and is constantly on the move. It inhabits open country and the margins of open woodland near water. The nest, lined sparingly with vegetation such as grass and leaves, is located in swamps, marshland and marshy sites on the shore. As a rule four eggs are laid in May or June, sometimes in July, and incubated by both partners for 21 to 24 days. The young remain in the nest for at the most two days, after which they wander about the neighbourhood foraging for food. When they are able to fly, they roam the countryside in flocks and soon after depart for the wintering grounds. Diet consists of small invertebrates, especially water boatmen, the larvae of the harlequin fly and worms.

Voice:
When courting
'tleea-tleea-tleea; in flight,
a sharp 'chiff-iff-iff'.

Length:
20 cm.

Male and female have
similar plumage.

Size of egg:
33.0–42.5
× 24.4–29.3 mm.

Migratory bird

Dunlin

Calidris alpina

The dunlin's breeding grounds are along the coasts of Scandinavia, Finland, Russia, Poland, Germany, Denmark, Iceland, Great Britain and Ireland. European populations winter mostly on the coasts of western Europe and North Africa. During migration the species is found throughout Europe on the muddy edges of ponds, lakes, and rivers. Some birds, however, are resident. The greatest concentrations of dunlin are found on tundra. Birds return to their breeding grounds in late March and in April. They inhabit the seashore, river deltas and inland waters, occurring on wet meadow, moor or marsh. Nests are located near water, usually concealed by a tussock of grass. As a rule, the female lays four eggs at the end of April or in May; in the extreme north of the range, as late as the beginning of June. Both partners take turns to incubate for 21 to 22 days. As soon as the newly hatched birds are dry, they leave the nest but remain in the neighbourhood. They can fly at 28 days, and, in the far northern tundras, even at 20 days. The birds then form flocks that roam the countryside seeking water. At this stage adult birds start migrating, whereas the young remain until the end of August. When the dunlin forages for food, it wades in shallows but sometimes it also swims. During the nesting season the diet consists mainly of the larvae of mosquitoes, other insects and small molluscs and crustaceans; in autumn the birds also gather seeds.

Size of egg:
31.2–38.3
× 22.4–25.8 mm.

Length:
18 cm.

Male and female have similar plumage.

Voice:
Flight note is
a high-pitched 'treer'; song
is a purring trill.

Migratory bird

Ruff

Philomachus pugnax

This remarkable species is found mainly on the tundras of Europe, Asia and northern North America, but in Europe it also breeds along the coasts of Poland, Germany, Holland, Belgium, France and Scotland. During the spring and autumn migrations there are large numbers throughout Europe on seashores and by lakes, ponds and rivers. The wintering grounds are in southern and eastern Africa, though some birds winter on the coasts of southern and western Europe. The ruff returns to its summer quarters in large flocks in April, or sometimes as late as May, favouring wet meadows, moors, marshland and seashores for its nest sites. The males engage in great courtship 'fights', chopping with their beaks and expanding their magnificent collars. The purpose is to settle without actual fighting who shall mate with the females. An interesting feature of the male's striking nuptial plumage is that no two birds are alike in colour. Outside the breeding season, the plumage of both sexes is identical. The nest, a shallow hollow lined sparingly with vegetation, is prepared by the female alone. In May or June she usually lays four eggs, which she incubates by herself for 20 to 21 days; she likewise rears the young alone. When they can fly they form flocks that roam the countryside seeking food near water. Diet consists of various invertebrates as well as insects, worms, molluscs and crustaceans, but ruffs also eat seeds and small berries.

Voice:	Length:	Size of egg:
Muttering sounds when courting.	Male 29 cm, female 23 cm.	38.9–48.6 × 28.0–32.8 mm.
	Sexually dimorphic.	

Migratory bird

Red-necked Phalarope

Phalaropus lobatus

The red-necked phalarope breeds in Iceland, northern and western Scandinavia, northern Finland, on the islands off Scotland, in northern Russia and also arctic North America. European populations migrate along the European coast, but may also be seen on inland waters. Winter quarters are African coasts, southern Asia and the Aral Sea. Eastern populations migrate as far as Australia and North American populations to South America. Outside the breeding season, both male and female are a drab grey colour. Red-necked phalaropes nest in small groups on marshes, shores of lakes and rivers and on the seashores. The female selects the site, which is a hollow in the ground lined with dry grass, leaves and small twigs taken from the dwarf willow. It is usually well concealed in a grass tussock. Generally four eggs are laid and the duties of incubating are left entirely to the male, who also tends the young by himself. These hatch after 20 to 21 days and leave the nest as soon as they are dry. For the first few days, they conceal themselves in vegetation but after about a week they venture out on the water. When grown, the birds spend most of their time on water, swimming buoyantly on the waves and swinging their heads from side to side as they pick food from the surface with their bills. The diet consists mainly of aquatic insects and their larvae, with flies, molluscs and crustaceans.

Size of egg:
26.7–34.5
× 19.6–22.2 mm.

Length:
16.5 cm.

The female is more brightly coloured than the male.

Voice:
Short scratchy notes such as 'whit' or 'prip'.

Migratory bird

168

Avocet

Recurvirostra avosetta

The avocet is found mainly on the coasts of Germany, Denmark and Holland, also south-east England, southern Spain, the Rhône delta, by the Black and Caspian Seas and also on the salt lakes of southeastern Europe. It favours marshy places, sandy shores and islands with bare, open areas. Some birds are migrant, flying for the winter to South Africa and southern Asia, but many individuals remain on the coasts of southwestern and southeastern Europe. Avocets leave breeding grounds between the end of August an the beginning of November, returning again in March to early May. They usually congregate in flocks and during the breeding season they often breed in large colonies. The nest is sited near water in muddy or sandy spots, on grass or in very low vegetation. It is a simple scrape, sparsely lined with dry grass and small twigs. Between the end of April and June, sometimes even as late as July, the female lays four eggs which both partners incubate for twenty-four to twenty-five days. The young abandon the nest shortly after they have dried out. This species obtains its food mainly in shallows, where it stamps its feet on the mud bottom to stir up countless small crustaceans and insects which are then captured with rapid sweeping movements of the beak. It also eats small molluscs, sometimes nibbles green vegetable matter and very occasionally takes seeds.

Voice:
A high-pitched, flutey 'kleep' or 'kloo-it'.

Length:
43 cm.

Male and female have similar plumage.

Size of egg:
43.0–56.3
× 31.2–40.8 mm.

Migratory or resident bird

Black-winged Stilt

Himantopus himantopus

This species is widely distributed in Africa, America, southern Asia, Australia and Europe, where it breeds regularly in Spain, Portugal, southern France and the whole of southeastern Europe. Very occasionally, it also breeds in central Europe and Holland. The favoured habitats are lagoons, seashores, river deltas, large marshes, the shores of lakes and rivers, shallow salt lakes and the steppes. European birds are migrant, wintering in Africa and southern Asia and on migration the black-winged stilt may be seen in Great Britain and Denmark. It generally returns to its breeding grounds in April, nesting in colonies, often together with other species. The nest is a mere scrape near water, lined sparingly with vegetation. Often it is flooded, in which case the birds build a new one. In April or May, the female lays usually four eggs, which she and the male take turns incubating for 25 to 26 days. The adult birds guard the nest zealously and when danger threatens, fly above it in large arcs, uttering shrill cries. The newlyhatched young scatter in the neighbourhood of the nest as soon as they are dry. The diet consists of water boatmen and other aquatic insects, small aquatic molluscs, crustaceans and worms. Occasionally the birds nibble the green parts of plants.

Migratory bird

Size of egg:
38.8—48.2
× 28.0—33.5 mm.

Length:
38 cm.

Sexually dimorphic.

Voice:
A sharp, loud cry that sounds like 'kyip, kyip, kyip'.

Stone Curlew

Burhinus oedicnemus

Open fields, but especially dry, sandy places are the favourite haunts of the stone curlew, a sturdy bird with large, yellow, owlish eyes, that inhabits southern, eastern and western Europe (including southeastern England) and sometimes central Europe. It is locally quite common but because of its nocturnal habits may easily escape notice. In more southerly areas it is a resident species. Northern populations migrate to Africa in September or October, returning to their breeding grounds in April. Some individuals also winter in southwestern Europe. The nest, without any lining, is built in a shallow depression on the ground. Two, sometimes three spotted eggs, are laid usually in May, an some pairs have a second brood in July. Both partners share the duties of incubating for a period of 25 to 27 days. Towards evening, the stone curlew ventures out to hunt beetles, locusts, worms and other invertebrates, and occasionally small lizards and rodents. It is a very active bird, capable of running rapidly on the ground and also an accomplished flier. Its call is heard mainly at dawn and dusk.

Voice:
A wailing 'coo-ree' or
a high shrill 'keerrr-eee'.

Length:
40.5 cm.

Male and female have
similar plumage.

Size of egg:
47.0–61.7
× 35.6–43.0 mm.

**Migratory, resident or
dispersive bird**

Great Skua

Stercorarius skua

The European breeding grounds of the great skua include Iceland, the Faroes, Shetlands, Orkneys and northern Scotland. Interestingly enough, it also breeds on the opposite side of the world from the Antarctic coast to Tierra del Fuego. During the breeding season the great skua is found in marshes near the coast, the nest being located on the ground. The great skua nests in colonies as well as singly. In May or June the female usually lays two eggs which she and her partner incubate for 28 to 30 days. If the clutch is lost she lays again. The young remain in the nest for 6 to 7 weeks, where they are fed by the parents. When they are grown the birds roam the open seas of the eastern Atlantic, often flying as far as the coast of Spain; vagrants may be encountered inland only in rare instances. The great skua feeds on anything it can get hold of, from worms and crustaceans to fish, birds and small mammals. It is particulary fond of the eggs of other birds. It also harasses gulls and terns until they drop or regurgitate their prey, which the great skua quickly picks out of the air and swallows. If nothing else is available it will even gather carcasses cast up by the sea. The great skua is a courageous bird and at the nesting site will often chase a falcon and even attacks man. Nowhere throughout its range is it particularly abundant.

Migratory bird

Size of egg:
62.0—78.5
× 44.5—53.2 mm.

Length:
58 cm.

Male and female have
similar plumage.

Voice:
A low-pitched 'uk-uk-uk',
when attacking, 'tuk-tuk'.

Arctic Skua

Stercorarius parasiticus

Widespread in the arctic regions of Europe, Asia and North America, in Europe the Arctic skua breeds on the coasts of Scotland, Iceland, western and northern Scandinavia, Finland and northern Russia. Outside the breeding season it keeps to the open seas or coastal waters. When migrating, European populations fly along the coast to western Africa, but single individuals often occur as vagrants inland, though rarely in central Europe. During migration the birds often occur in large flocks. They return to their breeding grounds in April or early May, nesting in colonies on tundra and marshes. The well-spaced nests are shallow depressions in grass without, as a rule, any lining. The female generally lays two eggs, which she begins to incubate as soon as the first is laid; the male relieves her at regular intervals. Hatching is after 25 to 28 days and the chicks are fed by both parents. They can fly at 32 days, when the birds set out together for their wintering grounds. The arctic skua feeds on small fish, invertebrates, small birds, mammals and the eggs of other birds. It harries gulls, terns and guillemots to rob them of their prey; it will also take carrion washed up on beaches and occasionally berries.

Voice:
A guttural 'eee-air'.

Length:
66 cm.

Both sexes have very variable plumage, ranging from a distinct light phase to a distinct dark phase.

Size of egg:
49.0–63.1
× 37.2–44.3 mm.

Dispersive or migratory bird

Great Black-backed Gull

Larus marinus

This rapacious-looking gull is widespread in Iceland, on the coasts of Scandinavia and Finland, in Ireland and on the west coasts of England and Scotland. Occasionally, it nests on the west coast of France and in Denmark. It also nests in Greenland and on the eastern coast of northern North America. The species is locally resident, but in winter many individuals roam the European coasts westwards from Poland and southwards as far as Spain. They are rarely encountered inland. Great black-backs nest in colonies, often with the lesser black-backed gull, as well as singly, choosing rocky coasts and islands as well as marshes and islands in lakes. The nest is built by both partners, usually on a rock ledge, less often on the ground. It is made of twigs, grass, seaweeds and other vegetable matter and lined with feathers. In May or June, very occasionally also in late April, the female lays two or three eggs which she and her partner take turns incubating for 26 to 28 days. The newly-hatched nestlings weigh about 80 grams. They soon leave the nest to scatter in the neighbourhood, concealing themselves in the vegetation. The adult birds bring them food for almost 50 days. Flight feathers grow in when the chicks are 45 days old, but they do not fly well until the age of two months. The diet consists of fish, small birds and their eggs, crustaceans, molluscs, and animal remains.

Resident or dispersive bird

Size of egg:
67.5—87.0
× 49.0—57.6 mm.

Length:
74 cm.

Male and female have
similar plumage.

Voice:
Usually a harsh
low-pitched 'owk'.

Lesser Black-backed Gull

Larus fuscus

The lesser black-backed gull has a comparatively limited range. It inhabits Scandinavia, Finland, Iceland, the British Isles, Ireland, Denmark, the coasts of Germany and western France, and also breeds in northern Siberia. Usually a migrant, only in England and Ireland it is generally resident. Winter quarters are the coasts of western and southern Europe and North Africa, sometimes western Africa. Young, non-breeding birds, however, roam far and wide even during the nesting period. The return to the breeding grounds is in April, the birds seeking out islands or rocky coasts, river deltas and freshwater near the sea. Lesser blackbacks breed in colonies, favouring grassy sites. The nest is made of sticks, seaweed and other vegetable matter, lined with fine plant remnants and feathers. The clutch is usually three eggs, which are laid in May or June. They are incubated by both partners for a period of 26 to 27 days. The young abandon the nest soon after hatching, though they sometimes remain there several days if not disturbed. They are fed mostly small fish by both parents. When fledged, groups of young birds roam the countryside in company with adult birds. The lesser black-backed gull feeds mostly on fish, especially herring, but it also catches small mammals and birds.

Voice:
A deep, loud cry sounding like 'goh-goh-goh'.

Length:
53 cm.

Male and female have similar plumage.

Size of egg:
57.5—77.1
× 43.0—52.1 mm.

Resident or migratory bird

Herring Gull

Larus argentatus

Herring gulls are widespread in Europe, Asia, North America and Africa. The species breeds along practically the entire European coast from the Baltic to the Mediterranean, and along the Black and Caspian Sea coasts. It is a migrant as well as a partial migrant. Outside the breeding season, the birds occur in large flocks in harbours, where they scavenge for fish dropped by fishing fleets. Nesting is in colonies on islands and cliffs or in reed beds, sometimes numbering several thousand pairs. Sometimes herring gulls nest on the roofs of houses. They build a structure of sticks and bits of vegetation; if in a reed bed it is mounted on a pile of flattened reeds. In May or June the female usually lays three eggs, and if the clutch is lost, she lays a new one. Both partners incubate for 26 to 28 days. The young birds scatter about the neighbourhood of the nest the day after hatching, concealing themselves in clumps of grass or among the reeds. They are fed by the adult birds even when they are able to fly, which is at 40 to 42 days. The herring gull eats various remnants cast up by the sea, including refuse and the eggs of birds and their young. Herring gulls multiply at the expense of other birds — particularly ducks and terns — so that in recent years measures have been taken to limit their numbers.

Resident or dispersive bird

Size of egg:
58.0—82.7
× 44.1—54.8 mm.

Length:
56 cm.

Male and female have
similar plumage.

Voice:
A ringing 'kyow', also
'gah-gah-gah'.

Common Gull

Larus canus

The common gull breeds on the shores of Scandinavia, Finland, Russia, Great Britain, Ireland, Denmark, Germany, Poland and, very occasionally, the shores of Holland, Belgium and France. Outside the breeding season it may be seen throughout practically the whole of Europe, but mostly by the sea. It often occurs as a vagrant inland in central Europe. Birds arrive at their nesting grounds in March or early April already paired. They breed in colonies, placing the nests on rock ledges or among vegetation and occasionally in a tree. It is constructed mainly by the female, while the male keeps his distance, now and then bringing a piece of building material to his mate. In colonies, the nests are generally spaced several metres apart. The clutch consists, as a rule, of three eggs, which the two partners take turns incubating at intervals of two to three hours. The young hatch after 25 to 26 days and leave the nest at one or two days, but remain in the vicinity. They are tended by both parents who bring them food — insects and small fish the first four days — which the young take from their beaks. At 20 days the young gulls forage for food by themselves, gathering insects and their larvae, worms and molluscs, but also continue to be fed by the parents. Not until 35 days are they fully independent. This gull's favourite fish are cod and herring.

Voice:
A high-pitched cry that sounds like 'gah-gah-gah'.

Length:
40 cm.

Male and female have similar plumage.

Size of egg:
50.0—67.2
× 35.9—45.4 mm.

Dispersive bird

177

Black-headed Gull

Larus ridibundus

The black-headed gull is one of the commonest European birds. It nests in central, western and eastern Europe, in Scandinavia and on the shores of Iceland. Northern and eastern populations fly south in July to August, whereas gulls from the other parts of Europe may stay the winter or migrate to the Mediterranean. During the winter months, the birds seek out unfrozen lakes and rivers and often occur in large groups in big cities. They return to their breeding grounds in flocks, already paired, during March and April, to nest on lakes, ponds and the seashore. Black-headed gulls breed in large colonies containing as many as a thousand birds. The nest is built by both partners on dry ground on an islet or as a floating structure on water. Three eggs, with marked variation in colour, are incubated by both partners for 20 to 23 days. The speckled offspring remain in the nest a number of days, abandoning it if disturbed, either concealing themselves in the surrounding vegetation or making their escape by swimming. Food is brought to the young by the male, who sometimes first passes it to the female for distribution. The young begin to fly at five to six weeks, after which they roam the countryside in flocks. The diet consists of insects, worms, molluscs, other invertebrates, small vertebrates, fish and frogs. Sometimes the birds eat green plant parts; they are also fond of visiting cherry orchards.

Resident, dispersive or migratory bird

Size of egg:
43.0—66.0
× 31.3—42.1 mm.

Length:
37 cm.

Male and female have similar plumage. The head is white in winter.

Voice:
A repeated 'kwarr' or short 'kroup'.

Little Gull

Larus minutus

Little gulls are widely distributed from the Baltic seacoast of Finland and southern Sweden east through Poland and Russia to eastern Siberia. They are also found in North America. Very occasionally, they breed along the coast of Denmark and the northern coast of the Black Sea. The habitats are generally seashores and river deltas, but also inland lakes. A large number of these birds winter in the Mediterranean, but many too in western Europe and on the Baltic Sea. During migration, the little gull may be seen regularly in central Europe. It nests in colonies numbering two to 50 pairs, often with terns and other gulls, usually in marshes. The nest, built by both partners, is placed on a mound of reeds or on the ground and is constructed of dry as well as of green plant parts. It generally measures 50 centimetres in diameter, the nesting hollow being about ten centimetres across, and the whole structure 20 centimetres high. At the end of May or in June, very occasionally in July, the female lays two to three eggs which she and her partner take turns incubating for 20 to 21 days. The young generally leave the nest on their first day and conceal themselves in the surrounding vegetation, where the parents bring them food. They begin to fly at 25 days. The little gull captures insects in the air or on the water; it also eats molluscs, crustaceans, worms and occasionally small fish.

Voice:
A not very loud
'kek-kek-kek'
or a whistling 'kay-ee'.

Length:
28 cm.

Male and female have
similar plumage.

Size of egg:
37.0–45.8
× 27.3–32.0 mm.

Migratory bird

Kittiwake

Rissa tridactyla

The kittiwake is found in Europe along the coasts of Norway, Iceland, the British Isles, Ireland and the Murmansk region. Occasionally it nests in Heligoland and on the coast of Brittany. Outside the breeding season, European birds stay on the open sea, mostly in mid-Atlantic. Only on rare occasions do young birds stray inland. The kittiwake breeds in large colonies on the narrow rock ledges of steep cliffs, but sometimes on the ledges of tall buildings in cities, particularly Norwegian ports. The nest, a sturdy structure with a deep hollow, is built by both partners of lichens, moss, seaweeds and other plant matter held together with clay or mud. As a rule, two eggs are laid in May or June, occasionally in July, and both partners take turns incubating them for 21 to 24 days. The young, unlike those of other gulls, remain in the nest for 33 to 37 days until they are able to fly, being fed by their parents the whole time. When they have fledged, the entire colony leaves the nesting site for the open sea. The diet consists mostly of marine animals, particularly fish, crustaceans and molluscs, but the kittiwake also eats plant food. It obtains its food in flight from the water's surface.

Dispersive bird

Size of egg:
47.1–62.5
× 35.3–44.5 mm.

Length:
40 cm.

Male and female have similar plumage.

Voice:
In the nesting grounds its call sounds like 'kitti-wack' or 'kaka-week'.

Black Tern

Chlidonias niger

Resembling a large swallow, the black tern is graceful to watch flying over water. It inhabits eastern, central, southwestern and western Europe and occasionally nests in the British Isles. It also occurs very occasionally in the south of Sweden. Definitely a migrant, the bird leaves for its winter quarters in August or the beginning of September, generally following a southwesterly course. Populations from western regions fly along the western coast of Europe and Iberia to tropical Africa; eastern populations travel to Africa via the Nile. They return to their breeding grounds quite late — not until the end of April or beginning of May — seeking out ponds and lakes with dense vegetation, peat bogs with small pools or swamps in lowland country. This is a gregarious bird which breeds in small colonies numbering several pairs. The nest of dry reeds is usually built on bent, flattened reeds in shallows or on small, floating islets of vegetation. Both partners share the task of construction. The female lays three, but sometimes only two eggs in May or June (if the nest is destroyed as late as July). Both partners take turns incubating for 14 to 17 days and both feed the young insects and their larvae as well as small fish, which they bring at frequent intervals. Flying insects are caught above the water's surface.

Voice:
A short 'kreek' or 'kitt'.

Length:
25 cm.

Male and female have similar plumage.

Size of egg:
30.5−40.2
× 22.5−27.4 mm.

Migratory bird

Caspian Tern

Hydroprogne caspia

Although the Caspian tern has a disrupted range, it is found practically throughout the world. In Europe it breeds on the eastern coast of Sweden, Finland, and the northern shores of the Caspian and Black Seas. Occasionally, it nests on the northern coasts of West Germany and in Sardinia. This is a bird of the seashore. After the breeding season it flies to winter quarters along the shores of tropical regions, rarely straying inland on passage. The return to the breeding grounds is in April and May. The Caspian tern breeds in large colonies on sandy beaches or small islands. The nesting hollow is only sparingly lined with plant matter. In May or June the female generally lays two eggs which are incubated by both partners for 20 to 22 days. Shortly after they have hatched, the young scatter throughout the neighbourhood, concealing themselves in vegetation, where the adult birds bring them food. At 30 to 35 days they are able to fly and fend for themselves. These birds feed mainly on fish, (mostly herring) but also eat various invertebrates and occasionally small birds and their eggs. When seeking fish they fly above the water, every so often stopping to hover, then plummeting downwards to the water.

Migratory bird

Size of egg:
55.0−72.3
× 40.5−46.5 mm.

Length:
53 cm.

Male and female have
similar plumage.

Voice:
A very deep 'kaah' or
'kraa-uh'.

Common Tern

Sterna hirundo

The common tern inhabits practically all of Europe except the far north. It is absent, however, in some areas, not breeding, for example, in central Spain. At the end of July, or in the south as late as September or October, it leaves for winter quarters in the Persian Gulf, on the shores of the Red Sea and on the west coast of Africa, sometimes flying as far as Madagascar. It is a strong and skilled flier. The end of April or beginning of May marks its return to breeding grounds, usually on large inland lakes or ponds, large rivers, islands and coasts. A gregarious species, it is usually seen in flocks and breeds colonially. The birds arrive at the nesting grounds in large groups and then form pairs which indulge in courtship flights. Small twigs, blades of grass, reeds and other green or dead plant parts are used to build the nest, which is placed in a shallow depression. The site is often muddy. In May or June the female lays three eggs, which are incubated by both partners for 20 to 24, sometimes 26 days. The young are fed insects, insect larvae, other invertebrates and small fish by both parents. When searching for food, the tern often hovers in one spot with head down, scanning the water's surface. As soon as it sights its prey it plunges into the water, often disappearing from sight, then reappearing again with the victim in its beak.

Voice:
Usually 'kree-err', also a short 'kirri-kirri'.

Length:
35 cm.

Male and female have similar plumage.

Size of egg:
35.3−48.0
× 25.0−32.8 mm.

Migratory bird

183

Arctic Tern

Sterna paradisaea

The arctic tern is widespread in the northern regions of the Old and New World. In Europe it breeds in Iceland, Scandinavia and on the coasts of Poland, Germany, Denmark, Holland, the British Isles, Ireland, Brittany and northern Russia. It is found chiefly on seashores and rocky islands, also on inland lakes in Iceland and Scandinavia. On passage, it flies along the continental shores as far as the tip of South Africa, whence many individuals continue on to the Antarctic. They return to their breeding grounds in April or early May. The nest is usually a shallow scrape without any lining; seldom is it decorated with small shell fragments. In May or June, the female usually lays two, very occasionally one or three eggs, which she and her partner take turns incubating. The young hatch after 20 to 22 days and soon abandon the nest to scatter in the neighbourhood. They continue to be fed by their parents, even when they are capable of flight, which is usually at four weeks. The arctic tern usually obtains its food in flight from the water, but very occasionally from the ground. It also eats small fish, molluscs, worms and crustaceans. This species has many enemies, especially the larger gulls, skuas, and predators. In colonies, its eggs and young suffer severe losses – usually only about 16 percent of the offspring reach maturity.

Migratory bird

Size of egg:
35.3–47.3
× 26.2–33.4 mm.

Length:
38 cm.

Male and female have similar plumage.

Voice:
A short call that sounds like 'kee-kee' or 'kria'.

Roseate Tern

Sterna dougallii

This beautiful tern is well distributed through the Atlantic coast of North America, the coast of Central America, the Antilles, the African coast and southeast Asia. In Europe it breeds mainly on the coasts of the British Isles and Ireland. At one time it also nested in the south of France and on the North Friesian Islands, but now no more. European birds winter on the islands of the Atlantic and on the western coast of Africa. When migrating they sometimes occur on the coasts of West Germany and Holland. The habitat is confined to the seashore. Roseate terns nest in large colonies on sandy or rocky peninsulas and islands, often with other terns. The eggs, usually two, very occasionally three, are laid in a shallow, unlined depression or merely on the bare, hard ground. In Europe they are generally laid in June and are incubated by both partners for 21 days. Both share the duties of feeding their offspring for over a month. After the young are grown, the birds roam the coast in large flocks, setting out for their winter quarters at the end of July or in August. Diet consists chiefly of small fish, but also water insects and their larvae and molluscs, crustaceans and worms. The roseate tern is particularly persecuted by the larger gulls, which steal its eggs and young from the nest.

Voice:
A long 'aak', soft 'chu-ick', also 'kekekekek'.

Length:
38 cm.

Male and female have similar plumage.

Size of egg:
38.0−47.0
× 30.0−32.0 mm.

Migratory bird

Little Tern

Sterna albifrons

Smallest and most delicately beautiful of the European terns, this species is found in the temperate zones of nearly all the continents. In Europe it breeds along practically the entire Atlantic coast and sometimes inland; it is absent, however, in Iceland, Scandinavia and the northern parts of Europe. The habitat is sandy places or marshy areas bordering lakes and rivers. A migratory bird, it leaves its breeding grounds by the end of July for winter quarters along the coasts of the Indian Ocean, returning again in late April or the beginning of May. It breeds in small colonies, the nests being spaced quite far apart, often in company with Kentish plovers. The nest is a shallow depression sparingly lined with small stones or shells. In the second half of May and in June the female usually lays two eggs, which are extremely well camouflaged. Incubation is mostly by the female, though the male relieves her now and then. The young hatch after 21 to 22 days and for the first few days of their life are kept warm by the mother while the male brings them food. Later they are fed by both parents. Diet consists of small fish and, to a lesser extent, invertebrates. Insects are taken both on the water and the ground, and fish by diving.

Migratory bird

Size of egg:
29.5—37.0
× 20.8—26.0 mm.

Length:
20 cm.

Male and female have similar plumage.

Voice:
A high-pitched 'kree-ik' or harsh 'kitt'.

Sandwich Tern

Sterna sandvicensis

The sandwich tern is widespread in Europe, by the Caspian Sea, as well as in Tunisia and North America, but its distribution is discontinuous and circumscribed. Regular European breeding grounds include southern Sweden, Denmark, Germany, Holland, Brittany, the British Isles, Spain and the shores of the Black Sea. In the autumn it departs for Africa, often flying as far as South Africa and the Persian Gulf. Only very occasionally does it stray inland. The sandwich tern forms dense colonies, sometimes numbering as many as a thousand pairs. It nests only on the seashore and on islands, being partial to locations covered partly with grass. The nests, shallow depressions only sparingly lined with varied plant material, are often spaced only ten to fifteen centimetres apart. In May or early June, the female usually lays two eggs which she and her mate incubate for 21 to 24 days. The young remain in the nest for 6 to 7 days, sometimes even a bit longer, and then scatter in the neighbourhood. At the age of 15 to 20 days the young birds join to form flocks and at the age of 35 days they are already able to fly. The sandwich tern feeds chiefly on fish, mainly herring, mackerel, etc. It hunts its prey by plunging headlong into the water from the air. Besides fish it also eats molluscs, crustaceans, worms and sometimes even small birds. On the rare occasion it will eat insects.

Voice:
A harsh cry that sounds like 'kirrik'.

Length:
40 cm.

Male and female have similar plumage.

Size of egg:
44.0—59.4
× 33.3—43.2 mm.

Migratory bird

187

Razorbill

Alca torda

Razorbills are found on the seacoasts of practically all of Scandinavia, the Murmansk region, Ireland, the British Isles, Iceland, Heligoland and Brittany. They also occur in Greenland and northern North America. A truly pelagic species, it roams the expanses of the Atlantic outside the breeding season. This is a gregarious bird which nests in large colonies on rock cliffs on islands or the shore, building no nest but laying its single egg on a rock ledge, under a boulder, in a rock crevice, or sometimes in the abandoned nest of a kittiwake. The egg, laid between mid-May and June, is incubated by both parents usually for 32 to 36 days. Both share the duties of rearing and feeding their offspring. When the young bird is between 17 and 21 days old it leaps into the water, often bouncing clumsily off the rocks as its falls, for at this stage it cannot yet fly properly. However, once afloat, it is immediately able to swim and dive. The diet consists chiefly of small fish in search of which the birds sometimes fly as far as 20 kilometres from the nest. In water the razorbill can hold several fish in its beak at the same time. It also takes crustaceans, molluscs and marine worms, and is an excellent diver.

Size of egg:
63.0—83.6
× 42.0—52.4 mm.

Length:
40 cm.

Male and female have
similar plumage.

Voice:
Long whistling notes.

Resident or dispersive bird

Guillemot

Uria aalge

Northern and western coasts of Scandinavia, the Murmansk regions, Iceland, the British Isles, occasionally Brittany, Portugal, Spain and some islands in the North and Baltic Seas are the European breeding grounds of the guillemot. Some young as well as adult birds stay the winter near the breeding grounds, but most roam the open seas of the Atlantic. The species occasionally visits inland areas. It arrives at its breeding grounds in December or January, but in the extreme northern parts of its range not till March, and nests colonially on cliffs. In the British Isles and the Baltic Sea area, the birds begin to lay in mid-May. The single egg, which is variable in colour, generally lies on the bare rock, but the female may place a small stone or bit of grass underneath or deposit it in a kittiwake's nest. The parents take turns incubating for 30 to 36 days and then feed their offspring which are covered with a thick coat of down, two to three times a day, mainly fish. At 20 to 25 days the young bird leaves the nest as yet unable to fly, merely spreading its wings and dropping onto the water, where it is fed by the parents for a short period longer. The diet consists mainly of small fish, with crustaceans, marine worms and molluscs.

Voice:
A long 'arrr' or 'arra'.

Length:
43 cm.

Male and female have similar plumage.

Size of egg:
74.0—93.0
× 46.0—55.0 mm.

Resident bird

Alcidae

Brünnich's Guillemot

Uria lomvia

The northernmost arctic regions of Asia, North America, Greenland and Europe are the home of Brünnich's guillemot. In Europe it breeds only in Iceland and on the Murmansk coast. During winter it may be seen along the northern coast of Norway and round Iceland, occasionally as far as the north of France and the Baltic Sea, rarely straying inland. It arrives at its breeding grounds in late March or early April, keeping to the water at first and then settling on steep cliffs. It nests in large colonies on rock ledges, laying a single egg on the bare rock. The young bird is covered with a thick, furry coat of down. It is fed as often as three times daily, the parents flying in search of food as far as 15 kilometres from the nesting site. At 18 to 25 days, the young bird drops down to the water, fluttering its wings in order to lessen the impact of the fall. Whole flocks of young then swim about uttering loud cries and calling to the adult birds, who fly after their offspring and continue to feed them at sea. Brünnich's guillemot hunts in flocks of 20 to 200 birds; its chief prey is fish five to 15 centimetres long, but it also eats crustaceans and molluscs. On land the bird walks upright and slowly; in water it swims buoyantly and dives expertly, but not to great depths.

Size of egg:
69.0–99.0
× 41.0–59.0 mm.

Length:
39 to 48 cm.

Male and female have
similar plumage.

Voice:
A whistling 'arr'.

Dispersive bird

Black Guillemot

Cepphus grylle

Black guillemots are widely distributed in Europe and in the northern parts of Asia and North America. Their European breeding grounds are the coasts of Scandinavia, Finland, the Murmansk region, Iceland, Scotland, Ireland and Denmark. Although mostly resident, in winter, flocks may be seen along the coast of Germany. Outside the breeding season the bird stays at sea, but inshore. Black guillemots start looking for suitable nesting sites when the ice and snow have thawed, and lay their eggs about a fortnight later. They nest singly or in small groups of under a hundred pairs. The nest is usually located in a rock crevice, under a rock ledge, sometimes even in a vertical burrow. Between mid-May and mid-June the female usually lays two eggs on the bare rock, sometimes placing several small stones underneath. Both partners take turns to incubate the eggs, which at this time register a temperature of 35°–37°C, though on the side resting on the ground the temperature is only 16°–19°C. The young hatch after 27 to 30 days. Lying on their bellies, they are fed by the parents from the second day onwards, being brought small fish three to five times daily. At 35 to 37 days they leave the nest, usually at night, venturing out onto the sea. The mainstay of the diet is small fish, other food being insects, molluscs and crustaceans.

Voice:
Whistling notes and twittering trills.

Length:
32 to 38 cm.

Male and female have similar plumage.

Size of egg:
57.0–65.0
× 38.0–44.0 mm.

Resident bird

Puffin

Fratercula arctica

The puffin is at home on the coasts and islands of the northern and middle Atlantic. In Europe it nests on the coasts of the Murmansk region, Norway, southwest Sweden, Great Britain, Ireland, Iceland and Brittany. It is a bird of the open seas and outside the breeding season keeps to the middle Atlantic waters. Before the nesting period it arrives on the coasts in large flocks seeking out soft grassy slopes in which it can dig its burrows more easily. However, it is also content with rocky locations where it can nest in cavities, crevices or rabbit holes. As a rule, with the aid of both feet and beak, it digs its own burrows; these have one or more nesting chambers and several corridors. The chambers are lined with dry grass, feathers or marine plants brought from the sea. The puffin nests in large colonies sometimes numbering more than a hundred thousand birds. The single egg, which is very large and often weighs more than one tenth of the body weight of the female, is usually laid in May and incubated by both partners for 40 to 42 days. The puffin feeds mainly on fish, but also eats molluscs and crustaceans. The adult birds often carry several fish in the beak at one time, sometimes as many as twelve. They obtain their food underwater, where they swim with the aid of both feet and wings.

Size of egg:
58.0−68.0
× 39.0−49.0 mm.

Length:
27 to 37 cm.

Male and female have
similar plumage.

Voice:
Heard only occasionally
on the breeding grounds,
the call consists of notes
that sound like 'ow' or 'arr'.

Dispersive bird

Stock Dove

Columba oenas

Deciduous and mixed woodland or less often thin conifer forests and old parks are the stock dove's habitats. This bird, widespread throughout Europe except for the most northern areas, is resident in the west and south. Inhabitants of other regions migrate to southwestern Europe and the Mediterranean in September and October. They return to their breeding grounds as early as the end of February, seeking out places with old trees which provide cavities for nesting. They sometimes take over an abandoned black woodpecker's hole, a hole in a sandbank or a nesting box. This species has disappeared from many forests where it was once plentiful because of the lack of suitable nesting cavities. The hollow is lined with dry sticks and small twigs, but some females will lay their clutch of two eggs without bothering to line the cavity. Incubation, shared by both partners, lasts 16 to 17 days, and both feed the young 'pigeon's milk' regurgitated from the crop. At three weeks, the young leave the nest, but continue to be fed half-digested seeds and grain by the parents for a short while longer. When their offspring are fully mature, the adult birds often have a second brood. The diet of the mature birds consists mostly of various seeds, but also includes small fruits, berries and green plant parts.

Voice:
A cooing note that sounds like 'coo-roo-oo'.

Length:
33 cm.

Male and female have similar plumage.

Size of egg:
33.0–43.0
× 26.0–31.0 mm.

Resident or migratory bird

Wood Pigeon

Columba palumbus

Around the middle of March, flocks of migrant wood pigeons return from winter quarters in the Mediterranean to their nesting grounds throughout most of Europe. Birds which inhabit warmer parts of the continent are either resident or transient migrants. The wood pigeon is found in all types of woodland, overgrown parks or in large gardens with thick ground cover. Early in spring one can hear the unusual clapping of the males' wings, this being a feature of their courtship antics. The nest is a flimsy structure of twigs, haphazardly laid on top of each other, generally located on the branch of a conifer, rarely a deciduous tree, at its junction with the trunk, some three to four metres above the ground or higher. Male and female take turns incubating the two eggs for 17 to 18 days, and both feed the young with 'pigeon's milk' regurgitated from the crop. The young birds leave the nest at 20 to 29 days, perching on nearby branches, where they continue to be fed by the parents. They are usually about 35 days old before they are capable of independent flight. There is usually a second brood in June to August and occasionally a third. The diet consists chiefly of seeds, green plant parts and, occasionally, even small invertebrates. During the day, flocks of wood pigeons may be seen on fields, where they often fall prey to the peregrine falcon. In September and October they again leave their nesting grounds.

Size of egg:
36.5—47.8
× 25.0—33.0 mm.

Length:
40.5 cm.

Male and female have similar plumage.

Voice:
A cooing note that sounds like 'cooo-coo, coo-coo, coo'.

Resident or migratory bird

Turtle Dove

Streptopelia turtur

The purring call of the turtle dove may be heard on a warm April or May day, announcing the bird's return from winter quarters in far-off tropical Africa. This species is plentiful throughout Europe, except Scandinavia, and is found also in northwestern Africa and western Asia. It frequents thin mixed woods with undergrowth, field groves, thickets alongside rivers, streams and ponds, and well-grown parkland. During the courtship flight, the male soars into the air, before gliding down with tail feathers spread wide. The nest is a simple structure of dry sticks and twigs arranged haphazardly on top of each other; it is built by both partners, generally between one and five metres above the ground, in bushes or treetops. The two eggs are incubated 14 to 16 days by both parents and both feed the young with 'pigeon's milk', regurgitated from the crop. Later, the diet consists of various half-digested seeds and grain. The young leave the nest at 14 to 16 days, but continue to be fed by the parent birds a short while longer. When the first brood is fully mature, the adult birds have a second, usually in June or July. The turtle dove leaves the woods to visit fields in search of food, and in late summer gathers in small groups in the fields before leaving for the south. In some countries this beautiful species is shot as a game bird. Agile and swift in flight, it is adept at darting between branches in the treetops, well capable of eluding a falcon in pursuit.

Voice:
A long-drawn-out 'roor-r-r'.

Length:
27 cm.

Male and female have similar plumage.

Size of egg:
27.0—34.6
× 20.0—24.6 mm.

Migratory bird

Collared Dove

Streptopelia decaocto

Before 1930 the collared dove's European range was confined to the Balkans. Today it inhabits the whole of Europe. It may be found in parks, gardens and avenues in large cities, even perching in a solitary tree in a town square. It is a resident bird, forming large flocks in winter wherever there is ample food, such as around farmyards, poultry farms and zoos. Highly commensal with man, the birds will perch on windowsills and accept scraps from the dinner table. Seeds form the principal item of diet, supplemented by insects, molluscs and worms. The nest is built in the branches of tall bushes or sometimes on a windowsill or the sheltered top of a nest box. It is a simple construction made only of dry twigs placed haphazardly on top of one another. The hen generally lays two eggs, which she and her mate take turns incubating for 14 to 15 days, the young nestlings fledging three weeks later. Like other pigeons, the collared dove may have as many as four broods a year, nesting right into the winter months. The main breeding season, however, is from April to September.

Size of egg:
27.5−33.8
× 21.8−25.0 mm.

Length:
28 cm.

Male and female have
similar plumage.

Voice:
A deep 'coo-coo-coo'; in
flight, a nasal ‚kwurr'.

Resident bird

Common Cuckoo

Cuculus canorus

As early as the middle of April the male cuckoo's familiar, melodius call is to be heard all over Europe. The females, who arrive from the African winter quarters a week or ten days later, do not make this characteristic call, but produce a sound resembling that of the woodpecker. Cuckoos often return to the same breeding grounds for several years in succession, and may be found in woods, field groves, large parks, overgrown graveyards as well as thickets beside water or even in large reed beds. The female roams her territory seeking small songbirds' nests and, when she finds one that is suitable, removes one egg, depositing her own in its place, which is usually similar in colouring to those of the host. From May to June, one hen lays 15 to 20 eggs, each in a different nest. An individual cuckoo lays eggs of similar colour, but often markedly different from those of other cuckoos. The period of incubation is 12 days and, on hatching, the young cuckoo soon tumbles all the eggs and even the rightful progeny of its foster parents out of the nest. A newly hatched cuckoo is completely naked, with very sensitive areas on its back which, during the first four days, react to contact with any foreign object in the nest, including eggs and the hatched offspring of the foster parents. Adult cuckoos feed on hairy caterpillars. Departure southwards is between early July and mid-September.

Voice:
The male's call sounds like 'cuc-coo', the female's like 'kwickkwick-kwick'; the young produce a 'tseetseetsee'.

Length:
33 cm.

Male and female have similar plumage.

Size of egg:
19.7—26.4 × 14.7—18.8 mm.
The eggs show marked variation in colour.

Migratory bird

Barn Owl

Tyto alba

The barn owl has taken a liking to built-up areas, preferring them to its original cliff habitats. It will build its nest in barn lofts, attics, dovecots, even church steeples or dark corners of a castle ruin, where its hoarse voice has frightened many a passer-by. It generally remains faithful to its chosen home, even in winter, but in times of severe frosts and lack of food it will migrate. The barn owl is one of the few cosmopolitan species with a distribution right around the globe. It is not particularly discriminating as to the time of nesting, and its clutch of four to six eggs may be found any time from March to November. When there is an abundance of mice it will have as many as three broods a year. It also hunts rats, bats, sparrows, amphibians and insects. The eggs, often laid in a bare scrape, are incubated for 30 to 32 days by the hen, fed meanwhile by the male. The young, which usually fledge after 52 to 58 days (this period sometimes being extended to 86 days), are fed by both parents. Shortly afterwards the young scatter about the countryside.

Size of egg:
34.8−43.0
× 28.6−33.5 mm.

Length:
34 cm.

Wing span:
About 80 cm.

Voice:
A long, wild shriek, also hissing, snapping and yapping notes.

Resident bird

Eagle Owl

Bubo bubo

This is the largest European owl, widespread throughout Europe except for the western parts. It is quite plentiful in some areas, numbers having increased in recent years, thanks to rigid protection laws. The species inhabits open woodland, rocky locations and scrub country. It is a resident bird or transient migrant and may be found in both lowland and mountain regions. Nesting is on cliff ledges, the walls of old castle ruins or simply the ground; in northern regions it often uses a tree cavity at ground level. The nest itself is simple, sometimes lined with only a few hairs and feathers from the owl's victims. Two to four eggs are incubated by the female for 32 to 37 days. During this time the male brings her food, which she takes from him at a short distance from the nest. The newly hatched nestlings are cared for by the hen, who also shelters them from rain and sun. At one to two months the young leave the nest and perch in its vicinity. By the time they are three months old they can fly well. The species requires a large territory, extending as far as 15 kilometres from the nest. It preys on vertebrates as big as hares or small foxes but will also feed on insects. The eagle owl is hated by predators and crows, a fact of which hunters once took advantage by using it as a decoy. This method of hunting is now forbidden in many countries with the object of protecting birds of prey.

Voice:
A penetrating note which sounds like 'coo-hu', and is sometimes followed by a guttural chuckle.

Length:
67 cm.

Wing span:
160 to 166 cm.

Male and female have similar plumage.

Size of egg:
51.2—73.0
× 42.0—53.7 mm.

Resident bird

Great Horned Owl

Bubo virginianus

The great horned owl is widely distributed throughout America, from Alaska across Canada and the USA to Peru and Rio de Janeiro. Within this vast range it occurs as several subspecies that differ in size as well as coloration. It inhabits various biotypes – forests, mountain regions, cliffs and thickets as well as prairies. It is usually a permanent resident and remains in its territory throughout the year, though it sometimes roams the countryside looking for food out of the breeding season. It often occupies a tree nest built and abandoned by another raptor or else nests in caves on cliffs or in tree cavities. The nest is usually lined only with the few odd hairs and feathers of its victims but occasionally the adult birds line it with bits of cloth or fine roots. The female lays two to three white eggs which she incubates by herself for about 34 days. During this period the male provides her with food, giving it to her a short distance from the nest. The young are covered with a thick layer of down feathers from birth. They are fed by the parents and remain in the nest about six weeks, after which they perch on branches or rocks nearby. They begin to fly at the age of three months. The great horned owl hunts food by night, chiefly ground squirrels, wild rabbits and mice. It also captures small birds and insects such as locusts.

Size of egg:
49.4–60.7
× 41.0–50.8 mm.

Length:
60 cm.

Wing span:
150 cm.

Male and female have
similar plumage.

Voice:
Characteristic hooting call
that sounds like
'oot-too-hoo, hoo-hoo'.

Resident bird

Snowy Owl

Nyctea scandiaca

This owl inhabits the arctic tundras of Europe, Asia, North America and Greenland, breeding in Europe on the coasts of Norway, the Murmansk region and in Iceland. Outside the breeding season it occurs in large numbers on sea and lake shores, straying very occasionally as far as central and western Europe. It is partial to open country and avoids woodland. On winter wanderings it perches on ice-floes or rocks. It makes no nest, but lays eggs in a depression on a hummock. Snowy owls require a hunting territory of about a square kilometre around the nest, or, when food is scarce, two square kilometres. Usually four to six eggs are laid, but in years when food is plentiful there may be as many as 15. Incubation is by the female alone for 32 to 34 days, during which time the male brings her food. After hatching, the young are covered with a thick layer of down. For the first few days, the female tears prey into pieces before feeding it to her offspring, who usually remain in the nest 57 to 61 days, at which time they are ready to fly. Snowy owls hunt near the ground with fluttering wingbeats, searching for lemmings, the mainstay of the diet. Two lemmings are the average daily consumption of a single nestling. In years when the lemming population is small, snowy owls may not nest at all, and rely on duck, geese, ptarmigan, alcids, gulls, squirrels and stoats for food.

♂

Voice:
A loud, repeated 'krow-ow' or a repeated 'rick'.

Length:
54 to 66 cm.

Sexually dimorphic.

Size of egg:
50.5–70.2
× 40.0–49.3 mm.

Dispersive bird

Pygmy Owl

Glaucidium passerinum

Smallest of the European owls, the pygmy owl inhabits conifer forests in lowland and mountain areas throughout Scandinavia, central and northeastern Europe, eastwards as far as the Amur. Inhabitants of central Europe are resident, those of northern regions are transient migrants. In central Europe the species occurs chiefly in mountain areas, such as the Black Forest, Bohemian Forest and the Alps, but it may also be found in deep woods at lower altitudes. The male's call and the female's lower pitched answering call may be heard as early as December. In April or May the pygmy owl seeks a place to nest, usually in a tree cavity, preferably one made by woodpeckers, but it will also occupy a nesting box hung up in its woodland habitat. The clutch generally consists of four to six eggs and the task of incubating them for a period of 28 days falls to the hen alone. The young are fed insects and small birds or mammals. Often, the pygmy owl stores part of its catch for future use, so the nesting cavity may contain several dozen mice, shrews, sparrows, buntings and other small birds. It hunts both night and day and is very agile, lying in wait for its victims, perched on a branch, darting out to eat a suitable bird, frequently on the wing. As a rule the pygmy owl does not hunt in open spaces, keeping to the cover of trees and thickets even when attacking.

Size of egg:
27.0–31.5
× 21.5–24.5 mm.

Length:
16.5 cm.

Male and female have similar plumage.

Voice:
A whistling note that sounds like 'keeoo', 'kitchick' or a bullfinch-like 'whee-whee-whee'.

Resident bird

Little Owl

Athene noctua

Sometimes, while walking in a park or on the edge of a forest, one is struck by the flurry and agitated cries of a group of small birds which suddenly converge on a particular spot in the bushes or in a tree. A moment later the cause of the furore is revealed: a little owl flies up and away, looking for a sheltered spot where it can hide from its pursuers. This predator is found throughout Europe, except Ireland and Scandinavia, on open, rocky country, in abandoned quarries, overgrown parks and on forest margins. It builds its nest chiefly in a tree hollow but will take over a wooden nest box. Four to eight eggs are laid on the bare, unlined floor and incubated by the hen for 26 to 28 days. On hatching, the young are covered with a thick coat of down; both parents feed them insects and small vertebrates. They leave the nest at 28 to 35 days, already capable of flight. The little owl hunts insects, mainly cockchafers, at dusk and fieldmice and rodents at night, so that it is genuinely useful to man. Sometimes, especially when rearing and feeding the young, it hunts during the day. This is a resident species, although sometimes it migrates locally, flying two hundred kilometres or more from its breeding ground.

Voice:
A shrill 'kiu', a sharp
'werro' and similar sounds.

Length:
23 cm.

Wing span:
About 50 cm.

Male and female
have similar plumage.

Size of egg:
31.5−37.1
× 25.7−31.0 mm.

Resident or dispersive bird

Tawny Owl
Strix aluco

This is one of the most common owls in Europe, and remains in its breeding grounds even during severe winters. A denizen of woods, it is found also in parks with old trees and sometimes in suburban quarters. In mild winters it often nests as early as February, otherwise usually in April. Even before this one can hear it hooting; it also produces odd sounds by the slapping of the wing quills against each other. His nest is usually located in a tree cavity, though the tawny owl will also occupy a large, man-made nesting box. Occasionally it will take over an abandoned raptor's nest and has also been known to use a hollow in the ground, though this is exceptional. The female incubates the three to five eggs for 28 to 30 days by herself, the male bringing her food during this period and occasionally relieving her on the nest. Since incubation begins as soon as the first egg is laid, the young hatch successively. For about ten days after the first nestlings have hatched, the hen does not leave the nest. The male supplies the whole family with food, mainly small mammals, but also other vertebrates such as bats, reptiles, amphibians as well as insects. Later the hen assists in hunting, but keeps an eye on the nest during the daytime. Sometimes she feeds the young in the daylight hours, supplying them from stores gathered during the night. At 28 to 36 days the young leave the nest, remaining in its vicinity and continuing to be fed by the parents. At 50 days they fly for the first time.

Resident bird

Size of egg:
43.0—51.7
× 34.4—43.3 mm.

Length:
38 cm.

Wing span:
92 to 94 cm.

Male and female have
similar plumage, which
shows marked variation in
colour.

Voice:
During the courting season
'hoo-hoo-hoo,
oo-oo-oo-oo'; sometimes
also 'kewick'.

Long-eared Owl

Asio otus

The long-eared owl is common throughout Europe except in the most northern parts. The habitat is chiefly small conifer and mixed woods, as well as field groves, large parks and overgrown gardens. It is faithful to its breeding grounds, but many birds, especially inhabitants of northerly regions, form groups that travel southwest in winter, staying in places where field mice are plentiful. At the end of March or in April the eggs are laid in the abandoned nests of crows, raptors, jays or the dreys of squirrels, which the owl may modify slightly to its own taste. The hen incubates the four to six eggs herself for 27 to 28 days, beginning as soon as the first is laid, so the young hatch successively. Her mate brings food for his partner and also the nestlings, which however are fed only by the hen. Often, the male stands beside the nest and claps his wings against his body with a sharp crack, thus revealing the nest's location. This owl hunts only after dusk, concealing itself in the thick branches of trees during the daytime. Pressed motionless against a branch, it often looks like a broken stump, escaping detection by all except an experienced ornithologist. Besides rodents, the long-eared owl hunts small birds and, when the young are being fed, it also captures countless insects, including such harmful pests as chafers. The young leave the nest at 21 to 26 days.

Voice:
During the courting season a penetrating 'oo-oo-oo'; also semi-whistling sounds.

Length:
34 cm.

Wing span:
85 to 90 cm.

Male and female have similar plumage.

Size of egg:
35.0−44.7
× 28.0−34.5 mm.

Resident or migratory bird

Short-eared Owl

Asio flammeus

Open, damp meadows near ponds, lakes, marshes and moorland are where the short-eared owl makes its home. This attractive bird, with its short 'ears' of longish feathers, inhabits all of northern, western, central and eastern Europe. In England it nests only in the northern half of the country and in Ireland it occurs only outside the breeding season. Birds of the northernmost regions are migrant, those that nest in more southerly parts are dispersive. The birds return to their breeding grounds from March to mid-April and make a nest of materials such as coarse plant stalks in a shallow depression in the ground, lining it with leaves and fine greenery. Four to seven eggs — but as many as 14 in years when rodents are plentiful — are normally laid at 48-hour intervals. The female incubates alone for 24 to 27 days, sitting on the eggs as soon as the first is laid: the young thus hatch successively. During this period the male stands guard close by and when the young have hatched, brings food for the whole family. The young leave the nest at three to four weeks and take to the air when they are about five weeks old. When hunting prey, the short-eared owl sometimes hovers motionless in the air over a single spot. Its victims are usually fieldmice and voles, though it sometimes captures small birds or amphibians and reptiles.

Size of egg:
35.1−45.0
× 29.0−33.0 mm.

Length:
37 cm.

Wing span:
103 to 107 cm.

Male and female have
similar plumage.

Voice:
A deep 'boo-boo' or
'kee-aw'.

Dispersive or migratory bird

European Nightjar

Caprimulgus europaeus

This weird and fascinating bird returns from its winter quarters in eastern and southern Africa in late April or in May. Widespread throughout Europe, it frequents light, dry conifer or mixed woods, favouring places where pines predominate, but also favouring forest edges and clearings. During the day it perches lengthwise on a tree branch, cryptic colouring making it practically invisible. When startled, it opens its bill wide and spreads its wings and tail in an attempt to frighten off any intruder. If disturbed on the nest it frequently flies up, hovering in the air with wide-open beak in an attempt to ward off the assailant and prevent any approach to the nest. Courtship behaviour includes wing clapping by the male, and both sexes have gliding, aerial displays. The female lays two eggs on the bare ground at the end of May or in June, and both partners take turns at incubating for 16 to 18 days. The young, which leave their 'nest' at 16 to 19 days, are fed insects for a full month. Among these will be chafers and other beetles, as well as moths. The nightjar leaves for its winter quarters in August or September. Outside the nesting season it is comparatively tame, and often visits pasture, flying close to humans and animals in its pursuit of airborne insects. This accounts for the belief that it visits grazing she-goats and sucks their udders; hence its exotic names in many languages, i. e. *Ziegenmelker*, the German for 'billy-goat milker'.

Voice:
The flight call is a soft 'goo-ek'; the alarm call a high 'quick-quick-quick' and the night song a loud rapid churring, rising and falling, which can last for as long as five minutes.

Length:
27 cm.

The female lacks the white patch on the primaries.

Size of egg:
27.0−36.5 × 20.0−24.0 mm.

Migratory bird

207

Swift

Apus apus

Swifts arrive in the skies over their European breeding grounds in May, shrill, piercing calls signalling their return from tropical and Southern Africa. These scimitar-winged birds can, if pressed, hurtle through the air at a remarkable speed − up to 160 km per hour. They also possess great endurance, probably capable of flying an unbelievable 800 km in a single day. In the evening they can be seen frolicking on the wing, and at night they fly to great heights even sleeping in flight. On the ground, however, they are totally inept because their legs are small and weak. The swift builds its nest on tall buildings, in wall crevices and holes beneath eaves, and in old castle ruins. It is constructed of material the bird catches on the wing, such as floating feathers and bits of straw, cemented together with sticky and rapidly congealing saliva. The clutch consists of two to three eggs, which the female incubates alone for 18 to 21 days, being fed meanwhile by the male who brings her insects caught in flight. The young generally leave the nest at 35 to 42 days and are immediately capable of flight.

Migratory bird

Size of egg:
22.8−28.0
× 14.3−17.6 mm.

Length:
16.5 cm.

Male and female have similar plumage.

Voice:
A shrill, piercing 'screech' uttered in flight.

Ruby-throated Hummingbird

Archilochus colubris

The ruby-throated hummingbird is one of the smallest species in the family. It is widespread throughout North America. In autumn it leaves its nesting grounds for winter quarters in Central America, returning again in spring. It prefers open places with plenty of flowering shrubs and trees or tall herbaceous plants. It is fond of forest margins and large parks. An expert flier, it flies at speeds of up to 80 kilometres per hour. It can fly backward as well as forward and can also remain hovering in one spot. It sucks the nectar of flowers on the wing and also eats small insects which it skilfully captures in the air. During the nesting period when the birds are paired the males are quarrelsome and chase away all potential rivals. The nest is placed saddle-fashion on a horizontal limb. It is an exquisite structure made of fine moss and plant fibres interlaced with bits of lichen and strips of bark from the tree on which it is located. The foundations are reinforced with grass stems. The female lays two all-white eggs, which are comparatively large in relation to the size of the bird, and incubates them by herself for about 14 days. The young nestlings are fed by both parents for about three weeks in the nest and a short while longer after they have fledged. The ruby-throated hummingbird is a brave creature and chases even much larger birds away from the nest or the vicinity of its offspring.

Voice:
A delicate but sharp piping note.

Length:
7.5 cm.

Sexually dimorphic.

Size of egg:
11.5—14.5
×7.8—9.1 mm.

Migratory bird

Kingfisher

Alcedo atthis

Kingfishers, among the most superbly coloured of birds, occur all over Europe except the far north. They are non-migratory, but roam the countryside during the cold months, seeking out water from fast-flowing rivers and streams. During the breeding season, the birds occur on still as well as flowing waters, as long as these are bordered by a steep bank in which the nesting hole may be dug. Both partners share the task of excavation, which takes several days, bills being used as digging implements, feet to scrape out the loosened material. The chamber (between 40 and 100 centimetres long) is unlined, but within a short time it becomes littered with rotting fish remains. There is one brood between April and June and a second between June and July. The clutch consists of six to seven eggs and the female begins incubating as soon as the first is laid. Hatching is after 18 to 21 days. During this period the male keeps his partner supplied with food and sometimes also relieves her on the nest. Both share the duties of feeding the young in the nesting chamber for 23 to 27 days, continuing to bring them food for a few days longer when they have fledged. The kingfisher feeds on small fish (caught by diving), crustaceans and water insects.

Size of egg:
20.3–24.8
× 16.7–20.0 mm.

Length:
16.5 cm.

Male and female have
similar plumage.

Voice:
In flight a lengthy 'che-kee'
or a short 'chee'.

Resident or dispersive bird

Bee-eater

Merops apiaster

This brilliantly coloured bird inhabits southern, southwestern and southeastern Europe and occurs very occasionally as a vagrant in England and Scandinavia. All the European breeding grounds are abandoned in late August and September, when the birds depart for winter quarters in Africa or Arabia, returning again in April to May. They are to be found in open country near rivers, ponds or lakes, where vertical mud or sand walls and banks and abandoned sand quarries are sought as nesting places. The bee-eater is a gregarious bird and breeds colonially. Each pair of birds digs a burrow some 1.2–2 metres long, the task taking 14 to 21 days. Between May and July the female lays five to six eggs directly on the bare earth. Later, however, these will rest on a bed of undigested food pellets regurgitated by the birds. Male and female take turns incubating for 20 to 22 days, and both feed the young for 20 to 30 days in the nest and a short while after they have fledged. The diet consists mostly of hymenopterous insects such as wasps, bumblebees and bees, also flying beetles, dragon-flies and cicadas. Stings are ground out on a branch before the prey is swallowed. The bee-eater is light and graceful in flight but awkward and clumsy on land. It is understandably unpopular with bee-keepers.

Voice:
In flight, 'prruip'.

Length:
28 cm.

Male and female have similar plumage.

Size of egg:
22.5–29.5
× 17.6–23.6 mm.

Migratory bird

European Roller

Coracias garrulus

This brilliant coloured bird may be seen in open places with old trees, in light deciduous woods, or in rows of trees alongside rivers. It inhabits southern and eastern Europe as well as the eastern half of central Europe and it is common in the southerly areas. When migrating it may make its way as far as Norway, Finland and Iceland. The winter is spent mainly in eastern Africa, from where it returns at the beginning of May to its breeding grounds — lowland dotted with woods and meadows. It is fond of perching on telegraph and telephone wires or poles. The male performs his courtship flight above the tree in which he has located the nest: a breathtaking performance in which he turns somersaults, darts skywards, rolls and plummets to earth. The female lays four to five eggs in the nesting cavity, incubating them herself for 18 to 20 days, though occasionally the male relieves her in this task. She begins incubating as soon as the first egg is laid. The young leave the nest at 26 to 28 days, but continue to be fed by the parents for a short while after. Their food consists of insects, which also form the major part of the adults' diet. The roller is swift and agile, generally catching its prey on the wing. Sometimes it will take a small lizard or mouse, beating it to death against the ground. In autumn it also nibbles soft fruits. The southward journey starts in August or the beginning of September.

Size of egg:
32.0—40.0
× 25.5—31.5 mm.

Length:
30.5 cm.

Male and female have similar plumage.

Voice:
A loud 'kr-r-r-r-ak' or 'krak-ak' like a crow's call, and a harsh chatter.

Migratory bird

Hoopoe

Upupa epops

Hoopoes are native to practically all of Europe except northeastern Scandinavia and the British Isles and do not breed in Denmark or Iceland. The species does, however, occur accidentally in England and Finland. European populations leave in September for winter quarters in tropical Africa, returning to their breeding grounds in April. The birds are found in open country with extensive meadows, especially near ponds and lakes, and also in light, deciduous woods. The nest is made in a tree hollow, sometimes as high as six metres above the ground. It may also be made close to the ground among rocks. In May to June, sometimes also in July, the female lays six to seven eggs, which she alone incubates for 16 to 20 days. Because the female starts incubating as soon as the first egg is laid, the young hatch successively. Both parents feed their offspring in the nest for 24 to 27 days, doling out the food in the following manner: one nestling awaits the adults' arrival at the entrance hole and as soon as it receives its ration, the one behind pushes to the front; and so it continues, each returning to the end of the queue until its turn comes again. The hoopoe exists mostly on insects and their larvae, which it digs out of soil or cattle droppings with its long bill. Surface prey, such as locusts and spiders, are also taken.

Voice:
The characteristic 'poo-poo-poo'.

Length:
28 cm.

Male and female have similar plumage.

Size of egg:
23.1–30.3
× 16.3–19.8 mm.

Migratory bird

Green Woodpecker

Picus viridis

The green woodpecker's range covers all of Europe except northern Scandinavia, Ireland, Scotland and Iceland. Mainly a resident species, but in winter is also a transient migrant. Light deciduous woods, field groves, parks, large gardens, orchards and overgrown graveyards are the favoured habitats. During the courting period the male and female pursue each other in the air or round the trunk of a tree, uttering loud cries. At the end of April the pair drill a hole in the trunk of a deciduous tree, usually where the wood is soft or has rotted. The pear-shaped cavity, about 50 centimetres deep, is completed in about two weeks. In addition to the proper nesting cavity, the green woodpecker also drills another for use as a sleeping quarter, both being used for several years in succession. Sometimes the green woodpecker will nest in a hole in a wall, especially in a city park. The female lays five to seven eggs, which she and the male take turns incubating for 15 to 17 days. The young are born naked and blind and the parents feed them mostly on ants and their pupae. Also included in the diet are the larvae of beetles which the woodpecker finds when raiding anthills. In winter the bird will excavate a deep tunnel in the ground to reach hibernating ants. Sometimes it visits beehives, splitting the wooden casing in its efforts to reach the bees.

Size of egg:
28.0–33.9
× 20.3–24.0 mm.

Length:
32 cm.

Sexually dimorphic.

Voice:
During the courtship period a very loud ringing 'laugh'; the female's note is shorter and does not have the same ring.

Resident or dispersive bird

Black Woodpecker

Dryocopus martius

Early in spring, often as early as March, wood-lands with old pine trees or beeches echo to the loud drumming of the black woodpecker. This sound, produced by rapidly striking a tree with the beak, advertises the male's possession of territory and his presence to the females. In the middle of April both partners drill a nesting cavity in a tree trunk, usually 35 to 55 cen-timetres, though sometimes as much as one metre deep, depending on the hardness of the wood. Usually the trunk of a pine or beech is selected, the task of drilling taking some ten to 15 days with the male doing most of the work. Large woodchips at the base of a tree betray the presence of such a cavity, and he also excavates other chambers in the vicinity, which he uses as sleeping quarters, all having an oval entrance hole. The four to five eggs are incubated by both partners for 12 to 13 days, the male sitting on them mainly at night. The young, which remain in the cavity for 23 to 28 days, are fed by both parents, primarily on ants and their pupae. They are fed only a few times each day, but in large quantities. Adult birds feed on the larvae of weevils and bark beetles. When the young have fledged, the parents remain in the neighbour-hood but their offspring wander as far as several hundred kilometres from the nest. The black woodpecker is widespread in central, northern and eastern Europe and may be found in both mountain areas and lowland country.

Voice:
A long drawn-out 'kleea',
a high, grating
'krri-krri-krri', and in flight
a ringing 'choc-choc-choc'.

Length:
45 cm.

Sexually dimorphic.

Size of egg:
31.0−37.7
× 22.0−27.0 mm.

Resident bird

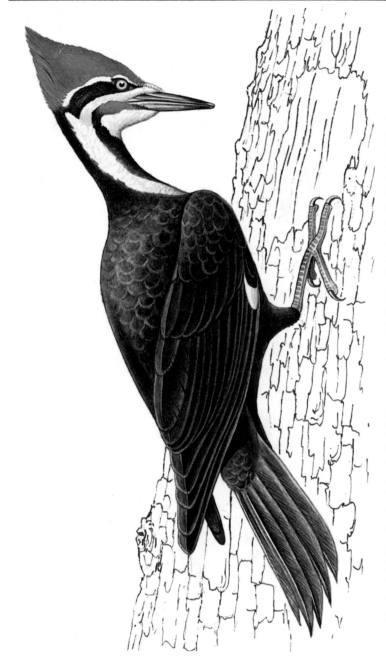

Pileated Woodpecker

Dryocopus pileatus

The pileated woodpecker is found in southern, southwestern and southeastern Canada and in the eastern and northwestern parts of the USA. It is not very abundant but is one of the best known of North American woodpeckers and one of the largest. It inhabits larger forests, preferring mixed forests in the lowlands but is also found in mountain forests. It does not leave its breeding grounds but roams far and wide throughout the countryside out of the nesting season. Paired birds begin building the nest in early spring. Selecting an old tree, usually a co-nifer, they start excavating a large cavity in the trunk, sometimes as much as one metre deep, with their strong beaks. The entrance hole is usually four to 25 metres above the ground. Rarely a tall tree stump may be used. The female makes little effort to line the nest and lays her three to six pure white eggs on the few chips remaining in the hollow. Both partners take turns incubating for about 14 days. At the early age of two weeks the young nestlings can be seen poking their heads out of the entrance hole in eager anticipation of their parents and the food they bring. They remain in the nest for 25 days and continue to be fed for a few days longer outside the nest. The diet consists of ants, their eggs and pupae, wood-boring beetles and their larvae and also berries and seeds from the cones of conifers.

Size of egg:
29.3−38.2
× 22.0−27.1 mm

Length:
42 cm.

Male and female
have similar plumage.

Voice:
A loud, tooting call.

Resident bird

Great Spotted Woodpecker

Dendrocopos major

♀

♂

All of Europe, except Ireland and the most northern areas, provides a home for this common woodpecker. It stays for the winter in most areas, though it is also a transient migrant outside the breeding season, and inhabitants of northern Europe sometimes journey south in large flocks. Why they undertake such a long trip is not yet understood. The great spotted woodpecker occurs in woodlands of all types, in mountains up to the tree line, in parks, large gardens, orchards and tree-lined avenues. In winter it often roams the countryside in the company of nuthatches and tits, and will visit bird tables to nibble sunflower seeds or suet. In spring both partners, though mainly the male, drill a hole about 30 centimetres deep in the trunk of a deciduous or coniferous tree, often using the same cavity for several years. The female lays five to six eggs, which she and the male take turns incubating for 12 to 13 days. The parents feed the young from the beak, and must consequently bring food to the nest much more often than the green or black woodpecker. At first they make about 40 trips a day, but when the young are some ten days old the daily trips can total 150 or more. For this reason, prey must be sought in the immediate neighbourhood of the nest. The diet consists mainly of insects and their larvae. At 21 to 23 days the young abandon the cavity but remain in the vicinity of the nest.

Voice:
A loud 'kik' or 'chick'. In spring it drums with its beak on the trunks or branches of trees.

Length:
23 cm.

Sexually dimorphic.

Size of egg:
20.0−29.5 × 15.4−21.8 mm.

Resident or dispersive bird

Lesser Spotted Woodpecker

Dendrocopos minor

The lesser spotted woodpecker is to be found throughout Europe, in Asia as far as Japan and in northwestern Africa; nowhere is it abundant. It frequents broad-leaved and mixed woodland in lowland areas, also visiting old parks, tree-lined avenues and orchards. Although mainly a resident species, individuals that breed in northern areas migrate to central Europe. In winter the birds roam the countryside, often in the company of tits. During the courting season (March to April), it often drums softly on dry stumps or branches. Both partners chisel a ten- to 14-centimetre-deep nesting cavity in rotting tree trunks or braches anywhere from near ground level up to 20 metres above ground. This task is undertaken afresh every year. Both share in incubating the four to seven eggs for a period of two weeks and in feeding the young; their diet consists of insects (mostly fall-flies) larvae, cocoons and, to a lesser degree, ants. The nestlings leave their shelter for the first time at three weeks. In winter, the lesser spotted woodpecker feeds principally on the eggs and cocoons of insects, which it finds in crevices in the bark of trees, and also seeds.

Size of egg:
17.0−21.0
× 12.9−15.6 mm.

Length:
14.5 cm.

Sexually dimorphic.

Voice:
A repeated, high 'pee-pee-pee'. It may be heard drumming from early spring until autumn.

Resident bird

Wryneck

Jynx torquilla

In the second half of April one can hear the monotonous, querulous call of the wryneck in gardens, orchards, parks, avenues and in deciduous and mixed woodland. Because the bird can vary the loudness of its call, one is led to believe that it is near one moment and far off the next; in fact it is probably perched motionless on a branch at the top of a nearby tree, on a telephone pole or on some other vantage point. Surprisingly, the female may be as vocal as the male. Both birds prepare a nest of a few shavings or small bits of rotting wood in a cavity selected by the hen. This may be in a tree hollow, an opening in loose masonry or a sparrow's nest box, the occupants of which may be unceremoniously dislodged. Male and female take turns sitting on the eggs, seven to ten in number, for 12 to 14 days; both share the duties of feeding the young, their diet being the same as that of adult birds — mostly ants and their cocoons. These are gathered by breaking up an anthill and collecting its inhabitants on the long, sticky tongue. The wryneck also feeds on other insects, and in autumn takes elderberries. When disturbed on the nest, it stretches its neck out and hisses like a snake, in order to frighten away the intruder. Departure for the winter quarters in northern or tropical Africa is in August or September.

♂

Voice:
A repeated 'kyee-kyee'.

Length:
16.5 cm.

Male and female
have similar plumage.

Size of egg:
16.2—23.0
× 13.0—16.7 mm.

Migratory bird

Woodlark

Lullula arborea

This species, which is distributed throughout the whole of Europe except the far north and in Ireland, frequents dry, sandy and stony localities with pine trees, shrub-dotted meadows and heaths. It is a migrant, but birds inhabiting western and southern Europe are resident, these areas being places where northern populations spend the winter months. The woodlark returns to its breeding grounds in March, but in central Europe this may be as early as the end of February. Birds pair immediately on arrival — if they have not already done so during the return trip. Shortly after arrival, they start building their nest on the ground amidst heather, beneath a young pine tree or in thickets. It is made of roots, plant stalks and moss and lined with hairs and plant fibres. The clutch, numbering four to five eggs, is incubated by the hen alone for 13 to 15 days. The young are fed by both parents with insects, insect larvae and spiders, usually for 13 to 15 days in the nest, and a short time after fledging. The woodlark then generally builds a new nest in another spot and lays a second clutch from June or July to August. On leaving the nest, the birds form flocks that roam the woods in search of seeds. The woodlark sings mostly at night or as twilight falls, but from early April until August its voice may also be heard during the day. Formerly much sought-after by trappers, it is now protected by law.

Size of egg:
18.0—24.0
× 14.5—17.4 mm.

Length:
15 cm.

Male and female have
similar plumage.

Voice:
A characteristic 'toolee' or
'toolooeet'.

Song:
Sounds like
'lu-lu-lu-lu'.

Migratory or resident bird

Skylark

Alauda arvensis

High in the sky, almost motionless, hovers the skylark, its sweet liquid song filling the air; then it plummets towards the ground, levelling out at the very last moment. This species makes a nest of roots and bits of leaves, lined with hairs, and placed on the ground in fields and meadows. Males guard their territory fiercely. The hen lays three to five eggs which she incubates alone for 12 to 14 days. Both parents feed the young with various insects and larvae, centipedes, spiders and small snails. Chicks leave the nest at nine to 11 days, as yet incapable of flight, and conceal themselves in clumps of grass. The species is double- and sometimes treble-brooded. By three weeks the young are able to fly and to feed themselves. Adult birds include in their diet the seeds of various weeds which they gather on the ground. In October to November, skylarks form small groups which fly off together to winter quarters in southern Europe, returning sometimes as early as the end of February, when winter is still in the air and snowfall not uncommon. Distribution includes the whole of Europe, a large part of Asia and northwestern Africa.

Voice:
A clear, liquid 'chir-r-up'.

Song:
Trilling and warbling; notes sometimes learned from other birds.

Length:
18 cm.

Male and female have similar plumage.

Size of egg:
19.4—28.0
× 15.0—19.5 mm.

Migratory bird

Sand Martin

Riparia riparia

The slender sand martin breeds all over Europe except Iceland. A migratory species, it leaves its breeding grounds in August and September for winter quarters in eastern Africa, returning again in late April or early May. It is found in open country where there are bodies or still of flowing water with vertical mud or sand banks, or abandoned sand quarries nearby. It is in these that the sand martin digs its nest. Excavation is very tiring for a bird ill-adapted to ground work. It starts by perching on a small ledge and digging a hole with its beak; later it uses its feet to remove the mud or sand, working until it has excavated a tunnel about 1 metre long terminating in a nesting hollow about 10 centimetres in diameter. This is lined with bits of straw and feathers, some of which are amazingly long. Five to six eggs are laid in May to June (and occasionally a second clutch in July), which both partners take turns incubating for 12 to 14 days (sometimes, though rarely, as long as 16 days). The young are supplied with food which the parents catch on the wing, for the 16 to 23 days they remain in the nest. When the young have fledged, the parents continue to feed them for two more weeks. The diet consists of various insects; while raising young, however, the birds also seek other prey in sand quarries and near the nest.

Migratory bird

Size of egg:
15.2–22.0
× 11.4–13.5 mm.

Length:
12 cm.

Male and female have similar plumage.

Voice:
In flight, a note that sounds like 'tcherip'.

Swallow

Hirundo rustica

Throughout Europe the graceful swallow has left its ancestral cliffside habitat and moved to the neighbourhood of man, where it has found more favourable conditions. The arrival from winter quarters is generally in early April, but the vanguard may appear at the end of March, often to be caught by an unexpected snowfall. The swallow's favoured nest-site is inside a building, with a preference for farm sheds; it builds an open nest of mud cemented with saliva and strengthened with plant stalks and straw. The female lines it with feathers before laying the eggs, five as a rule, which she incubates alone for 14 to 16 days, being fed meanwhile by the male. The young, which first leave the nest after 19 to 23 days, are fed by the parents on insects caught adroitly on the wing. When the young have fledged, all the birds form large flocks that fly to neighbouring ponds each evening, where they roost in thick reeds. One fine day in September or October, the whole flock suddenly takes off on its long journey to tropical or even South Africa. In Transvaal, for instance, a million swallows were once counted roosting in a single place.

Voice:
A much-repeated 'tswit, tswit'.

Song:
Delicate, long and short twittering and warbling notes.

Length:
18 cm.

Male and female have similar plumage.

Size of egg:
16.7—23.0
× 12.2—15.0 mm.

Migratory bird

223

House Martin

Delichon urbica

The house martin inhabits all of Europe, Asia as far east as Japan and northwestern Africa. It is found everywhere in the neighbourhood of human habitation. Unlike the swallow, it builds its nest on the outside, rather than inside walls of houses and sheds and under balconies, cornices and eaves, frequently in large colonies, the nests being placed tightly one against the other. The nest itself is made of soft mud, which the house martin collects beside puddles, ponds and rivers; the birds gather it in their beaks, mixing it with saliva and pasting little balls of the sticky mass in rows one above the other to form a covered nest with a small entrance hole at the top. The lining is of straw and feathers, often large ones such as those of a hen. The five eggs are incubated for 12 to 14 days by both birds, who then feed the nestlings flies, aphids, mayflies and small spiders caught floating through the air on their webs. The nestlings fly for the first time at 20 to 23 days, but they return to the nest each night to roost for several more days. In September or October the house martin departs for its winter quarters in Africa south of the Sahara, returning to its breeding grounds at the end of April or in early May.

Size of egg:
16.1–21.6
× 11.5–14.7 mm.

Length:
13 cm.

Male and female have
similar plumage.

Voice:
A clear 'tchirrip' or
'tchichirrip'.

Song:
Twittering notes.

Migratory bird

Yellow Wagtail

Motacilla flava

These attractively coloured birds are distributed all over Europe except in Ireland and Iceland. They leave in August or September for winter quarters in tropical and southern Africa. In the autumn, flocks numbering as many as a thousand birds may be seen beside ponds and lakes, where they roost in reeds. On the return trip at the end of March or beginning of April, they form smaller flocks, which soon break up into pairs which stake out their nesting territories, the males defending them against all comers. The yellow wagtail is partial to extensive, damp or swampy meadows, the grass-covered banks of rivers, ponds and lakes, especially in lowland areas. However, it may also be found on the edges of fields near water. In May or June, the female builds a nest on the ground, well concealed in a clump of grass which often forms a kind of roof. The structure is made of grass stems and is lined with animal hairs, sometimes also with plant wool and occasionally small feathers. The clutch usually consists of four to five eggs, which the female incubates alone for 13 to 14 days, the male meanwhile staying close by. The young are fed by both parents. They leave the nest at seven to 11 days, though still incapable of flight, and continue to be fed by the parents some two weeks longer. The diet generally consists of locusts, small species of beetles, caterpillars, spiders and small gastropod molluscs.

Voice:	**Length:**	**Size of egg:**	
A ringing, monosyllabic note, 'tsweep'.	16.5 cm.	16.3–21.0 × 12.0–15.3 mm.	
	The female is not as brightly coloured as the male and her head is olive-green.		**Migratory bird**

Grey Wagtail

Motacilla cinerea

This handsome bird with a strikingly long tail, which it continually wags up and down, is to be found running about on the boulder-strewn banks of brooks and streams, searching the shallow water for small water-beetles and insect larvae. It also frequents farmyards, looking in manure heaps for insects, mainly flies, which it captures skilfully on the wing. The nesting site, however, is always near water, perhaps on a beam beneath a bridge spanning a brook, in a hole in a wall, in a pile of stones, a cavity in a rock face or a nest box. Both partners take turns incubating the five to six eggs for 12 to 14 days and both share the duties of feeding the young for 12 to 13 days in the nest, and for a short time after they have fledged, after which the parents often raise a second brood. The grey wagtail is distributed throughout Europe, except for Scandinavia, and is mostly resident.

Size of egg:
16.1—21.7
× 12.7—16.0 mm.

Length:
18 cm.

Sexually dimorphic.

Voice:
Call-notes are more metallic than the pied wagtail's, alarm is a shrill 'see-eet'.

Song:
Chirping, with flutey notes.

Resident or migratory bird

Pied Wagtail

Motacilla alba

This species is distributed throughout the continent and may occur near human habitation particularly in northern Europe; its natural habitat is by a brook or pond. It may also be seen in places where livestock is kept — beside stables and on pasture, also in abandoned quarries and on ploughed fields. Individuals from northern Europe move south in winter, but in western Europe this is a sedentary species. In autumn and winter it forms large flocks that roost in rushes, trees lining busy streets and in greenhouses. During the nesting season it is highly territorial and individual pairs vigorously chase out any intruder. However, should a sparrow-hawk make its appearance every bird in the neighbourhood will join forces to mob the dangerous intruder. The pied wagtail builds its nest in a sheltered crevice, producing five to six eggs which are incubated for 12 to 14 days by the hen alone; both parents share the duties of feeding the young for 13 to 15 days, bringing them insects and their larvae gathered near water.

♂

Voice:
A lively 'tchizzik'; alarm is an abrupt 'tchik'.

Song:
Made up of similar notes to voice.

Length:
18 cm.

The female has more grey plumage than the male.

Size of egg:
16.7—22.3
× 13.1—16.2 mm.

Migratory bird

Tawny Pipit

Anthus campestris

The tawny pipit inhabits dry, open country — stony slopes, abandoned sandpits, steppes and sandy heaths. Nowadays its range includes the whole of Europe except Scandinavia and the British Isles, although it did once nest in southern England in 1905—6. The bird can also be found in northwestern Africa and in Asia. It returns to its breeding grounds at the end of April or in early May, building its nest on the ground in a depression beneath a clump of heather, dwarf shrub or behind a large mound or stone. The structure of moss and roots is lined with a soft layer of hairs and well concealed by overhanging grass. Only the female does any building work and it is she who incubates the four to six eggs for 13 to 14 days, relieved on rare occasions by the male. The diet consists mainly of insects and larvae, with a partiality for beetles and locusts, hunted on the ground. The young leave the nest at 14 days, but remain in the neighbourhood. In August or September tawny pipits migrate to northern Africa or Arabia, where they feed mainly on various kinds of grasshopper.

Migratory bird

Size of egg:
19.0—23.8
× 14.2—17.1 mm.

Length:
16.5 cm.

Male and female
have similar plumage.

Voice:
Rare and variable call notes
such as 'tsweep', 'chup'
and 'chirrup'.

Song:
A repeated, metallic
'chivee-chivee-chivee'.

Tree Pipit

Anthus trivialis

Tree pipits are widely distributed throughout Europe, except in Spain and Iceland, and also occur in parts of Asia as far north as Siberia. It spends the winter in Africa south of the Sahara, returning in April to its nesting grounds in thin woodlands, open glades, meadows with scattered pine trees, woodland margins and forest clearings, both in lowland country and mountains. Birds do not pair until the end of April, when the males begin their trilling, which is similar to the canary's song. As he sings, the male flies up from his perch at the top of a tree, spreads his wings and tail and descends slowly in a spiral, not stopping his song until he alights. In May to June the female hatches her four to six eggs in a nest, usually located in a hollow in a clump of grass or heather. It is built of plant stalks, moss and lichens and lined with grass and hairs. The young, hatched after 12 to 13 days, are fed by both parents with insects, mostly mosquitoes and butterflies, various larvae and small spiders. They leave the nest at the age of ten to 14 days, as yet incapable of flight, and conceal themselves in the immediate vicinity where the parent birds continue to feed them a further two weeks. When the young have fledged, they and the adult birds roam fields in search of leaf beetles, weevils, the caterpillars of moths and aphids; thus these birds are among the most beneficial to man.

Voice:
When courting, a long drawn-out 'teeze'; the alarm note is 'sip sip sip'.

Song:
Sounds resemble 'chew chew chew chew' followed by a long drawn-out 'seea-seea-seea'.

Length:
15 cm.

Male and female have similar plumage.

Size of egg:
18.0−23.5
× 14.7−17.2 mm.

Migratory bird

Meadow Pipit

Anthus pratensis

The meadow pipit is widespread throughout all of western, central, northern and northeastern Europe and is also found in Italy. It inhabits swampy meadows, places near water where there is short grass, and also mountain meadows. Birds from northerly regions are migrant. Some winter in western Europe, but most travel to the Mediterranean, leaving their breeding grounds in September to November. March or April is the time of the birds' return to summer quarters, their arrival soon being announced by the song-flight of the male, in which he rises to about 100 feet, then descends either directly, or in a glide like the tree pipit's. In May or June, occasionally as early as the end of April, the meadow pipit builds a nest on the ground, well concealed in a clump of grass. The materials used are grass stems, reeds, moss and lichens, the lining nearly always being animal hairs. The clutch generally consists of four to five eggs, which the female incubates alone for 12 to 14 days. The young are fed by both parents – mostly insects, insect larvae and small spiders. They leave the nest at 11 to 13 days. About 14 days later the young are fully independent and the adult birds usually prepare to raise a second brood. The diet consists chiefly of hymenopterous insects, small beetles, spiders and other small invertebrates, in autumn and winter also small seeds.

Resident, dispersive or migratory bird

Size of egg:
17.2—21.4
× 13.0—15.7 mm.

Length:
14.5 cm.

Male and female have similar plumage.

Voice:
Song sounds like 'tseep....'; call resembles 'tissip'.

Water Pipit

Anthus spinoletta

The water pipit inhabits barren, rocky places with screes above the tree line, on high mountains, preferring large spaces with a great many scattered boulders and clumps of grass. Its range includes southern and southeastern Europe, parts of central Europe (the Alps and Carpathians), England and the coast of Scandinavia. Northern populations migrate south to central Europe in winter. Central European populations are on the whole resident. Water pipits nesting in high mountains descend to lower altitudes during the winter, forming small groups that roam the countryside in the vicinity of water or marshes. In April they return to their breeding territories and, in May or June, build nests among clumps of grass under an overhanging bush or stone. The structure itself is of fine plant stalks, lichen and moss lined with fine hairs, with usually thick walls — as much as 5 centimetres. The female lays four to six eggs, which she incubates herself for 14 to 16 days. The young, which leave the nest at two weeks, are fed by both parents with insects and their larvae, spiders and worms. After fledging, the whole family roams the countryside, often keeping close to human habitation. The water pipit is an active bird that continually runs about on the ground, flits here and there, hops up on a rock, looks about and then resumes its search for food.

Voice:
Courting note that sounds like 'tseep-eep'.

Song:
In flight, comprises notes resembling 'tsip' and 'jeep'.

Length:
16 cm.

Male and female have similar plumage.

Size of egg:
18.9—24.0
× 14.0—16.5 mm.

Resident, migratory or dispersive bird

Red-backed Shrike

Lanius collurio

In hedgerows and forest margins one may sometimes come across a grisly collection of beetles, grasshoppers and other insects impaled on the spikes of thorny shrubs. This is in fact a 'larder' prepared by the red-backed shrike for leaner days. The nest is built in a place with thorny shrubs, well concealed in the undergrowth, and made of roots, dry stalks and other plant material, lined with a soft layer of hairs and plant wool. The major share of the work is undertaken by the male and is complete within three to four days. The three to eight eggs are incubated chiefly by the hen for 14 to 15 days. The male only relieves her on rare occasions. Both partners, however, share the duties of feeding the young, chiefly with insects and larvae. At two weeks the young can already perch neatly beside one another on a branch outside the nest, but continue to be fed by the parents for three weeks more until they are fully independent. On approaching the nest, one may hear the bird's distinctive warning call, but the male's song is hard to distinguish for he is an excellent mimic of other birds. In August the red-backed shrike leaves for winter quarters in tropical and southern Africa, returning fairly late, in mid-May.

Size of egg:
18.3—26.1
× 14.0—19.0 mm.

Length:
18 cm.

Sexually dimorphic.

Voice:
A harsh, grating
'shack-shack' or 'chee-uk'.

Song:
A soft chatter with
melodies learned from
other birds.

Migratory bird

Great Grey Shrike

Lanius excubitor

The great grey shrike is the only shrike that stays the winter in its breeding grounds, which include most of Europe except for the British Isles and Italy. It is also found in Asia, North Africa and North America. During the winter months, it roams its neighbourhood, frequenting shrubberies, fields and meadows and feeding chiefly on fieldmice, often sighting its prey by hovering in the air. Its habit of establishing a larder of spare food by impaling it on sharp thorns has earned the species, along with other shrikes, the name of butcher bird. In summer it takes lizards, various insects and sometimes even young birds. The nest of dry branches and roots, lined with feathers and hairs, is built in April or May, usually in a tree two to five metres above the ground. The hen lays three to six eggs which she incubates for 15 to 16 days mostly by herself, the male relieving her only occasionally. Should a crow or magpie appear in the vicinity of the nest during this period, both partners quickly chase the intruder away. The young remain in the nest until they are 19 or 20 days old but continue to be fed by the parents for another three weeks.

Voice:
A characteristic 'shek-shek'.

Song:
Croaking and whistling notes as well as those learned from other birds.

Length:
25 cm.

Male and female have similar plumage.

Size of egg:
23.0–30.5
× 18.0–20.7 mm.

Resident bird

Waxwing

Bombycilla garrulus

This strange-looking, but nonetheless beautiful bird is a native of the coldest, northernmost parts of Europe and Asia. It also occurs in North America, where it is known as the Bohemian waxwing. The species inhabits coniferous and mixed woodland where it builds nests of twigs and moss in the branches of trees, usually in the Arctic summer, i. e. June or July. The clutch comprises four to five eggs incubated by the female for 14 days, during which she is fed by the male. Both parents feed the young with insects and larvae. At 16 to 18 days the young leave the nest and form flocks which sometimes number as many as several thousand birds. As a rule, they set out for central Europe in October where they remain until March. In some years, fair numbers move as far west as the British Isles, when they may be seen in tree-lined avenues, and in parks and gardens feeding especially on the berries of shrubs such as viburnum and cotoneaster. An observer may approach a flock of waxwings quite closely without their taking wing, for these are fearless, inquisitive birds. They have an enormous appetite − food passes through the alimentary canal very rapidly − and spend most of the day hunting for food, only occasionally taking time to rest.

Size of egg:
20.7−28.3
× 15.6−18.8 mm.

Length:
18 cm.

Male and female have similar plumage.

Voice:
Call note is a weak trill, 'zhree'.

Migratory bird

Dipper

Cinclus cinclus

Dippers breed all over Europe except southeastern England, Denmark, and some northerly parts of Germany, Holland, Belgium and France. The species is usually resident, and rarely found away from rapidly-flowing rivers. In mountainous regions it occurs above the tree line. During April or May the birds start looking for a suitable territory, often establishing themselves there for years, and start building a nest – in a wall beside a brook, in a crack under a footbridge, in a hole between rocks, sometimes even behind a waterfall. The size of the nest depends on the size of the cavity, for the dipper fills the entire space with moss and pieces of vegetation. It is interesting to note that the bird dives underwater for this material and that it dips the moss in water before using it for building. Both partners construct the nest, which is a domed structure with the entrance at the side. The female lays four to six eggs and in all probability incubates them alone for 14 to 17 days. Both birds tend the young for 18 to 24 days in the nest and for a short while longer after fledging. When foraging for food, the dipper walks (or sometimes dives) into the water and gathers insect larvae and small crustaceans on the bottom, even catching small fish now and then. This remarkable feat is apparently achieved by continual wing movements to force the body down.

Voice:
A short 'zit'.

Song:
Similar to that of the wren, consisting of piping and chattering notes.

Length:
18 cm.

Male and female have similar plumage.

Size of egg:
23.8–27.7
× 17.4–20.1 mm.

Resident bird

Wren

Troglodytes troglodytes

Nearly the smallest European bird (weighing only eight to nine grams), the wren makes its home in woods throughout most of Europe. It is also found in parts of Asia, northwestern Africa and North America. It is an agile, restless bird, which remains in its breeding grounds throughout the year; only individuals from the north travel south for the winter. The favourite habitat is woodland with thick undergrowth, though it also likes thickets alongside ponds, ditches and streams. Sometimes it is found in parks and, in winter, frequently enters villages. In spring the male stakes out his nesting territory, which he stoutly defends and, at the end of April, begins building several 'cock' nests, which are made of plant stalks, small twigs and moss and provided with a tiny side entrance. His mate then selects the one she considers best; it is then lined with animal hairs and feathers. The nests are located in the branches of spruce trees, stacks of wood, between roots, in piles of brushwood and similar sites, and the ones not chosen by the female are used by the male as sleeping quarters. Incubation of the five to seven eggs is by the female alone for 14 to 16 days; 15 to 17 days later the young leave the nest. In June the parent birds often have a second brood, the male taking the first to roost in one of the rejected nests while the female is occupied with incubation. A wren's diet consists of insects, insect larvae, spiders and small seeds.

Size of egg:
14.7—18.9
× 11.5—13.5 mm.

Length:
9.5 cm.

Male and female have similar plumage.

Voice:
A loud 'tit-tit-tit' and twittering 'tserr'.

Song:
Loud and frequent, even in winter.

Resident bird

Dunnock

Prunella modularis

One can chance on a dunnock's nest in parks, gardens, cemeteries or deciduous and coniferous woods. It is large, and located in dense undergrowth or in the branches of a spruce or pine. In woodland, the basic building material consists of dry spruce branches, in gardens long bean stalks, and elsewhere the stems of nettles; failing these, the next resort is green moss, of which the lining will anyway be made. The four to five blue-green eggs blend so well with it as to be practically invisible. The task of incubating the eggs falls mainly to the hen, though the male relieves her at regular intervals during the 12- to 14-day period. When they are between 12 and 14 days old, the young birds leave the nest, and are fully able to fend for themselves soon afterwards. Dunnocks are common, but surprisingly easy to overlook if concealed in a thicket. The staple diet consists of insects, larvae and spiders with berries and seeds in autumn. In September or October dunnocks from the more northerly regions of Europe leave for the western and southern parts; occasionally they also winter in central Europe. The return to the breeding grounds is in March or April.

Voice:
A high, piping 'tseep' and trilling note.

Song:
Sharp, loud, metallic notes.

Length:
14.5 cm.

Male and female have similar plumage.

Size of egg:
17.5—21.2
× 13.0—15.5 mm.

Migratory bird

Grasshopper Warbler

Locustella naevia

The inconspicuous grasshopper warbler is distributed throughout most of Europe from northern Spain to southern Sweden and Finland. It does not nest in Italy or the Balkan Peninsula, but does inhabit the British Isles. Its favourite haunts are tall, dense shrubberies, stands of willow and alder with thick grass cover, marshy meadows and thickets bordering lakes, ponds and river backwaters. This is an especially retiring bird; its presence is most likely to be revealed by the song of the male, who perches on a raised stem as he emitts his unique, high-pitched trilling song, sometimes continuing without interruption a full three minutes. Grasshopper warblers are migratory, leaving for winter quarters in northern Africa or southwestern Asia in August or September and returning to their breeding grounds in late April or the beginning of May. The nest, well concealed under a grass tussock or in a thick shrub, is built in May or June by both partners. Made of grass blades or reeds, it is fairly deep. The clutch consists of four to five eggs, which are incubated 12 to 14 days mostly by the female. The young are cared for by both parents, who bring them various small invertebrates. The adult's diet is the same. The young leave the nest after nine days but continue to be fed by the parents a further two weeks.

Size of egg:
16.0–20.3
× 12.5–14.8 mm.

Length:
12.5 cm.

Male and female have
similar plumage.

Voice:
Courting call is a note that
sounds like 'twhit'.

Song:
Resembles a 'seerrrr...'

Migratory bird

Sedge Warbler

Acrocephalus schoenobaenus

The sedge warbler inhabits all of Europe except the Iberian peninsula and Iceland. A migrant, it leaves its breeding grounds in September or October for winter quarters in tropical Africa, flying south as far as the Transvaal, and returns in the second half of April. It is found in abundance on the banks of lakes and ponds in reeds, tall grass, nettles and thickets. Even though normally well concealed in thick vegetation, its presence is revealed soon after arrival by the song. The sedge warbler sings in flight, ascending with widespread wings and tail, then descending in a shallow dive. In May or June, the paired birds build a fairly large nest in thickets, reeds, or tall grass near water, sometimes directly above water. The structure is made of plant stalks, roots and moss, lined with plant fluff, animal hairs, and similar materials. It is erected by both partners, but the major share of the work falls to the female, who, when it is complete, lays four to five, sometimes as many as seven eggs, which she incubates alone for 12 to 13 days. Both partners, however, care for their offspring, feeding them insects, insect larvae, spiders and small gastropod molluscs. The young leave the nest at ten to 13 days, to hide in the surrounding vegetation where their parents continue to bring them food for another ten to 14 days.

Voice:
Song similar to that of the reed warbler, but the sequences are more frequently repeated and sound like 'tuc tuc tuc'.

Length:
12.5 cm.

Male and female have similar plumage.

Size of egg:
15.7—20.5
× 11.9—15.0 mm.

Migratory bird

Marsh Warbler

Acrocephalus palustris

Moist, overgrown ditches and fields are the marsh warbler's habitats. This is a widespread species in western Europe (though restricted to the southern counties of England), central and eastern Europe, and in Asia as far as western Siberia. In Scandinavia it occurs rarely, and then only on the south coast. It returns from its winter quarters in east Africa in mid-May. Shortly after arrival, it starts building a nest of grass and other plant stalks in tall grass, clover, or cereal crops bordering rivers. This is placed very close to the ground, either among tall, standing plant stems, or dwarf shrubs and dense growths of tall nettles, but never over water. In May or June the hen lays four to seven eggs, which she and the male take turns in incubating for 12 to 13 days. The nestlings, which leave their shelter at 11 to 13 days, are fed with small insects and larvae, these also being the staple diet of adult birds. After hatching, the young are fed by the parents for some ten days more. The marsh warbler's song may be heard by day or night.

Size of egg:
16.7–21.5
× 10.0–14.9 mm.

Length:
12.5 cm.

Voice:
A loud 'tchuc', 'tweek', and similar sounds.

Song:
Resembles that of the mocking-bird; no chirping notes.

Migratory bird

Reed Warbler

Acrocephalus scirpaceus

This species is among the commonest of European warblers. Its breeding range includes most of the continent except Ireland and Holland; in Scandinavia it occurs only in the south and in Finland only in the southwest. A migrant, it leaves its breeding grounds in late September or early October, wintering as far away as tropical Africa, mainly in the east. In the second half of April or beginning of May it returns to nesting sites in reeds bordering ponds, lakes and swampy places. The nest is not built necessarily above water. It is usually woven around several strong reed stems, and made of finer material than that of the great reed warbler; the cup itself is very deep so that neither the eggs nor the young nestlings can fall out if the reeds are swayed by a strong wind. The female lays four to five eggs in May or June (in rare instances July or August should the first nest be destroyed) and she and her partner take turns incubating for 11 to 12 days, sometimes as long as 14 days. Both likewise share the duties of feeding the young — 11 to 14 days in the nest and a further two weeks after fledging. They also shield the young with their bodies against rain and the heat of the sun. The food is generally insects and insect larvae, spiders and small gastropod molluscs.

Voice:
Not a very loud song — something like 'chirruc-chirruc, jag-jag-jag'.

Length:
12.5 cm.

Male and female have similar plumage.

Size of egg:
16.3—21.4
× 12.4—14.7 mm.

Migratory bird

Great Reed Warbler

Acrocephalus arundinaceus

By far the largest of the European warblers, the great reed warbler, has a wide distribution embracing the entire continent except for the British Isles and Scandinavia, though it does occur in rare instances on the southern tip of Sweden. It leaves in August and September for winter quarters in equatorial and southern Africa, returning at the beginning of May. Favourite haunts are large reed-beds in ponds, pools, lakes and river deltas. Plentiful throughout its range, the species is easily identified from a distance by the male's distinctive strident note, whose loudness few other birds can match. Between May and July the female, unaided by the male, builds a fairly large nest of reed stems woven round two to six tall reeds which serve as supporting 'pillars'. She either pulls the old reed leaves from which the nest is made out of the water, or else thoroughly soaks them so that they are pliable, and thus more easily woven. The nest is generally located some 50 to 100 centimetres above the water's surface. The clutch consists of four to five eggs, which both partners take turns incubating for 14 to 15 days; both also care for the young. These are fed 12 to 14 days in the nest and a further two weeks after fledging. The diet consists basically of small invertebrates, mostly insects and insect larvae, spiders and small molluscs, which the great reed warbler gathers on water.

Size of egg:
19.5—26.3
× 15.1—17.6 mm.

Length:
19 cm.

Male and female have
similar plumage.

Voice:
Alarm note 'karrr karrr'.

Song:
A loud and strident
'karra karra, krik, krik, gurk'.

Migratory bird

Icterine Warbler

Hippolais icterina

This species is widespread in central, northern and western Europe, except the British Isles. In the east, the distribution extends as far as western Siberia. It does not return to its breeding grounds until mid-May, from when the loud, varied and pleasant song may be heard among bushes in parks and gardens, or in deciduous woods, at almost any time of day. The male changes his perch every now and then, moving from a low bush to the branch of a tall tree and back again. Both partners build the deep, tidy, semi-spherical nest of grasses strengthened with bast and spider webs, generally selecting a damp locality near a stream or pond. Its outer walls are often camouflaged with bits of bark, usually from birches, and the elevation tends to be between two and four metres above the ground; it may well be placed in an elderberry bush. The three to six eggs (pink, spotted with black) are incubated by both partners, the male, as a rule, taking over at mid-day. The young hatch after 12 to 13 days and leave the nest about two weeks later. Food consists of aphids, flies and other insects. At the end of August icterine warblers travel via Italy and the Balkans to winter quarters in Africa.

Voice:
A musical 'deederoid' or 'hoocet'.

Song:
Very loud, and includes phrases in which one can distinguish the songs of other birds.

Length:
13 cm.

Male and female have similar plumage.

Size of egg:
17.0−21.5
× 12.4−14.7 mm.

Migratory bird

Garden Warbler

Sylvia borin

The garden warbler inhabits parks with thick undergrowth, thickets alongside rivers, streams, ponds, as well as hardwood and mixed forest with dense undergrowth. Its distribution covers almost all of Europe, extending eastwards as far as western Siberia. Arrival from winter quarters in Africa is at any time between late April and mid-May. The fairly large nest may be situated in a thicket close to the ground, perhaps a raspberry or blackberry bush. Both partners share the task of collecting the long, dry plant stalks used as nesting material; an inner lining is laced from spider and caterpillar webs. Both share the task of incubating the four to five eggs for 12 to 14 days and rearing the young, feeding them insects, insect larvae and spiders. They are just as conscientious in caring for a young cuckoo hatched from one of the eggs frequently deposited by this parasitic species in their nest. At around 11 to 14 days (perhaps earlier), the young leave the nest, still incapable of flight. Besides insects, the garden warbler feeds on various berries. It leaves for its winter quarters at the end of August or beginning of September.

Size of egg:
17.0—23.2
× 13.0—16.5 mm.

Length:
14 cm.

Voice:
Call-note 'check-check' also 'tchur-r-r' and a faint 'whit'.

Song:
Lengthy, pleasant, loud, and flutey.

Migratory bird

Blackcap

Sylvia atricapilla

This warbler is common throughout Europe, in Asia as far as western Siberia, in the Middle East and on the coast of northwestern Africa. European blackcaps winter in southern Europe and equatorial Africa, returning in April to their breeding grounds in hardwood or pine forest, groves, parks and overgrown gardens, in both lowland and mountain regions. They build a carelessly woven nest of stalks in the fork of a bush close above the ground, lining it with horse or other animal hair. The male also builds a special nest for himself where he will perch and sing. Both parents take turns to incubate the four to six eggs for a period of 13 to 14 days, and both feed the young with hairless caterpillars for 11 to 14 days in the nest, and for a few extra days after they have fledged. In July the blackcap often has a second brood. Adult birds feed chiefly on insects, insect larvae and spiders. They also like woodland berries, especially blueberries and raspberries and, in the autumn, elderberries. The southward migration starts in late August or early September.

Voice:
An emphatic 'tac-tac'.

Song:
Flutey notes ending in
a loud whistle.

Length:
14 cm.

Sexually dimorphic.

Size of egg:
17.0–22.2
× 13.0–15.8 mm.

Migratory bird

Whitethroat

Sylvia communis

Places with thick growths of brambles and nettles are the chosen habitat of the whitethroat, which is found throughout Europe. In the east its distribution extends to Lake Baikal, and it is also widespread in northwestern Africa. Its arrival at the end of April or in early May is publicised by the cock, who displays by flying upwards in an oblique line, warbling as he goes, then hurtling down again, continuing his song after landing in a thicket. At other times he sings while perched on a high branch, thistle or other tall plant. The nest is built close to the ground in a thicket, hedge (whitethroats are particularly fond of brambles, blackthorns and nettles), in a grove of trees or on a rock slope. Sometimes it is placed directly on the ground; a loosely woven construction of grasses and rootlets, the edges are sometimes lined with spiders' webs. The whitethroat has its first brood in May and a second in June. The female lays four to six eggs, which both partners take turns to incubate, usually for 13 days. The nestlings are fed with the type of food eaten by the adults — insects, their larvae and small spiders. The young abandon the nest at 11 to 13 days and in September the birds depart for their winter quarters in Africa.

Size of egg:
16.0—20.9
× 12.0—15.2 mm.

Length:
14 cm.

Sexually dimorphic.

Voice:
A quiet but fast
'wheet-wheet-whit-whit-whit',
also a repeated 'check'.

Song:
A short, repeated melody
composed of whistling and
flutey notes.

Migratory bird

Lesser Whitethroat

Sylvia curruca

This species is found from mid-April throughout Europe, except Spain and Ireland. In the east, its range extends all the way to northern China. Females arrive at the breeding grounds about a week after the males, who find the nest site. The birds are most commonly found in parks, cemeteries, overgrown woodland edges and in hedgerows, but will only breed in large rambling gardens. The nest is superbly woven from long, thin rootlets plucked from the ground. Both partners share the duties of incubating the four to six eggs for ten to 12 days. They have one brood in May or June and frequently a second one in July or August. At ten to 15 days the young leave the nest, continuing to be fed by the parents on small insects, caterpillars and spiders a short while longer. In autumn, the lesser whitethroat also feeds on various berries. Departure for winter quarters in tropical Africa is in September.

Voice:
Call notes like 'tcharr' or 'check'.

Song:
Begins with a subdued warble, then becomes an outburst of unmusical rattling.

Length:
13.5 cm.

Sexually dimorphic.

Size of egg:
14.0–18.9
× 11.5–14.5 mm.

Migratory bird

Chiffchaff

Phylloscopus collybita

Often as early as mid-March, one can hear the monotonous song of the chiffchaff emanating from tree-tops in parks, gardens and woodland. The species breeds throughout most of Europe after spending the winter months in the Mediterranean. Its distribution also includes northwestern Africa and Asia as far as northern Siberia. Though basically a tree dweller, it builds a nest on the ground in grass, on gentle slopes, in ditches, beside forest trails and in clearings. This is an enclosed, circular construction made of dry leaves and grasses and is so excellently camouflaged that it is very difficult to spot. The entrance, built by the female alone, is a small opening at the side. The six to seven eggs are incubated for 13 to 14 days generally by the hen alone and the task of rearing the young is also mainly her responsibility, though the male sometimes assists. On reaching 13 to 15 days, the young hop out of the nest, but the parents still continue to feed them insects, larvae and spiders a short while longer. Departure for winter quarters is usually in late September, though some individuals do not leave until November.

Size of egg:
13.0—17.7
× 10.3—13.7 mm.

Length:
11 cm.

Male and female have
similar plumage.

Voice:
A soft 'hweet'.

Song:
Monotonous, continually
repeated
'chiff-chaff-chiff-chaff'.

Migratory bird

Willow Warbler

Phylloscopus trochilus

The loud, rippling song of the willow warbler can be heard in April when the bird has returned from its winter quarters in tropical and southern Africa. It nests in thick deciduous or mixed woods with thick undergrowth, or less often in coniferous forest. The species is distributed throughout Europe, except the south and the Balkans. In the east its range extends as far as northeastern Siberia. A small bird, it hops and flits restlessly from branch to branch, collecting small insects and their larvae, as well as small spiders. In the warm days of May or June the female builds a neat, dome-shaped nest in a clump of grass, or close to the ground in a blueberry bush or heather. The nest is made of grass stems, dead leaves, moss and lichens and lined with fine materials. Its entrance is located at the side so that the clutch is out of sight. Six or seven eggs are incubated by the hen alone, usually for 13 days, but the male helps share the duties of rearing the young. They leave the nest after 12 to 16 days, but continue to be fed by the parents for a further 14 days. A cuckoo often lays its eggs in the willow warbler's nest, and on hatching the young cuckoo will be reared by the willow warblers and fed by them for far longer than their own nestlings. In September or October the willow warbler leaves for winter quarters. It is one of the most plentiful species of woodland birds.

Voice:
A bright 'hooeet'.

Song:
Resembles that of the chaffinch but is a softer and more rippling 'sooeet-sooeetoo'.

Length:
11 cm.

Male and female have similar plumage.

Size of egg:
13.2 – 18.8
× 10.9 – 13.8 mm.

Migratory bird

Wood Warbler

Phylloscopus sibilatrix

The wood warbler is found throughout Europe as far as western Siberia, except in Spain, Portugal, Ireland and Scandinavia. By the end of April or the beginning of May, this small bird returns from its winter haunts in tropical Africa to nesting grounds in thin, deciduous or mixed woodland in lowland and hilly country. It may also be found in coniferous forests, but only in places where there is the occasional broad-leaved tree and some thick undergrowth. The round, covered nest, with a fairly large side entrance, is built by the female in a tussock on the ground. Considering the bird's small size, it is a fairly large structure, and the side entrance far larger than those in the nests of other warblers. By the end of May, or beginning of June, the nest already contains the full clutch of five to seven eggs, which are incubated by the hen alone. The young hatch after 12 days and are fed by both parents, the mainstay of the diet being insects and their larvae, gathered mostly from deciduous trees and the undergrowth. Fledging is at 12 days. The wood warbler differs from other warblers in having a bright yellow throat and breast and a broad stripe above the eye, but these features can be recognized in the wild only with the aid of powerful field glasses. Wood warblers set out for their winter quarters in Africa between the end of August and middle of September.

Size of egg:
14.0–18.3
× 11.4–13.5 mm.

Length:
13 cm.

Male and female have
similar plumage.

Voice:
'Pru' or 'whit whit whit'.

Song:
Chattering, beginning with
a repeated 'piu', followed
by a lengthy 'stip stip stip'
and ending with 'shreeee'.

Migratory bird

Goldcrest

Regulus regulus

Smallest of the European birds, a goldcrest weighs only five to six grams. It inhabits most of Europe except Iceland and the northernmost parts of Scandinavia, and in Spain is found only in the central parts of the country. It may be seen in pine and spruce woods, from lowland to mountain altitudes, up to the tree line. In winter it sometimes appears in parks. Though mostly a resident species, some individuals from northern localities travel to southern or western Europe in winter. During the winter months, flocks flit about in the treetops. At the end of April, and often for a second time in June, pairs of goldcrests weave a fairly large nest from small twigs, stalks, moss, lichen, spiders' webs and hairs. Rounded, and narrowing towards the top, it is carefully concealed in the thick branches of a coniferous tree and, when viewed from above, appears to be closed except for a very tiny opening. There is good reason for this — goldcrest nests are plundered by squirrels, dormice, jays and predators generally. The eight to 11 eggs are incubated by the hen for 14 to 16 days and the young are fed small caterpillars, spiders and flies by both parents. When they are about 14 days old, the chicks leave the nest and pass the night among thick branches with their parents. In winter, the goldcrest feeds on insect eggs and cocoons collected from branches. It is a very active bird with a good appetite.

Voice:
A soft 'zee-zee-zee' or louder 'whit'.

Song:
Composed of similar notes.

Length:
9 cm.

Sexually dimorphic.

Size of egg:
12.1—14.6
× 9.2—11.0 mm.

Resident bird

♂

Spotted Flycatcher

Muscicapa striata

From a high vantage point, such as a cottage roof, wooden fence post or jutting branch, the spotted flycatcher darts out to catch an insect on the wing, immediately returning to its perch. This agile bird may be seen throughout Europe in sparsely wooded regions, parks and gardens. It arrives from its winter quarters in tropical and South Africa at the end of April or beginning of May and builds a nest of rootlets, plant stalks and moss lined with vegetable fibres, fine hairs and feathers. The spotted flycatcher particularly favours a nest box, but it will build on a rafter in a shed, over a doorway, or even on a horizontal branch jutting out over a well-used path. The four to six eggs are incubated for 12 to 14 days, generally by the hen. The parents provide the young with insects, one at a time; a family may consume more than 500 a day with the result that the adults are kept frantically busy. Spotted flycatchers leave for their winter quarters at the end of August.

Size of egg:
16.4—21.4
× 12.5—15.6 mm.

Length:
14 cm.

Male and female have
similar plumage.

Voice:
A rapid 'tzee-tuc-ruc' and
a grating 'tzee'.

Song:
Soft, thin, high notes that
are rarely audible, like
'sip-sip-see-sitli-see-see'.

Migratory bird

Pied Flycatcher

Ficedula hypoleuca

The black and white male pied flycatcher is quite common in thin woodland from as early as the beginning of April. He flies impatiently from one tree to another, seeking a suitable nesting cavity, his choice generally being an abandoned woodpecker's nest, though a nest box is also acceptable. The sober-coloured female then lines the nest with quantities of silky moss, finishing it with soft animal hairs. From mid-May until June she lays from five to eight eggs, which she herself incubates for 13 to 15 days. The male helps feed the young with small insects, which the parent birds capture on the wing; additional food items are small caterpillars and spiders. Fledging is 14 to 16 days, but the young continue to be fed by the parents for a further two weeks or so. The whole family then roams the countryside around the nest until setting out on the long journey to tropical Africa in late August or early September. The pied flycatcher inhabits most of Europe, except Italy and Ireland, and is only seen in north- and southwestern Germany and western France during migration. It has a somewhat patchy distribution and in some areas only nests sporadically.

Voice:
A short 'whit'.

Song:
Clear 'zee-it zee-it zee-it' sounds.

Length:
13 cm.

Sexually dimorphic.

Size of egg:
15.5 – 19.5
× 12.0 – 14.4 mm.

Migratory bird

Nightingale

Luscinia megarhynchos

Bushes on the edges of damp, deciduous woods, overgrown parks, gardens, hillsides and thickets, bordering rivers and ponds are favourite haunts of the nightingale. Its song, famed for strength, clarity and purity, is mostly heard at night, but also at intervals during the day. Not all nightingales have the same sweet song, and some are markedly more accomplished than others. They return to their breeding grounds, which embrace all of Europe except Scandinavia, Ireland and Scotland, from mid-April onwards, flying, as a rule, by night. First to arrive are the males, who immediately burst into song. The females arrive several days later. A nest is built of grass, rootlets and dry leaves, close to the ground or on a pile of leaves, well concealed in thick undergrowth. The female lays three to six eggs which she incubates herself for 14 days. However, in rearing the young, which hop out of the nest at the tender age of 11 days (as yet incapable of flight), she is aided by the male. Both parents feed the young with insects, larvae and spiders. In late August or early September the nightingale leaves for its winter quarters in tropical Africa.

Migratory bird

Size of egg:
18.2–24.7
× 13.9–17.0 mm.

Length:
16.5 cm.

Male and female have
similar plumage.

Voice:
A liquid 'wheet', short 'tuc'
and similar sounds.

Song:
Beautiful, rich and varied
melodies alternating with
joyous bubbling phrases;
the song often includes
phrases learned from other
birds.

Bluethroat

Luscinia svecica

The bluethroat is widespread in eastern and northern Europe, but also nests in a few places in central and western Europe excluding England. It is also found in several places in central Spain. There are two subspecies that differ from each other in colour. One is *Luscinia svecica svecica,* which inhabits Scandinavia, Finland and the USSR up to about 60° north: this has a russet patch in the centre of the blue throat-patch. The other is *Luscinia svecica cyanecula,* which lives elsewhere in Europe and has a white spot in the centre of the throat-patch. During autumn and spring migration, the former subspecies appears in large numbers in central Europe. Winter quarters for both subspecies are in northern Africa. The birds leave their breeding grounds in late August or September and return again between mid-March and mid-April. The nest is built in May or June, well concealed in undergrowth or thickets. It is made of plant stems and fine roots and is apparently built by the female. Whether she is aided by the male is not known. The clutch consists of five to six eggs, which the female generally incubates alone for 12 to 14 days. The young are fed in the nest by both parents for 13 to 14 days and a further two weeks after they have fledged. The diet of both young and adult birds consists of small invertebrates.

Voice:
Courting call 'tac'; the song is a warbling 'wheet'.

Length:
14 cm.

Sexually dimorphic.

Size of egg:
16.4–20.7
× 12.5–15.1 mm.

Migratory bird

Robin

Erithacus rubecula

Deciduous, mixed and coniferous woods with thick undergrowth, from lowland to mountain altitudes, are the home of the robin over practically the whole of Europe except Iceland and northern Scandinavia. Its range extends eastwards as far as western Siberia, and it is also found in northwestern Africa. In western and central Europe it is plentiful in parks and cemeteries, preferring thickly overgrown, dimly lighted spots, which accounts for its conspicuously large eyes. Northern and eastern populations migrate in September and October to winter quarters in western and southern Europe, and northern Africa. Birds often fly to England in the autumn, sometimes catching a ride on ships crossing the channel. March marks the return to the breeding grounds, where in April the females begin building their nests of roots, plant stalks and moss. These are well concealed between stones, under protruding roots, in piles of underbrush or less frequently in a hollow stump, and are lined with thin roots, fine plant parts and sometimes with animal hairs. The three to six eggs are incubated by the hen only for 13 to 14 days, but the male assists her in feeding the young with insects, larvae and spiders. The young leave the nest at the age of 12 to 15 days, though as yet incapable of flight, and conceal themselves on the ground, where the parents bring them food.

Size of egg:
16.9—22.2
× 13.8—16.3 mm.

Length:
14 cm.

Male and female have
similar plumage.

Voice:
A ringing 'tic' or 'tsip'.

Song:
Loud and melodious.

Migratory or resident bird

Redstart

Phoenicurus phoenicurus

During the first half of April the redstart returns to its breeding grounds throughout Europe. The winter quarters are in tropical Africa, for which it starts out in September or early October. The species frequents sun-dappled woods but is mainly to be seen in parks and occasionally suburban gardens. A very agile bird, hardly still for a moment and continually twitching its tail, its presence is noticeable almost immediately. The male, with his rasping song, is seen on the roofs of houses, sheds and similar buildings. A nest is begun in May and sited in a wall crevice, among the rafters beneath a shed roof, or in the free spaces between stacked wood. Failing these, the redstart will make use of a nest box. The nest is made of roots, plant stalks, moss and leaves, lined with hair and feathers. Five to eight eggs are incubated by the hen alone for 13 to 15 days. On hatching, the ever-hungry nestlings tax their parents to the limit, who are seemingly tireless in bringing them young caterpillars, butterflies, bed bugs, beetles and other insects, many caught on the wing. The young leave the nest after 12 to 16 days and soon afterwards the parents begin to prepare for a second brood.

Voice:
A sharp 'tooick', a liquid 'wheet' and 'whee-tic-tic'.

Song:
Lengthy high note followed by two lower-pitched, short sounds — otherwise varies according to the individual.

Length:
14 cm.

Sexually dimorphic.

Size of egg:
16.1–21.0 × 12.3–15.1 mm.

Migratory bird

Black Redstart

Phoenicurus ochruros

In late March black redstarts return to their European breeding grounds. The species was originally a native of cliffs and mountain regions, where it still occurs but has since adapted to the industrial landscape. In England it is confined in very small numbers to the southeast. Nests are built in wall crevices, behind drainpipes, on windowsills, in a nestbox and, on rare occasions, a tree cavity. The bird remains faithful to its nesting ground, returning there every year throughout its lifetime. The nest itself, built in practically the same spot each time, consists of bits of twigs, roots, plant stalks, dry leaves and mud, and is lined with fine hairs. The hen usually lays five eggs, incubating them herself for 13 to 14 days, while the male rasps his song from a high perch nearby. The neighbourhoods of stables, sties and rubbish dumps are the black redstart's favourite hunting grounds offering an abundance of insects to be caught on the wing and fed to the young. These often leave the nest as early as 12 days after hatching, as yet unable to fly, and conceal themselves on the ground. The black redstart leaves during October for its winter quarters in the Mediterranean; only individuals inhabiting western and southern Europe are resident.

Size of egg:
17.0–21.5
× 13.2–16.2 mm.

Length:
14 cm.

Sexually dimorphic.

Voice:
A stuttering 'tititic' and a brief 'tsip'; warning 'fuid, teck-teck'.

Song:
Rasping and chirping, sometimes with flutey notes.

Resident or migratory bird

Stonechat

Saxicola torquata

Dry open meadows with low shrubs, barren, stony places and heathland are the favoured habitats of the stonechat. This is a widespread species in western, central and southern Europe and in many places in Asia and Africa. Birds inhabiting central Europe migrate to the Mediterranean for the winter; western and southern populations are resident. At the end of March the stonechat may already be seen back in its breeding grounds, the male perching on a large stone or horizontal branch of a bush, singing his spring song. Nest-building begins in April or May, the structure being fashioned of rootlets and stalks, lined with animal hairs and other soft materials, excellently concealed in a clump of grass, the overhanging stems forming a kind of roof. The three to seven eggs hatch after 14 to 15 days, incubated by the hen alone. The young leave the nest at 12 to 13 days, as yet incapable of flight, and conceal themselves among stones in the surrounding grass. In June or July many pairs have a second brood. The diet consists of small insects, larvae, spiders, worms and small molluscs. In winter stonechats frequent fields and meadows.

Voice:
'Wheet-tsack-tsact' resembling two pebbles being knocked together.

Song:
A short repeated, grating 'wheet-wheet'.

Length:
12.5 cm.

Sexually dimorphic.

Size of egg:
15.6–20.0
× 13.2–15.5 mm.

Resident or migratory bird

Whinchat

Saxicola rubetra

At the end of April or in early May the whinchat, which winters in North Africa, returns to its breeding grounds in fields, meadows and moors showing a preference for hilly country with isolated trees and bushes. In spring one may see it perching on a telephone wire, the top of a shrub or any piece of high ground where there is a good view. The instant it spots a fly or other insect, it swoops to the attack. Its nest is built in a shallow depression in the ground, well concealed in a thick clump of grass or under a low bush. Four to seven eggs, usually blue-green, are incubated by the hen alone for 12 to 14 days. The young hop out of the nest when they are about 12 days old, as yet incapable of flight, and conceal themselves in various nearby places. Even when they have fledged, however, they continue to be fed by the parents who teach them how to catch insects on the wing. At the end of August or beginning of September, the whinchat journeys south again for the winter. This is a widespread species throughout nearly all of Europe, and in Asia ranges as far as the western parts of Siberia; it is also found in southwestern Asia.

Size of egg:
15.2–21.5
× 12.9–15.4 mm.

Length:
12.5 cm.

The female's plumage is more sober than the male's.

Voice:
A short 'tic-tic' or 'tu-tic-tic'.

Song:
Whistling and grating notes somewhat reminiscent of the black redstart's.

Migratory bird

Wheatear

Oenanthe oenanthe

This species is found on open steppes, in mountain areas, among rocks and dunes, in abandoned sandpits and quarries, and on railway embankments. Its range includes all of Europe and Asia, northern Africa and even Greenland. European birds migrate in late August or the beginning of September to northern Africa, returning at the end of March or beginning of April. The wheatear is essentially a ground bird, running about with agility or perching on a large stone which affords a good view of the surroundings. In May or June it builds its nest in a pile of stones in a rock crevice, a hole in the ground or even between railway sleepers. Made of roots, plant stalks and small twigs, and lined with animal hair and feathers, it generally contains five to seven eggs which hatch after 13 to 14 days. They are incubated mostly by the hen, the male assisting only occasionally and for a short time. However, both partners share the duties of rearing the young, bringing them beetles, butterflies, caterpillars and other invertebrates. The diet of the adult birds is the same. The young hop out of the nest when they are two weeks old, but do not begin to fly until a few days later.

Voice:
A hard 'chack' or 'weet-chack'.

Song:
Simple, grating, seemingly suppressed notes, heard only rarely.

Length:
14 cm.

Sexually dimorphic.

Size of egg:
18.4—23.2 × 14.0—16.5 mm.

Migratory bird

Mistle Thrush

Turdus viscivorus

Mistle thrushes are regarded as heralds of spring because they arrive at their breeding grounds and start singing as early as the end of February. Distributed throughout all Europe except Iceland, their range extends also to northwest Africa, the Middle East and western Asia. Individuals from western and southern Europe remain there the year round, being joined in October and November by migrant populations from other parts of Europe. The mistle thrush is found in coniferous and mixed woods, at lowland as well as mountain altitudes, and in western Europe frequents parks. It generally builds its nest high in the fork of a tree at the end of March and, for the second brood, again in June. The nest is constructed of twigs, grass, roots and moss, lined with a layer of mud and fine grasses, a task performed by the female. Four or five eggs are incubated by the hen alone for about 14 days. The young leave the nest at 14 to 16 days, still incapable of flight. In the autumn mistle thrushes roam the countryside, migrant populations usually flying southwest. The species generally seeks its food at the edges of forests or in forest clearings, taking insects, worms, small molluscs, and, in the autumn, fruits and berries. In spring, the mistle thrush delivers its loud song from the top of a tall conifer.

Dispersive or migratory bird

Size of egg:
25.8 – 35.8
× 19.6 – 24.4 mm.

Length:
26.5 cm.

Male and female have similar plumage.

Voice:
A hard 'tuc-tuc-tuc' and a thin 'see-ip'.

Song:
Resembles that of the blackbird but louder and with pauses between individual phrases.

Fieldfare

Turdus pilaris

Northern Europe is the home of the fieldfare, one of the few songbirds that were once prized as game birds. It was shot mostly during the migration season, and its meat considered a great delicacy. However, in most European countries it is today no longer taken as game. The fieldfare nests in many parts of central Europe, which it has been invading from the north in increasing numbers since the end of the nineteenth century, in some places breeding regularly in fair numbers. Fieldfares return to their breeding grounds in flocks at the end of March, nesting together in small colonies in woods, parks and thickets alongside brooks and ponds, as well as in thin birch or pine groves. There the individual pairs build nests close to one another in thickets, usually at a height of three metres. In tundra, nests are only 30 to 50 centimetres above the ground. The structure itself is made of dry twigs, roots and stems with a small amount of mud, lined with fine stems. The clutch comprises four to six eggs and these are incubated, primarily by the hen, for 13 to 14 days, the young leaving the nest after the same period of time. The fieldfare feeds on insects, worms, small molluscs, beetles and caterpillars; in the autumn and winter months mostly on berries, especially the rowanberry. In October, fieldfares from the north arrive in large flocks to winter in central, western and southern Europe.

Voice:
A loud 'tchak-tchak-tchak', also 'see see'.

Song:
Semi-loud and pleasant.

Length:
25.5 cm.

Male and female have similar plumage.

Size of egg:
25.0−33.5
× 19.0−23.4 mm.

Migratory bird

Redwing

Turdus iliacus

The redwing is a typical thrush of northern Europe and Asia. In rare instances, it nests in central Europe in cool, mountain areas near streams. On migration, it occurs abundantly during the winter months in central Europe on its way to western and southern Europe, or as far south as northwestern Africa. At this time redwings form large flocks that alight in beech and mountain ash woods to feed on rowan berries. Between the middle of March and the beginning of April, the redwing returns to its breeding grounds in thin birch woods or coniferous forests with thick undergrowth and, in Scandinavia, also in large parks. The nest is found in deciduous and coniferous trees at a height of about three metres, in tundras only 30 to 50 centimetres above the ground, and sometimes actually on the ground. Made of dry twigs, roots, stalks and mud, it is plastered inside with a layer of mud mixed with mucous secretions. The female lays four to six eggs from May to July, which both birds take turns incubating for 13 to 15 days. The young are fed mostly on insects and their larvae by the adult birds for 11 to 14 days in the nest, plus a further three weeks after fledging. When the young have fledged, the redwings gather in flocks, which set out on their southward journey at the end of October or the beginning of November.

Migratory bird

Size of egg:
22.0−29.1
× 17.2−20.7 mm.

Length:
21 cm.

Male and female have similar plumage.

Voice:
‚Tchack tchack', when alarmed; also 'terr terr', at night and in flight a clear 'see-ip'.

Song:
Loud, flutey tones interspersed with chattering and rasping sounds.

Ring Ouzel

Turdus torquatus

Ring ouzels live in the mountain areas of the west coast of Scandinavia, in England, Ireland, the Alps, Pyrenees and the Carpathians. The species frequents light woods at the dwarf-pine level but in northern Europe and England it is to be found on moors and rocky places with thickets. Its favourite haunts, however, are mountain slopes sparsely dotted with dwarf-pine and short spruce trees, where it is most often found in the vicinity of swift mountain streams. In more southerly parts of Europe it is resident, but inhabitants of northern areas fly to countries bordering the Mediterranean in September to November, returning again in mid-March to April. The somewhat untidy nest of twigs, plant stalks and grasses is built low down in trees, often among dwarf-pine; occasionally the birds nest on the ground between stones by a mountain stream. Usually the structure itself is well concealed by lichen gathered in the vicinity. The four to five eggs are incubated for 14 days, mostly by the hen, though sometimes the male takes a turn. Both, however, feed the nestlings for 15 to 16 days. On leaving the nest the young conceal themselves in the neighbourhood, usually between stones, and the parents continue to feed them for a further two weeks or so. When their offspring are fully independent, the parent birds often build a new nest and rear a second brood. The ring ouzel feeds chiefly on insects and their larvae, small molluscs and worms, and, in the autumn, also on berries and soft fruits.

Voice:
A clear, piping 'pee-u' and a 'tac-tac-tac' like the blackbird's.

Song:
Includes ‚tcheru', 'tchivi', 'ti-cho-o' and chuckling.

Length:
24 cm.

Sexually dimorphic.

Size of egg:
28.9–34.0
× 20.3–24.0 mm.

Resident or migratory bird

Blackbird

Turdus merula

The blackbird is found in all but the northernmost parts of Europe. In the central and western regions it is mostly resident, but more northerly populations winter in the Mediterranean. During spring, at dawn and even while it is still dark, one may hear the melodic song of the male perched on a rooftop, a tall post or a tree. His song may be interspersed with various unexpected passages for the bird is an expert mimic. As soon as the thickets show the first hint of green, he begins building his nest of roots, grass stems, bits of paper and rags, often using mud as well. The nest may be found in many different places — in thickets or trees, on a windowsill, wall or in a woodpile. In the latter part of April the hen may already have started incubating her four to six eggs. The young hatch after 13 to 15 days, leave the nest two weeks later as yet incapable of flight, and conceale themselves on the ground. The parent birds are tireless providers of food, mainly earthworms, which they are very adept at pulling out of the ground. Blackbirds also feed on caterpillars, molluscs and, in autumn and winter, berries and household scraps. In winter they are frequent visitors to suspended feeders and bird tables in parks and gardens.

Size of egg:
24.0—35.5
× 18.0—23.6 mm.

Length:
25.5 cm.

Sexually dimorphic.

Voice:
'tchink, tchink, tchink';
an anxious 'tchook'.

Song:
Loud flutey, very melodic.

Resident or migratory bird

Song Thrush

Turdus philomelos

If on a cold morning in March one hears a loud flutey song, it is likely to be the male song thrush just returned from winter quarters in north Africa or southern Europe. The birds perch on the branches of trees, as yet still bare, making themselves all the more conspicuous, emphatically proclaiming their ownership of nesting territories. Not until several days later are they joined by the females who select their mates with nesting grounds already staked out. The song thrush may frequently be seen not only in parks and gardens but also in woods. By mid-April the nest of dry plant stems may be found in trees, among thickets and on rafters in sheds. It is easily recognized by the interior of mud and rotting wood cemented together with saliva to form a smooth layer that soon dries and turns hard. It is provided with no further lining. The four to six eggs are incubated by the hen for 12 to 14 days, the nestlings being fed in the nest by both parents for two weeks. Then they hop out of the nest, but remain on the ground and continue to be provided with food by the adults. This consists of worms, snails, caterpillars and berries. The song thrush, whose range covers almost all of Europe, leaves for its winter quarters in late September or early October.

♂

Voice:
A liquid 'tchuck' or 'tchick', sometimes 'dag-dag'.

Song:
Flutey, whistling, very distinctive varied phrases, repeated two to four times, between brief pauses.

Length:
23 cm.

Male and female have similar plumage.

Size of egg:
23.0–31.8
× 18.6–23.00 mm.

Migratory bird

American Robin

Turdus migratorius

The American robin is one of the best known and also one of the most numerous of North American birds. Its range extends from Alaska across Canada and the USA to northern Mexico. In the autumn it leaves its northern nesting grounds to winter in the southern parts of the USA and in Mexico, sometimes flying as far as Cuba. Birds from southern regions remain in their breeding grounds throughout the year. A few individuals remain throughout the winter in cities, even in more northerly parts. The American robin inhabits parks, gardens and open woodlands or their margins. It is also found in large cities. The nest is built in early spring on the branch of a fruit tree near the trunk, in the fork of a branch, on a low construction, on the jutting ledge of a cabin, etc. It is made of grass stems and mud, bits of paper and other materials. The female lays three to six blue-green eggs which she incubates by herself for 13 to 15 days. Both parents bring food to the young. After about two weeks the young birds leave the nest and conceal themselves in the surrounding area, where the parents continue to bring them food. When the first brood is fully independent the adult birds embark on a second brood. The American robin feeds on insects and their larvae, worms, molluscs and in large part also on berries, particularly in autumn. It often visits parks and gardens where it hunts earthworms and insects in turf.

Migratory or resident bird

Size of egg:
24.0–32.5
× 17.5–22.8 mm.

Length:
25 cm.

Male and female have similar plumage.

Voice:
'Kwik, kwik, kwik' like blackbird.

Song:
A series of six to ten whistling notes.

Eastern Bluebird

Sialia sialis

The eastern bluebird belongs to the thrush family. It inhabits a vast range extending from southeastern Canada down the USA to east and south of the Rockies, northern Florida, also as far as southern Mexico. In the mid-eastern and eastern states it stays the winter; birds of more northerly regions fly south in autumn to their winter quarters in Mexico and also the Greater Antilles. April usually marks the eastern bluebird's return to its nesting grounds; in more northerly regions this may not be until early May. It inhabits open woodlands, forest margins, shrubby areas with occasional trees as well as orchards and farmers' gardens. During the nesting period the male perches on the branch of a tree and warbles loudly, often for as long as 40 minutes without pause. Because of its lovely song it was often captured and sold as a cage bird. Today, however, it is protected by law. The nest is located in tree cavities, generally ones abandoned by woodpeckers. It is usually situated one to ten metres above the ground and is lined with leaves, moss, small twigs, feathers and hairs. The female lays three to seven eggs which are usually pale blue-green in colour, though they may sometimes be all-white. They are incubated for 16 days, mostly by the female. The young are fed by both parents who bring them insects and their larvae, spiders, etc. In autumn adult birds also feed on various berries which they seek out even in parks and gardens.

Voice:
Song composed of various melodies and whistling notes.

Length:
17 cm.

Male and female have similar plumage.

Size of egg:
18.0—23.1
× 15.3—17.8 mm.

Migratory or resident bird

Bearded Tit

Panurus biarmicus

Thick reed-beds are the haunt of the lovely bearded tit, which is widespread in south-eastern Europe and eastern Spain. It also nests locally in central Europe, France, Holland, Belgium and the east of England. Bearded tits are usually resident, but some individuals from northerly regions move southwards. The birds spend their entire lives in the reed-beds bordering lakes and large ponds, and in swamps. The nest is build in April or May (and for a second brood in June to July) among thick reed-beds, rushes or in a clump of grass often just above the water's surface. Both partners build, bringing in their bills bit of reed stems and the long leaves of marsh plants which they weave firmly together. The hollow is lined with feathers. Five to seven eggs are the usual clutch, which both partners take turns incubating for 12 to 13 days, though sometimes the young hatch after ten days. They are fed insects, which the parents catch amongst the reeds, for ten to 13 days in the nest and a further 14 days or so after they have fledged. The family remains together for about three weeks, after which the young fly off and the adult birds start building a new nest preparatory to the second brood. Diet consists of small invertebrates and, in autumn and winter months, mostly of the seeds of water and marsh plants.

Size of egg:
14.5—19.2
× 13.0—15.0 mm.

Length:
16.5 cm.

Sexually dimorphic.

Voice:
Courting note 'cheen', alarm note 'tching'.

Song:
A soft chattering.

Resident bird

Long-tailed Tit

Aegithalos caudatus

The long-tailed tit ranks among the smallest of European birds, weighing a mere eight to nine grams. Unlike other tits, it builds an elaborate nest. This is a closed, oval structure made of moss, lichen and spiders' webs about 20 centimetres high, with a small entrance at the top. The outside is camouflaged with bits of bark and the inside is lined with masses of assorted small feathers, sometimes numbering more than a thousand. Both partners share the task of building the nest, the male bringing the material and the female shaping it, the work taking from 15 to 20 days. When it is complete, the hen lays six to 12 small eggs which she incubates alone for 12 to 13 days. The young are fed small insects by both parents while they are in the nest and for a while after fledging. As a rule, the adult birds then have a second brood, though the young of the first brood remain in their company. The latter have even been seen assisting their parents in feeding the new nestlings. On fledging, long-tailed tits form small groups that roam the countryside, flitting from tree to tree. They remain in their breeding territory throughout the winter.

Voice:
A repeated 'tsirrup' and a weak 'tsee-tsee-tsee' which may be heard even in flight.

Length:
14 cm.

Male and female have similar plumage.

Size of egg:
12.8−16.0
× 10.0−12.0 mm.

Resident bird

Crested Tit

Parus cristatus

The lovely crested tit is plentiful throughout Europe but absent from England, Ireland, Italy and the far north. It makes its home in tall, evergreen forests from lowland to mountain altitudes, though in western Europe it is interesting that it now occurs in deciduous woods, where it finds more cavities suitable for nesting. During the courting season, the male displays by spreading and closing his headcrest and executes various bows while singing his serenade. He often has trouble finding a suitable cavity in which to build his nest, and sometimes has to be satisfied with an abandoned squirrel's drey, an old overturned tree stump or a man-made nest box. On rare occasions, he excavates his own hole in rotten wood. The female lays the first clutch of seven to ten eggs in April, incubating them herself for 15 to 18 days. The young, which leave the nest after 20 to 22 days, are led by both parents. When these have fledged, the parent birds generally raise a second brood in June, often using the same nest. In the autumn, crested tits join groups of other tits, often acting as leaders of a flock as it roams the countryside. Their diet consists mainly of small insects, especially aphids, bark beetles and weevils and, in winter, various seeds. The crested tit is adroit at squeezing between the thick branches of conifers in search of food, and if it does not find enough there it often seeks fallen seeds on the ground.

Size of egg:
14.3–17.8
× 11.8–13.3 mm.

Length:
11.5 cm.

Male and female have similar plumage.

Voice:
A characteristic 'tzee tzee tzee', but often only 'choo-r-r'.

Resident bird

Coal Tit

Parus ater

Coal tits favour tall but not very dense coniferous forests, from lowland to mountain altitudes, and are distributed throughout the whole of Europe except the far north. Their range extends eastwards as far as Kamchatka and southern China and they are also found in northwestern Africa. They prefer to inhabit pine woods but are plentiful in spruce stands. In some parts of Great Britain and Ireland they may also be found in mixed woods and in the mountainous areas of southern Europe among beechwoods. Individuals from central, western and southern Europe are usually resident, whereas populations from eastern and northern Europe migrate in vast numbers to central Europe for the winter. Such journeys, however, are not undertaken regularly. At the end of April, the coal tit builds its nest of moss in a tree cavity; if there is a scarcity of these it will use hollow tree stumps, ground burrows or rock crevices, lining the inside with hairs. It also takes happily to a nesting box. The female lays seven to 11 eggs, which she alone incubates for a period of 14 to 15 days, rarely a day more or less. The young are fed insects, insect larvae and spiders by both parents. They leave the nest at 16 to 17 days, but continue to be fed by the adult birds for another two weeks. Having reared one brood the coal tit has a second, usually in July. Following the nesting period the birds form flocks, roaming the woods of the surrounding countryside together with other tits.

Voice:
In spring a characteristic 'seetoo seetoo seetoo'; the courting call is a soft 'sissi-sissi-sissi' and a scolding 'chi-chi-chich'.

Length:
11 cm.

Male and female have similar plumage.

Size of egg:
13.3—16.8 × 10.5—12.1 mm.

Resident or migratory bird

Willow Tit

Parus montanus

Willow tits are found in damp, evergreen forests, and to a lesser extent in mixed woods, both in lowland and in mountainous country, throughout most of Europe, except Spain, Ireland and Italy. Although generally a resident species, individuals from the north occasionally form large flocks and travel to central and southern Europe, but this does not happen regularly and is not considered to be true migration. The willow tit's range extends eastward as far as Japan and it is found also in North America. Pairs stay together permanently, even after the breeding season, forming flocks that roam the countryside. In spring, the female laboriously excavates a hole for her nest in a rotten tree stump; the male does not assist in this task, which often takes more than three weeks, although if the wood is well rotted the hole can be excavated in about two. Often, however, the female uses a natural cavity. In May she lays six to nine eggs, which she incubates alone for 14 days. The task of feeding the young, however, is shared by both partners — 17 to 18 days in the nest and a further two weeks after the nestlings have fledged. The parent birds make about 20 trips an hour, bringing caterpillars, aphids, flies, small beetles and spiders. After the young have fledged, willow tits roam the countryside far and wide in search of food. Additional winter food items are the seeds of various conifers.

Size of egg:
14.4—16.3
× 11.8—12.4 mm.

Length:
11.5 cm.

Male and female have similar plumage.

Voice:
Courting and alarm note is a repeated 'eez-eez-eez' with a short 'zi-zi-zi' in between. The male also makes a loud 'day' sound.

Migratory or resident bird

Great Tit

Parus major

Great tits are to be found in all parks and gardens including those in the immediate vicinity of buildings, as well as in woodland. Their distribution includes the whole of Europe and a large part of Asia and North Africa. Most do not leave their nesting grounds even in winter and only birds inhabiting the northernmost regions fly southwest in small flocks in the autumn. As early as April, and then again in June or July, it builds its soft-lined nest in tree cavities, wall crevices and nest boxes. First it gathers bits of moss and lichen, then lines a deep hollow with fine hairs and feathers. When all is ready the hen lays one egg a day until there are eight to ten, at which stage she begins incubating. The male gives no assistance, but does bring her a juicy caterpillar at intervals to satisfy her hunger. The naked, helpless nestlings hatch after 13 to 14 days, whereon the parent birds are kept busy supplying them with food, mainly caterpillars. To begin with they make as many as 500 trips a day and before the nestlings are fledged even 800 a day. The young tits abandon the nest at 16 to 21 days but perch on branches close by for several more days, continuing to be fed by the parent birds. In winter the great tit is one of the commonest visitors to bird tables.

Voice:
A clear 'tsink, tsink', 'tchair, tchair' or 'chi-chi-chi'.

Song:
A ringing 'teechew, teechew, teechew'.

Length:
14 cm.

Male and female have similar plumage.

Size of egg:
14.4—20.1
× 11.3—14.8 mm.

Resident bird

275

♂

Blue Tit

Parus caeruleus

The charming and familiar blue tit is an inhabitant of the whole of Europe, except northern Scandinavia. It remains in the neighbourhood of its nest throughout the winter and is a frequent visitor to bird tables, being especially fond of beef fat and peanuts; its truly acrobatic feats while feeding are a delight to watch. In early April pairs of birds may already be seen impatiently flying from place to place in gardens, parks and sun-dappled woods, seeking a suitable nest site. If there is no nesting box or tree cavity in the vicinity they will be content with a crack between the boards of a shed, a hollow tree stump or letter box, where they build the nest of moss, well lined with feathers and fine hairs. Ten to 16 eggs are incubated for 12 to 14 days by the hen alone. The newborn young are fed countless small caterpillars and insects by both parents. It is no mean feat keeping all these hungry mouths filled, and more remarkable that the parents often raise a second brood in July. The young leave the nest after 17 to 20 days, but continue to be fed by the parents for a short while longer.

Size of egg:
14.0−17.8
× 10.1−13.2 mm.

Length:
11.5 cm.

Male and female have similar plumage.

Voice:
Varied call-notes like 'tsee-tsee-tsee-tsit'.

Song:
A high 'tsee-tsee', followed by a long trill.

Resident bird

Marsh Tit

Parus palustris

Most of Europe, except the far north, supplies habitats for the agile marsh tit, an all-year resident. Favourite haunts are parks and large gardens, but it also inhabits deciduous and mixed woodland. The individual pairs remain together even during the winter months often joining groups of other tits to roam the countryside. In early spring, usually the beginning of April, the marsh tit claims its nesting ground and at the end of the month or the beginning of May the hen lays six to 12 eggs. The nest, made of moss and thickly lined with hairs, is generally located in a cavity, the bird being satisfied with a hollow in a tree stump or rotting branch or, if nothing else is available, a nest box. The eggs are incubated for 14 days by the hen alone; the young leave the nest at 18 to 19 days, but continue to be fed insects and larvae by the parents for a short while longer. Adults have a similar diet, but also take various invertebrates, and in autumn and winter, small seeds. In winter the marsh tit is a frequent visitor to parks.

Voice:
A loud 'pitchew' or 'piti-chewee', sometimes also 'chick-adeedee-dee'. It is, however, rarely heard.

Song:
Melodic warbling.

Length:
11.5 cm.

Male and female have similar plumage.

Size of egg:
14.6—17.1
× 11.5—13.1 mm.

Resident bird

Nuthatch

Sitta europaea

Nuthatches are common in thin deciduous, mixed and coniferous woodland, as well as parks and large gardens. They are found throughout Europe, except Ireland and northern Scandinavia. A resident bird, the nuthatch remains in its breeding grounds throughout the winter, when it may often be seen around houses on visits to the bird tables. Sunflower seeds are the favourite food. Picking one up in its beak, it will fly off with it to a nearby branch, wedge it in the bark, crack the seed coat and swallow the kernel, after which the same process is repeated. In spring, either at the end of April or the beginning of May, the female lays six to ten eggs in a tree cavity lined with pine bark chips or dead leaves. If the entrance is too large, the female narrows it by plastering the edges of the hole with mud mixed with mucous secretions. Incubation is by the hen alone for 13 to 14 days, but both parents share the duties of feeding the young. The male sleeps in another cavity nearby, having first ensured that his mate is comfortably settled for the night. Nuthatches often venture several hundred metres from the nest. The young leave after 22 to 24 days and soon learn to clamber up and down tree trunks with great adroitness, hunting insects and spiders in the bark like their parents, often head downwards. In winter they also feed on seeds, which are often stored in cracks.

Size of egg:
17.2—22.5
× 13.5—15.4 mm.

Length:
14 cm.

Male and female have
similar plumage.

Voice:
In early spring a loud
whistling that sounds like
'chwit-shwit-chwit'.
Courting note is 'tsit-tsit' or
a long trilling 'chi-chi-chi'
or 'qui-qui-qui-qui'.

Resident bird

Tree Creeper

Certhia familiaris

This is an inconspicuous bird with a long, slightly downcurved bill, which it uses to collect small insects, their eggs, larvae and pupae from crevices in the bark of trees. Like the nuthatch and woodpecker, it climbs trees, but travels upwards and around the trunk in a spiral, using its tail as a prop. It is found chiefly in coniferous forests from lowland to mountain altitudes, but occurs also in mixed, and sometimes in deciduous woodland. Except for southwestern Europe and northern Scandinavia, it is widespread, and extends eastwards as far as Japan, and occurs also in North and Central America. It does not leave its nesting grounds even in the most severe winters, but remains flitting about the woods in search of food. In the middle of April it builds its nest under a piece of loose bark, in a cranny, pile of wood, or other similar niche. The nest is woven of dried grass, rootlets, lichens and moss on a layer of small dry twigs, and lined with a thick layer of feathers and hairs. The five to seven eggs are incubated by the hen for 13 to 15 days. The nestlings are fed by both parents with small insects and their larvae, as well as spiders, leaving the nest after 15 to 16 days, but fed by the adult birds for a short while longer. Often the tree creeper has a second brood, usually in June. Young birds roam the neighbourhood and the following year raise their own families in the vicinity.

Voice:
Sounds resemble 'tsee' or 'tsit' but uttered only rarely.

Song:
Resembles the trill of the blue tit; similar to the song of the wren.

Length:
12.5 cm.

Male and female have similar plumage.

Size of egg:
14.0—16.7
× 11.0—13.0 mm.

Resident bird

♂

Yellowhammer

Emberiza citrinella

From April to July, throughout Europe one can hear the monotonous yet pleasant wheezing song of the yellowhammer as he perches high in a thicket, hedgerow or woodland edge. When courting, the male hops about, circling the hen with drooping wings and ruffling his bright chestnut rump, sometimes enhancing his attractiveness by picking up a stem and prancing about with it in his beak. The nest of plant stems, stalks and roots is built in the grass or close to the ground, almost always lined with horsehair, though it is a mystery how the birds find this material. The clutch comprises three to five eggs incubated mostly by the hen, though the male occasionally assists. The young hatch after 12 to 14 days and leave the nest 12 to 14 days after that, continuing to be fed by the parents for another ten days. Yellowhammers have two broods. About 30 per cent of the diet consists of insects, worms and spiders; the rest is seeds. After fledging, the birds gather in small groups to visit fields and meadows. In winter they often frequent the outskirts of cities.

Size of egg:
18.0–25.9
× 14.3–17.8 mm.

Length:
16.5 cm.

The female is more soberly coloured than the male.

Voice:
A metallic 'chip'.

Song:
Monotonous
'chi-chi-chi-chi-chi-chweee'
(a little bit of bread and no cheese).

Resident, dispersive or migratory bird

Cirl Bunting

Emberiza cirlus

This bunting, distinguished by its handsome colouring, inhabits western and southern Europe and the southern half of the British Isles. It stays the winter in its breeding grounds, gathering in flocks that visit fields and meadows. The habitats are open country with isolated shrubs and trees, cultivated areas, vineyards, woods and tree-lined thoroughfares. The female builds the nest of stalks in a concealed spot on or just above the ground (a clump of grass or a thicket) and lines it with material such as fine stems and horsehair. She incubates the three to five eggs for 11 to 13 days, raising one brood in April and often a second one in June. The young leave the nest at ten to 15 days. They are fed chiefly on insects and larvae. In addition to these, adults feed on various small seeds and berries in the autumn and winter. In places where the species is common, it is the male that usually attracts noise, for he is fond of singing on a high perch.

Voice:
A weak 'sip-sip'.

Song:
Twittering syllables, 'cirrrl'.

Length:
16 cm.

Sexually dimorphic.

Size of egg:
19.2–24.0
× 15.0–18.0 mm.

Resident bird

Corn Bunting

Emberiza calandra

The corn bunting inhabits all of Europe except the north and northeast and in Scandinavia is found only in the southwestern part of Sweden. Throughout most of its range it is resident but birds may wander in winter. First to return to the nesting grounds — open meadows in the vicinity of rivers or fields dotted with bushes — is the male, who selects and establishes his nesting territory. This often takes place as early as the end of March, but the beginning of April is more usual. He sings from the tip of a tall plant or some other elevated spot. The female arrives several days later and shortly afterwards begins building a nest in a shallow depression in the ground underneath a clump of overhanging grass. The structure is made of roots and dry grass stems, lined with small stems, animal hairs and also plant wool. In May or June, four to five eggs are laid, which the female incubates alone for 12 to 14 days. On hatching, the young are fed by the female for the first four days, after which she is aided by the male. Sometimes the male has several mates. The young leave the nest at nine to 12 days, as yet incapable of flight, and conceal themselves nearby in clumps of grass, being sought out by the parents, who continue to bring them food. During the nesting season, the corn bunting's diet consists mostly of small invertebrates; later, it feeds chiefly on grass seeds, grain kernels and greenery.

Size of egg:
19.0—28.6
× 16.0—19.5 mm.

Length:
18 cm.

Male and female have similar plumage.

Voice:
Courting note that sounds like 'chip'.

Song:
A rapid, dry jingle, resembling a bunch of keys being rattled.

Resident or dispersive bird

Reed Bunting

Emberiza schoeniclus

All of Europe except Iceland is home to the reed bunting. In western, southern and southeastern Europe it is resident, whereas northern and eastern European populations migrate southwards in October, as a rule passing the winter in the Mediterranean area. In central Europe, some birds are resident and some are migrant, the latter wintering in Italy, France or Spain. The reed bunting is found in marshland and swampy places, beside ponds and lakes where there are large reed-beds and also grassy areas. It may be seen in its nesting grounds from March. In April or May, the female, unaided by her mate, builds a nest in a dry spot in a clump of grass or dry reeds, or perhaps on the dam of a pond or in a field near water. The well concealed structure is made of dry grass stems, reed leaflets and other vegetation, lined with fine stems and animal hairs. The clutch usually consists of four to six eggs, which the female incubates for 12 to 14 days mostly alone. Both parents feed the young, bringing them mainly insects and insect larvae. The young leave the nest at 11 to 13 days, but continue to be fed by the parents a further two weeks or so. When their offspring are fully independent, the adult birds have a second brood, generally in June or July, though occasionally as late as August. Adult birds feed also on the seeds of various plant and on parts of green shoots.

Voice:
A courting note that sounds like 'tseek'.

Song:
A short
'tseek-tseek-tseek-tississisk'.

Length:
15 cm.

Sexually dimorphic.

Size of egg:
17.5 – 23.3
× 13.1 – 15.7 mm.

Resident or migratory bird

Snow Bunting

Plectrophenax nivalis

Snow buntings inhabit the far northern parts of Europe, arctic Asia and North America, occasionally nesting high in the mountains of northern Scotland. Every year, in September or October, they migrate south in huge flocks, and at this time may be seen inland, but not for long. The main wintering areas border the coasts of the North Sea, the Atlantic, the Baltic and the Mediterranean. In April the snow bunting returns to its breeding grounds, frequenting the rocky valleys of rivers and streams and mountainsides up to the snowline. The female usually builds the nest well hidden between stones, in a rock crevice or among shrubs and growing on a rock face. It is made of moss, lichen and grass and lined with hairs, horsehair, feathers and plant wool. Four to six eggs are laid during the brief arctic summer (June or July) and incubated by the hen for about 15 days. The young leave the nest after the same length of time. The staple diet consists of insects, larvae and other invertebrates, but adults also feed on small seeds. The snow bunting is fond of hunting mosquitoes near water, catching them on the wing.

Migratory bird

Size of egg:
19.5–25.1
× 14.3–18.0 mm.

Length:
16.5 cm.

Sexually dimorphic.

Voice:
A loud 'tsweet' and 'ten'.

Song:
A high, rapid
'turi-turi-turi-tetitui'.

Solitary Vireo

Vireo solitarius

The solitary vireo inhabits North America from the middle of Canada southwards across the whole of the USA, its range extending as far as Mexico. It is a migratory bird and in autumn leaves its breeding grounds to pass the winter in the southern USA and Mexico; populations living in these parts are resident. Early spring marks its return to its nesting grounds, usually in mixed and coniferous forests. The solitary vireo prefers open woodlands and is found in both lowland and mountain regions. The nest is built in broadleaf trees in the forks of low, slender side branches. It is an ingenious construction of grass blades and plant fibres, interlaced with strips of bark, spiderwebs or occasionally a caterpillar web. It is lined with hairs and fine grass. The nest is well masked and very difficult to find. The female lays three to five spotted eggs and begins incubating when the last one is laid. The male does not assist her in this task. The young hatch after 13 to 14 days and are fed by both parents, who bring them small caterpillars, spiders, and the like. Adult birds forage for food on the leaves and branches of trees. The young leave the nest after about 14 days and are fed by the parents for a further ten days. Adult birds feed chiefly on the caterpillars of various butterflies, some of which are plant pests, and the solitary vireo is therefore regarded as a beneficial bird and is protected by law throughout its range.

Voice:
A series of short, whistled notes.

Length:
13 cm.

Male and female have similar plumage.

Size of egg:
9.5 × 13.5 mm.

Migratory bird

Bobolink

Dolichonyx oryzivorus

The migratory bobolink nests in the eastern and central parts of the USA and in southern Canada, departing in autumn for its winter quarters on the coast of Central America and the Antilles, sometimes travelling as far as the Galapagos. The male's non-breeding plumage resembles that of the female, which has the upper feathers coloured yellowish-olive-brown tipped with black, the underparts yellowish-grey, and the wings and tail a blackish brown. Large flocks of these birds inhabit mainly wet, open grassland. The bobolink is a social bird even during the breeding season and pairs live close together. The nest is located in a depression in the ground, usually in a meadow. It is made of dry leaves, grass stems, and the like, and lined with fine grass. The female lays four to seven eggs which she incubates by herself for 11 to 13 days. The young are fed by both parents who bring them insects and insect larvae at first, later spiders, small molluscs, etc. and still later chiefly various seeds. Adult birds feed mainly on seeds and grain but also berries and green plant parts. In summer the diet may include insects and their larvae. When the young are fully grown family groups join up to form large flocks that feed on crops; for this reason they are disliked and much persecuted by farmers.

Migratory bird

Size of egg:
22.0 × 16.0 mm.

Length:
17.5 cm.

Sexually dimorphic.

Voice:
Tinkling song — long, rapid and bubbling.

Baltimore Oriole

Icterus galbula

The Baltimore oriole breeds in the eastern and central parts of North America, from southern Canada all the way to northeastern Mexico, flying south as far as Colombia and Venezuela for the winter. It inhabits open woodlands but often visits parks, gardens and plantations. The male's lovely, flute-like song is often heard in the treetops during the breeding period but the birds themselves are rarely seen, for they are extremely wary and shy at this time.

The unusual, deep, bag-shaped nest is hung from the tip of slender branches. It is made of long plant fibres interwoven with bits of animal fur and is open at the top. The female lays four to six eggs and begins incubating when the last one is laid. The male does not assist in incubation. When the young birds hatch after 12 to 15 days both parents feed their offspring for three weeks in the nest and a further two weeks after they have fledged. They bring them insects and insect larvae and spiders. When the young are fully independent the adult birds usually raise a second brood. After the nesting period families form flocks that roam the countryside, visiting also orchards with ripe fruit. They are fond of mulberries, figs and other soft fruits. They are also skilful at catching insects on the wing, but gather them on twigs as well. Often they eat wasps. In autumn the birds fly south to their winter quarters.

Voice:
Song – flute-like, whistling notes repeated in series.

Length:
18.5 cm.

Sexually dimorphic.

Size of egg:
23.0 × 16.0 mm.

Migratory bird

Chaffinch

Fringilla coelebs

One of our commonest birds, the chaffinch is found not only throughout Europe but also in northwestern Africa, the Middle East and Asia as far as western Siberia. Birds inhabiting northerly regions migrate to the Mediterranean in the autumn. Elsewhere they are resident or migrate only locally. The males stake out their breeding territory in February or March, the females arriving somewhat later to select a nesting site, usually in the fork of a tree, then building the nest, mostly alone, males assisting only for brief intervals. The nest itself is a neat, compact cup of moss, lichen and spiders' webs, often camouflaged with bits of bark from the tree in which it is placed. The chaffinch has one brood in April or May and a second in June or July. A clutch usually comprises five eggs, incubated for 12 to 14 days by the hen alone. Both partners, however, share the duties of rearing the young, feeding them mainly on insects and spiders for about two weeks in the nest, and for a short while after they abandon it. The diet of adult birds consists mainly of seeds. Outside the breeding season chaffinches form groups that roam the fields with other seed-eating birds or frequent parks and gardens where there are feeding trays or bird tables. They are also plentiful in thin woodlands.

Size of egg:
17.0—22.8
× 13.2—15.8 mm.

Length:
15 cm.

Sexually dimorphic.

Voice:
The familiar
'chwink-chwink'.

Song:
Short, melodious and rattling; terminates in a well defined flourish.

Resident or migratory bird

Brambling

Fringilla montifringilla

Every winter the brambling migrates from its breeding grounds in Scandinavia and northern Asia in huge flocks, sometimes numbering several thousand individuals. They often begin heading south by the end of September, and at this time bramblings may be seen in central and southern Europe where, together with other finches, they visit stubble and ploughed fields and meadows. They also feed on the berries of the mountain ash, or on the seeds of alder and birch. When snow covers the ground, solitary bramblings will visit feeding trays, even in built-up areas. In March and April, the bird returns to its breeding grounds in the coniferous forests of the far north. The nest of moss and plant stalks is camouflaged with lichen taken from the tree in which it is placed. In June, the female lays four to seven eggs, incubating them alone for 14 days. The nestlings are fed with insects and larvae by both parents, leaving the nest at 13 to 14 days but continuing to be fed for a short time after fledging. Soon after, the birds congregate in large flocks.

Voice:
A metallic 'tsweep';
also 'tchuc'.

Song:
Chattering and ringing
notes.

Length:
15 cm.

Sexually dimorphic.

Size of egg:
18.1—22.2
× 13.5—15.6 mm.

Migratory bird

Cardinal

Richmondena cardinalis

The cardinal inhabits practically the whole eastern half of the USA and is also widespread in central and southwestern USA as well as the northwestern and northeastern parts of Mexico. It has also been introduced to the Hawaiian Islands. Originally a bird of forest margins it has since moved to parks and gardens. It is often found also on farmlands with trees in which it can build its nest. The nest is built only by the female who constructs it of twigs, blades of grass and moss, and lines it with hairs and fine fibres. If there are no trees in the neighbourhood the nest may be placed in a tall shrub. It is interesting to note that though the male does not assist in nestbuilding he is constantly by the female's side, bringing her food and also singing loudly at frequent intervals. When the nest is complete, which takes only two to three days, the female lays three to four eggs and incubates them alone for 12 to 14 days. The nestlings grow fast and often leave the nest by the time they are ten days old, though they continue to be fed by the parents. They are fully grown at the age of about four weeks. The cardinal feeds on various seeds, berries, green shoots and also insects and their larvae. Food is gathered both in trees and on the ground. When the young are fully grown the birds often form small flocks that roam the countryside.

Size of egg:
25.0 × 18.0 mm.

Length:
22 cm.

Sexually dimorphic.

Voice:
Song — a repeated slow whistling note of several tones.

Resident or dispersive bird

Serin

Serinus serinus

Serins inhabit most of Europe, but are not yet established properly as a breeding species in the British Isles and Scandinavia. The end of March marks their return to the breeding grounds. In towns, especially in parks and gardens, the pleasant, twittering song may be heard daily. Favourite song-points of the male are slender branches or telegraph wires. As soon as the trees and bushes are covered with leaves, the hen begins building the small nest on a horizontal branch. It is made of rootlets, plant stems, bast and leaves, and lined so expertly with feathers and plant fluff that the three to five small eggs are practically invisible. Incubation, which lasts 11 to 13 days, falls to the hen alone but the male feeds her regularly. The young leave the nest at 11 to 14 days, having by this time trampled it flat. Outside the breeding season, flocks roam the countryside feeding on the seeds of thistle, alder and birch after first removing the husks. In October they migrate to winter quarters in southern Europe.

Voice:
A rapid 'si-twi-twi-twi'. or a hard 'chit-chit-chit'.

Song:
Chirping and twittering.

Length:
11.5 cm.

The female is paler than the male with more streaking on its plumage.

Size of egg:
14.4–17.6
× 11.0–12.7 mm.

Migratory or resident bird

Greenfinch

Carduelis chloris

The greenfinch is a fairly common bird, occurring in parks, large gardens, avenues, orchards, forest margins and sun-dappled groves. It is usually resident, though northern populations migrate south and west. Sometimes the birds form flocks with other finches that roam the countryside until returning to their nesting grounds in early April. The nest of twigs and roots, with a soft lining of feathers and hair may be found in thick hawthorn bushes by the roadside, in conifers or even in fruit trees. The five to six eggs are incubated by the hen, which is fed by the male during the 13- to 14-day period. Both parents share the duties of rearing the young, feeding them mostly with crushed seeds and an occasional caterpillar or spider. Adult birds feed principally on the seeds of various plants, shrubs and trees. The young leave the nest at 14 days, incapable of flight, and perch on nearby branches to be brought titbits by their parents for a few more days. There is frequently a second brood in July or August. In winter the greenfinch is a frequent visitor to feeding trays.

Size of egg:
17.2–24.1
× 12.2–16.1 mm.

Length:
14.5 cm.

The female is greyer than the male.

Voice:
A repeated short 'chup' or 'ten', also a rapid trill.

Song:
Various ringing notes.

Resident or dispersive bird

Goldfinch

Carduelis carduelis

The goldfinch is one of the most attractively coloured songbirds. Its range includes all of Europe except the northernmost parts. Although it nests in parks and gardens, it is an extremely wary bird, seldom seen during the breeding season. Sometimes only the song betrays its presence. The nest, built by the hen, is likewise well hidden, and needs an expert to find it. Usually it is woven of lichen and leaves but if located in a pine tree, pine needles are also used. In gardens the goldfinch likes to site its nest on the branch of a plum, apple of cherry tree; in parks on a maple or poplar. The duties of incubating the five to six eggs are performed by the hen alone for 12 to 14 days, fed on the nest by the male. Both parents feed the newly hatched young on aphids and, later, partially digested seeds. After fledging they form small flocks that roam the countryside during the winter months. Thistle and burdock are favourite food sources, from which goldfinches expertly extract the seeds; they are also fond of alder and birch seeds.

Voice:
A frequently repeated, liquid, twittering 'swilt-witt-witt-witt'.

Song:
Composed of similar notes to call.

Length:
12 cm.

The female is paler than the male.

Size of egg:
15.6—20.0 × 12.3—14.3 mm.

Dispersive bird

Siskin

Carduelis spinus

The siskin, one of the smallest members of the finch family, inhabits coniferous, mainly spruce, woodland, in lowland and mountainous country. It is found in central Europe, Scandinavia, Italy, southern France, Ireland and northern England, its range extending eastwards as far as western Siberia. The species particularly favours the vicinity of a brook, in which it loves to bathe. It leaves the woods in winter to form flocks which roam in birch and alder groves, or near brooks and streams, feeding on birch and alder seeds. The diet also includes the seeds of thistles. Occasionally it nips the buds off evergreens, and will sometimes feed on small berries. It is a very agile forager, clambering swiftly to the tips of branches, often hanging head downwards, employing antics similar to those of the tit family. Individuals from northern Europe frequently travel in large flocks to more southerly areas, often as far as the Mediterranean, returning to their breeding grounds at the end of March. The female builds the nest at the tip of a branch in a coniferous tree, generally more than 20 metres above the ground. It is made of slender twigs, bits of bark, lichen and moss and lined with feathers, down and hairs. The three to five eggs are incubated for 13 days by the hen alone, but she is assisted by the male in feeding the young, primarily with aphids and small caterpillars. Fledging is after two weeks and before long, usually in June, a second clutch is laid.

Size of egg:
14.7–18.5
× 11.1–13.6 mm.

Length:
12 cm.

Sexually dimorphic.

Voice:
A sound resembling 'tsy-zi'; in flight often 'tsooeet'.

Song:
Pleasant soft chirps and twitters.

Dispersive bird

Redpoll

Acanthis flammea

This is primarily a bird of the arctic tundra, from where it invades central and southern Europe in large numbers every autumn. It is also found in alpine regions at the dwarf-pine limits, especially the Swiss and Italian Alps, and in England and Ireland, where it occurs even in lowland country. More recently it has turned up in many places in central Europe, breeding in mountains and hill country. Its characteristic habitat is pure birch stands or mixed woods with birch. In May it builds a nest of slender twigs, stalks and grasses, lined with hairs and horsehair, usually located in bushes in the mountains, in dwarf-pine or short trees, generally 1.5 to 3 metres above the ground. In arctic regions it usually does not nest until June. Frequently, several pairs join to form a large nesting colony. The five to six eggs are incubated for ten to 12 days by the hen, while the male brings her food. The young, which leave the nest at ten to 14 days, are fed insects and insect larvae by both parents, who continue to feed them for a further ten to 14 days after they have fledged. The mainstay of the adult birds' diet is seeds, especially those of alder, birch and conifer. When the offspring are sufficiently independent, the parent birds may rear a second brood. In winter, groups of redpolls often visit parks and gardens which have birch or other seed-bearing trees and bushes.

Voice:
The characteristic flight call is a rapid 'chuch-uch-uch' or 'tiu-tiu-tiu'. Alarm note is a plaintive 'tsooeet'.

Song:
A sustained series of brief trills.

Length:
12.5 cm.

The male has a redder throat and rump than the female.

Size of egg:
14.3–17.5
× 10.0–13.2 mm.

Migratory bird

Hawfinch

Coccothraustes coccothraustes

Thin deciduous woodland, from lowland to mountain altitudes, and large parks and gardens are the hawfinch's habitats. The bird's most obvious characteristic is its parrot-shaped beak, with which it can crack cherry stones and similar hard seeds. The species is widely distributed throughout Europe, except in Ireland and Iceland, and in Scandinavia occurs only in the southeast. Its range extends eastwards as far as Japan and it is also found in northwestern Africa. Individuals from central Europe, generally transient migrants, wend their way in a southwesterly direction during the winter months, whereas populations from western and southern Europe remain at their nesting grounds all year. The hawfinch builds its nest at the end of April or the beginning of May, generally in broadleaved trees and often in fruit trees, from two to ten metres above the ground. Made of roots, plant stalks and grass, it rests on a thick layer of twigs and is lined with hairs or fine roots. The four to six eggs are incubated by the hen alone for 14 days, during which time she is fed by the male. The young leave the nest at two weeks. In spring and summer the hawfinch occasionally feeds on insects which it catches on the wing, but the mainstay of its diet is various seeds and kernels. At first the young are fed insects, later soft seeds.

Dispersive bird

Size of egg:
19.8—27.6
× 13.1—19.5 mm.

Length:
16.5 cm.

The female is not as richly coloured as the male.

Voice:
Sharp 'ptik'; also
a two-syllable 'ptik-it'
or 'tzecip'.

Song:
Soft and unobtrusive.

Bullfinch

Pyrrhula pyrrhula

During the winter months, especially when there is plenty of snow, one can come across a large number of brightly coloured birds in rowan woods, at the edges of forests, or in parks and gardens. They are bullfinches, which at this time fly to central and southern Europe in vast numbers from their homes in the north. Elsewhere, the bullfinch is distributed throughout most of Europe, except Spain, and in many places is a resident bird. It is found chiefly in coniferous forests with dense undergrowth, both in lowland country and in mountains, though it also frequents overgrown parks and large gardens. At the end of April, the female begins to build the nest in thick hedges or coniferous trees, quite close to the ground. It is woven of twigs and the hollow lined with hairs and lichen, or sometimes with fine roots. The male keeps his mate company during this period, both of them staying very quiet and unobtrusive, concealing themselves with some skill. The clutch, numbering five eggs, is incubated by the hen for 12 to 14 days; only sometimes is she relieved by the male. The young are fed in the nest by both parents for 12 to 16 days, chiefly on insects, and for a short while longer after they have fledged. In June or July there is usually a second brood. Bullfinches feed on seeds and berries, and in early spring devour the buds of flowering trees, especially fruit trees, which makes them extremely unpopular with gardeners.

Voice:
A soft, piping sound resembling 'wheeb'.

Song:
Composed of piping tones, including 'teek-teek-tioo'.

Length:
14.5—17 cm.

Sexually dimorphic.

Size of egg:
17.0—22.2
× 13.0—15.4 mm.

Resident bird

299

House Sparrow

Passer domesticus

This species is one of the commonest birds of Europe and Asia, but it has been very successfully introduced to all other parts of the world. It is essentially a city bird and can often be seen performing its courtship antics as early as February — the male hopping about in front of the female with drooping wings and a gallant air. The birds start building a nest of plant stalks, straw, bits of paper and feathers as early as March. Finding a site is no problem, the round, untidy structure (with side entrance) being placed in the branches of a tree, behind a drainpipe or beam, in a tree cavity, wall crevice or nest box. Sparrows are often colonial nesters. The female lays three to eight eggs on the thick feather lining and both partners take turns incubating for 13 to 14 days. The young fledge within 17 days, and after they have left the nest the parents prepare to raise further broods — sometimes as many as four. The diet consists chiefly of seeds, buds and the green parts of plants, supplemented in summer by insects. The sparrow is mostly resident, although in autumn flocks may form which roam around the locality.

Size of egg:
19.1−25.4
× 13.0−16.9 mm.

Length:
14.5 cm.

Sexually dimorphic.

Voice:
A loud 'cheep', 'chissis', and various twittering and chirping notes.

Resident bird

Tree Sparrow

Passer montanus

The tree sparrow is widespread throughout Europe and Asia, its range extending as far as Japan. Birds inhabiting southern regions or localities with mild climates are resident; northern and eastern populations are migratory. In winter, groups of tree sparrows roam the countryside, often in the company of siskins, seeking various seeds. During this period they roost in piles of twigs, thick treetops and cavities of various kinds. At the beginning of spring, often as early as February, the female perches on the branch of a tree, fluttering her wings, uttering soft cries and thus enticing the male to her side. Nests are built in tree hollows in orchards, parks and forest margins or in a nestbox, a hole in a wall or even the lower part of a stork's or eagle's nest. The species frequently breeds colonially. Both partners share the duties of building the nest which is typically made of straw, hair and feathers. The clutch comprises five to six eggs, incubated in turns for 13 to 14 days by both parents. In spring and summer the birds feed on insects and larvae, later on plant seeds.

Voice:
A short 'chick' or 'chop'; in flight, "tek tek".

Song:
Similar to voice.

Length:
14 cm.

Male and female have similar plumage.

Size of egg:
12.5—22.3 × 10.4—15.5 mm.

Resident or migratory bird

Starling

Sturnus vulgaris

Early in spring one often hears strange and varied sequence of notes, including sounds resembling the cackling of a hen and flutey trills emanating from the top of a tree or from beside a nest-box. All are made by the starling, an excellent imitator of other birds' songs. It has almost entirely abandoned the deciduous woods that were its ancestral habitat and moved instead to towns and suburbs. There, from April to June, the female builds the nest of rootlets and dried grass, sometimes assisted by the male. Both share the duties of incubating the four to six eggs for two weeks, alternating at regular intervals, and both feed the hungry nestlings who welcome each meal of insects and their larvae, molluscs and worms with a harsh, rasping call. The older nestlings literally fight to be among the first to get to the entrance hole with their wide-open beaks. Not until three weeks do they find courage to venture from the nest for the first time. After they have fledged, starlings assemble in flocks that visit cherry orchards and in autumn they are frequent and unwelcome visitors to vineyards. Flocks roost in spinneys, reed-beds or on buildings, and move south and west to escape the cold weather. Some individuals winter in southern Europe and North Africa; Scandinavian populations winter in the British Isles.

Size of egg:
26.2–34.1
× 19.7–23.2 mm.

Length:
21 cm.

The female's plumage has a less metallic sheen than the male's and is more spotted.

Voice:
A harsh, descending 'tcheer'.

Song:
Whistling and squeaky notes as well as imitations of the songs of other birds.

Resident or migratory bird

Golden Oriole

Oriolus oriolus

In late spring, when the nights are already warm, one can hear the melodious song of the golden oriole, just returned from its winter quarters in far-away tropical Africa to its breeding grounds in the large parks and deciduous woods of Europe. The golden oriole is distributed throughout most of Europe, but absent from Scandinavia, the British Isles and Iceland. It frequents mainly oak and other broad-leaved woods, more rarely field groves or thin pine woods, and is sometimes found in nature parkland. At the end of May or the beginning of June, the golden oriole weaves its hammock-shaped nest of long thin stalks and grasses, which it suspends between the forks of terminal tree branches about four metres above the ground. The upper edge of the nest is firmly woven around boughs on either side. Three to five eggs are incubated 14 to 15 days mostly by the hen alone. The young leave the nest at 14 to 15 days. Golden orioles feed chiefly on insects and their larvae, sometimes catching bees and other hymenopterous insects on the wing; spiders and molluscs are also eaten. The diet also includes berries and soft fruits, the birds being fond of visiting orchards where they eat ripe cherries, grapes, red currants and other fruits. In August they set out for their winter quarters. This is a very shy and wary bird which, though often heard, is rarely seen among thick foliage.

Voice:
Harsh, croaking calls like the jay's.

Song:
Flutey whistling notes that sound like 'weela-weeo' or 'chuck-chuck-weeo'.

Length:
24 cm.

Sexually dimorphic.

Size of egg:
27.8—36.0
× 19.9—23.5 mm.

Migratory bird

Jay

Garrulus glandarius

All of Europe, except Iceland and northern Scandinavia, provides a home for the jay, which frequents woodlands with undergrowth from lowland to mountain altitudes. It is most abundant, however, in woods where oak stands predominate. Mostly a resident bird, it roams the countryside after fledging, but inhabitants of northern Europe sometimes fly in large flocks to central Europe during the winter. The nest is built in April or May, generally among the dense branches of spruce trees on a forest margin at a height of four metres or more above the ground. It is usually constructed of dry twigs and a layer of plant stalks and roots, but is sometimes made of moss and lined with grass. The clutch, consisting of five to seven eggs, is incubated by the female for 16 to 17 days. Both parents feed the young until they are 20 to 21 days old, when they leave the nest and roam the countryside. Several families will later combine to form a flock. When crossing open territory a flock breaks up and the birds fly singly and spaced far apart, converging again only after they have reached a forest. The diet consists of both vegetable and animal food, and the jay is fond of other birds' eggs. In the autumn, flocks visit oak woods, where they collect acorns. The jay is an extremely wary bird and, on sighting a human being, immediately utters a loud cry. In the vicinity of the nest, however, it is very quiet and cautious. The jay can imitate various sounds.

Size of egg:
28.2—36.0
× 21.0—25.6 mm.

Length:
34 cm.

Wing span:
54 cm.

Male and female have similar plumage.

Voice:
A penetrating 'skraaak' and sometimes a mewing note.

Resident or dispersive bird

Blue Jay

Cyanocitta cristata

The blue jay inhabits the eastern and central parts of the USA, ranging southwards as far as Florida and the Gulf states. It is also found in southern Canada. It is one of the most attractively coloured and best known North American birds. It prefers dense mixed woods both in lowland and mountain regions and is particularly fond of forests with large numbers of red cedar. Sometimes it visits gardens if they are close to the forest. It does not migrate for the winter but roams the countryside out of the breeding season, usually in small flocks. The blue jay is an extremely wary bird and notices approaching danger from afar. The birds form pairs and stake out their nesting territory in early spring, by the end of March. The nest is fashioned from twigs and sticks, usually in conifers, preference being given to red cedar. The cup is lined with fine roots and hairs and contains three to five eggs. Before approaching the nest the birds watch the vicinity a long time for signs of possible danger and when they do so they are very quiet and wary. The young hatch after 17 days and are fed in the nest by both parents for about three weeks. After fledging the young roam the countryside with their parents. In the autumn blue jays fly in small flocks into forests where they gather forest fruits and seeds. In summer they also feed on insects, molluscs, worms, and the occasional small vertebrate. The blue jay is able to mimic the voices of other birds and various other sounds.

Voice:
A two-syllable, oft-repeated call that sounds like 'jay jay'.

Length:
28 cm.

Male and female have similar plumage.

Size of egg:
27.0 × 20.0 mm.

Resident bird

Magpie

Pica pica

The magpie is notorious for its habit of collecting glittering objects, which it then conceals in various places. Whereas wild magpies are very shy and wary, individuals reared in captivity are quickly tamed and grow into entertaining companions, though one must be careful to keep objects such as spectacles, rings and spoons out of sight. The species is widespread not only in Europe but also in Asia, northwestern Africa and North America. It is always resident, roaming the countryside far and wide in small flocks of ten to 20 individuals. In Europe, its favourite haunts are shrub-covered hillsides, woods and the edges of ponds. In early April, individual pairs choose a tree or tall shrub in which to build their nest made of dry, mostly thorny twigs, lined with turf and loam with an inner layer of hairs and fine stalks. It is additionally protected by a dome of thorny twigs. The hen lays three to ten eggs which she incubates for 17 to 18 days, mostly on her own. The young are fed in the nest by both parents for 24 days and for a further short period after fledging. The diet consists of mice, fieldmice, lizards, insects and other invertebrates, as well as seeds, fruits and berries.

Resident or dispersive bird

Size of egg:
27.3–41.9
× 21.2–26.4 mm.

Length:
46 cm.

Male and female have
similar plumage.

Voice:
Raucous, barking cries
such as 'chak-chak-chak'.

Nutcracker

Nucifraga caryocatactes

Arctic taiga was the nutcracker's original habitat, but it now frequents conifer forest in the mountain areas of southern Scandinavia and central and south-eastern Europe. It is both a resident species and a transient migrant; populations from as far away as Siberia invade Europe during some winters. The nutcracker generally nests at altitudes above 300 metres, but in the Alps it may be found at anything between 800 and 2000 metres above sea level. In northern Europe it is found also in lowlands. The deep nest is built at the end of February or the beginning of March, among thick branches in spruce trees, generally between four and 15 metres above the ground. The structure comprises a foundation of broken twigs on top of which is a layer of moss, lichens and rotting wood, the hollow being lined with soft grass, leaves, and feathers. The three to five eggs are incubated by the hen alone for 17 to 19 days, during which time she is fed by the male. The young leave the nest at 23 days and, in the company of their parents, roam woods where there is an abundant crop of pineseeds and nuts. These the parents will store in a base of a tree trunk for use especially during the next breeding season. Sometimes the birds visit orchards where they pick the seeds from ripe pears; they also eat insects. Nutcrackers have been known on rare occasions to take the young of songbirds.

Voice:
Cry like that of the jay; call in spring sounds like 'kror'.

Length:
32 cm.

Wing span:
59 cm.

Male and female have similar plumage.

Size of egg:
30.3—37.5
× 21.5—26.0 mm.

Resident or dispersive bird

Chough

Pyrrhocorax pyrrhocorax

Britain, France, Switzerland, Italy, Sicily, Spain and the Alps are the chough's European range. This bird, with its brightly coloured bill, may be seen in large numbers on coastal cliffs or high in the mountain, generally at about 1,500 metres, but also as high as 3,500 metres above sea level. It is faithful to its breeding ground, remaining there even in winter, but descending into valleys when cold weather sets in. Choughs congregate in groups and are colonial nesters, a single colony comprising 40 to 60 pairs of birds. The nest of twigs, roots, dry grass, wool and hair is built at the end of April or in May in rock cavities or crevices, sometimes on a church steeple, castle ruin or the roof of a tall building. The female usually lays three to six eggs, and these may show marked variation in colour. The period of incubation is 17 to 21 days, the task falling solely to the hen. The young are fed insects and their larvae by both parents, who make only seven trips a day between eight in the morning and three in the afternoon. Adult birds occasionally capture small vertebrates, and in winter will feed on seeds if a more normal diet is scarce. The young leave the nest at 32 to 38 days, but remain in the company of their parents. They can be distinguished from the adult birds by their orange beaks. On fledging, the chough shows little fear of man and groups often visit mountain chalets where they are fed by the guests. Groups of choughs regularly visit water to drink.

Size of egg:
34.3–42.0
× 21.5–29.5 mm.

Length:
38 cm.

Male and female have
similar plumage.

Voice:
'Kyaw', like a jackdaw,
a characteristic 'tchuff' and
a gull-like 'kwuk-uk-uk'.

Resident bird

Jackdaw

Corvus monedula

The jackdaw may site its nest in old castle ruins, a large park with plenty of old, hollow trees, a tree-lined avenue, an abandoned quarry, on a cliff edge or in a church steeple. A gregarious bird, it breeds in loose colonies, occasionally very large ones. In April or May, individual pairs start building their nests of twigs in various hollows and crevices, the lining being a layer of straw, hairs and feathers. The clutch usually comprises five or six eggs and the parents share the duties of incubating for 17 to 19 days, though the male sits on the eggs only for brief periods. Diet consists of insects, especially beetles, worms and molluscs, as well as frogs and other small vertebrates. The adults also feed on seeds and are fond of visiting cherry orchards and gardens, especially if the latter contain ripe strawberries. When seeking food they fly close to the ground. At one month the young leave the nest and a few days later may already be seen flying about the neighbourhood. Outside the breeding season jackdaws frequently flock with rooks. The species is distributed throughout Europe except northern Scandinavia. Northern populations winter in central and western Europe.

Voice:
A clear, repeated 'chak' also 'kya'. Imitations of other bird calls and even human words.

Length:
33 cm.

Wing span:
65–68 cm.

Male and female have similar plumage.

Size of egg:
30.0–40.9
× 21.6–29.7 mm.

Dispersive bird

309

Rook

Corvus frugilegus

Skies filled with clouds of migrating rooks are a typical early winter sight in many parts of Europe. These are birds from the north and east – populations inhabiting the central and western parts of the continent migrate only locally. Outside the breeding season they visit fields and meadows by day and at night roost together in woodland treetops. In early spring these huge communities break up into smaller flocks that fly to their regular breeding grounds or 'rookeries'. The nest, built in the top of an old tree, is made of twigs. Sometimes the birds repair the previous year's nest instead of building a new one. Often as early as the end of March, the hen lays four to five eggs which she incubates alone for 18 days. The male brings her food during this period and sometimes she flies off the nest to meet him. When the young hatch, the male feeds the whole family for several days on his own, but about six days later the hen is also sharing the task. Almost 90 per cent of the diet is insects, especially cockchafers, carried by the adult birds in a special throat sac, but rooks also eat various seeds.

Dispersive bird

Size of egg:
32.3–47.4
× 25.2–30.4 mm.

Length:
46 cm.

Male and female have
similar plumage.

Voice:
Usual notes 'kaw' or 'kaaa'.

Crow

Corvus corone

The crow is widespread throughout the whole of Europe. There are two subspecies: the carrion crow *(Corvus corone corone)* (1), inhabiting western and southwestern Europe and part of central Europe; and the hooded crow *(Corvus corone cornix)* (2), which inhabits the remaining territory including Scotland and Ireland. Where their distribution overlaps, the two races may interbreed. The crow is a resident bird or a transient migrant, large flocks flying to central and western Europe from the north and east in winter. During the breeding season it frequents open woodlands, field groves and thickly overgrown parks in cities. It builds its nest in March, usually in trees at a height of five metres or more. The structure is made of dry twigs, mud and turf, and lined with moss, grass, hairs, sheep's wool and rags. A new nest takes some eight to ten days to build, but crows often use old nests. The female incubates the four to six eggs herself for 18 to 21 days, fed by the male. He only feeds the nestlings for the first five to seven days, after which both partners share the duties of attending the young. At 28 to 35 days they leave the nest. Flocks of crows visit the edges of ponds, lakes and rivers, where they find plentiful food remnants. They are omnivorous birds, collecting seeds, berries, beech nuts, insects and their larvae, molluscs and carrion, besides which they also hunt fieldmice and other small vertebrates.

Voice:
A deep 'kraa' or croaking 'keerk'.

Song:
Composed of similar notes and heard in the spring months.

Length:
47 cm.

Wing span:
95 to 100 cm.

Male and female have similar plumage.

Size of egg:
35.5—52.7
× 26.0—29.7 mm.

Resident or dispersive bird

Index of Common Names

Index
of Latin Names